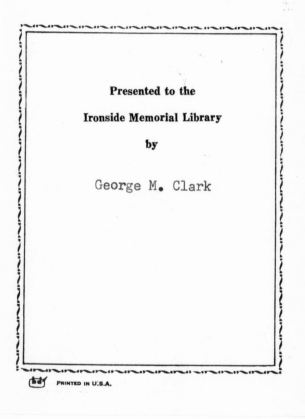
W9-BYT-877

Freedom
and
Federalism

BY FELIX MORLEY

Freedom

and

Federalism

BY FELIX MORLEY

A GATEWAY EDITION
HENRY REGNERY COMPANY
CHICAGO

TO MY GRANDCHILDREN

*Hoping that they, and their posterity,
may also continue to enjoy
the blessings of liberty*

"*The error . . . seems to owe its rise and prevalence chiefly to the confounding of a republic with a democracy. . . . A democracy . . . will be confined to a small spot. A republic may be extended over a large region.*"

JAMES MADISON

Contents

Foreword

This book is a conscientious attempt to repay a part of the heavy debt I owe, to my country and to the State of which I am a citizen; therefore a personal note of introduction is permissible.

Brought up in the United States as the child of English-born parents, in a border city with deeply divided opinions on the then sharply remembered Civil War, I early developed an appreciation of the great variety of means by which mankind seeks to attain the objective of stable government. This interest in political theory was steadily strengthened by academic study of governmental forms, both past and present, and enlivened by many years of political reporting, locally, from Washington, and from other national capitals.

Gradually I learned that the art of government, in all times and for all sorts of societies, may be reduced to very simple elements. It is at bottom nothing more than the reconciliation of two conditions—one essential for cooperative achievement, the other necessary for individual fulfillment. The social condition is Order, without which men cannot work together effectively. The more personal condition is Freedom, without which some men cannot work either happily or at their best.

I further came to realize that the outstanding

virtue of federalism, which is the distinctively American contribution to political art, is its facility in combining these naturally antagonistic conditions. Since the reconciliation of freedom and order is anything but easy a federal system requires both complicated governmental machinery and a high degree of interest and understanding among its citizens. These factors make federalism a distinctly experimental system, especially vulnerable in periods of upheaval.

The survival of federalism in the United States was first seriously called in question not by the Civil War, in which both sides favored the system, but during the period immediately following the fall of the Confederacy. No serious consideration of whether it is likely to continue or disappear in this county is therefore possible without examination of historical background. The approaching centennial of the outbreak of the War Between the States would therefore itself be an appropriate time to consider the probable longevity of this Republic, as conceived by its founders. And such a study is made more timely, if not imperative, by man's sudden achievement of mastery both over the atom and over the force of gravity—though not, unfortunately, over his own passion and prejudice.

These scientific achievements have overnight revolutionized military problems and procedures. What is not so obvious, though certain to be profound, is their effect on the political arrangements of mankind. The purpose of this book is to consider that issue, with particular reference to the impact on individual liberty as centralized government takes more and more authority into its hands.

There is a prima facie case for thinking that our federal system, having at least survived the enormous changes since its establishment in 1787, will continue to serve for a future now unusually unpredictable. If so, it could be that federalism, under American leadership, will be the device whereby men everywhere will bring their political institutions in line with the urgent necessity of peaceful co-existence on a compact and shrunken planet. Indications to that effect will be examined in the following pages.

At least equally possible is the alternative that federal theory will be discarded, even without war, by the voluntary actions of Americans themselves, in favor of that highly centralized, managerial form of government which to many now seems demanded by the complexities of modern civilization. Somewhat paradoxically it is argued that dictatorship, the simplest form of government, is best suited for highly diversified societies, although it does seem psychologically desirable to call such dictatorship "democracy." Indications that the era of the American Republic is in this manner drawing to its close are also closely considered here.

This judicial method of examination obviously requires a critical, even iconoclastic, attitude towards political dogma of every kind, our own especially. But it may be that such close analysis, though liable to arouse emotional resentments, will by its very objectivity help to disclose the advantages of the political system under which so many Americans have so long had the opportunity to live full and fruitful lives.

In preliminary form, much of what follows has

been presented to political science discussion groups at Buck Hill Falls, Pa.; Princeton, N. J.; Chapel Hill, N. C., and Claremont, Calif. Portions of a few chapters have also been printed in *Modern Age*, *Nation's Business*, and *Barron's Weekly*, to the editors of which thanks are due for permission to reprint. Mr. Walter Leckrone, editor of the Indianapolis *Times*, has graciously permitted me to excerpt an article of his therefrom.

Unquestionably the content of this book has been greatly improved by the forthright criticism it has received during its slow development. Gratitude for this is owing to so many that only a blanket acknowledgment is possible. I must, however, express something of my debt to Edith Hamilton, and to Roscoe Pound. Both have read the manuscript critically and carefully, making many helpful comments. With characteristic generosity the former Dean of the Harvard Law School has labored to save me from false steps when I have ventured in the intricate field of jurisprudence. Where conclusions remain open to reasonable criticism at any point, responsibility is mine alone.

FELIX MORLEY

Gibson Island, Md.
July 4, 1959

Freedom
and
Federalism

ONE

Our Federal Republic

The United States of America was not the first, but has unquestionably been the most successful, attempt to reconcile the presumable desideratum of general freedom with the necessity of social discipline.

Even if this unusually experimental form of government is doomed to eventual failure, the record of its tangible accomplishment will have proved unprecedented. During its lifetime, now approaching two centuries, the political system of this representative Republic has done more for its people as a whole than any other ever devised. The reason lies in a simple paradox. By the adoption of arrangements strongly negative towards the power of government, the Republic has so far permitted and encouraged its citizens to act affirmatively in their own interests. Many Americans do not realize that when first attempted this political plan was extraordinary, indeed revolutionary in the full sense of the word.

The United States, as the name implies, are a union of sovereign States, federal in nature. Certain characteristics, herewith enumerated, are common to all federations. First and foremost, federalism involves dispersion of political power. There will, of course, be some delegation of overriding authority

1

to the general or central government. This requires the establishment of a national capital, the presence of which itself distinguishes a federation from a mere league or alliance of independent sovereignties. The seating of the central government is the material reflection of the process of federation, whereby the component parts—while reserving certain powers to themselves—have permanently surrendered some prerogatives of sovereignty to a common national pool.

This division of sovereignty between the central government and the constituent states must be defined. In consequence, a constitution is prerequisite to any federation, and it is in practice necessary that this should be a written contract so that both the state and central governments may have reasonably precise understanding of their respective functions and authority. Even when this division of governmental authority is meticulously set forth there will be disputes as to the allocation, especially if economic or social development seems to require uniform national regulation. This certainty of changing circumstance gives rise to two other essential features of a federation. The written constitution must, as a practical matter, be subject to amendment by some prescribed process. And there must be a supreme court, empowered to decide just where the division of sovereignty lies in any contested case, at any particular time.

Flexibility is an outstanding asset of the federal form of government. By the device of keeping certain governmental powers under strictly local control, people with great diversities may be encouraged to unite under one flag. Thus the Swiss Confederation has successfully joined together German-speaking, French-speaking and Italian-speaking cantons. In Canada federation has united communities which are distinctively English and French in their linguistic, religious and cultural backgrounds. The German Empire, from 1871 to 1918, was a federation of monarchies. A mixed federation, of both republics and monarchies, could now conceivably be developed by those Western European nations which have subscribed to both the Common Market and Euratom treaties. Of the six states attempting to pool their sovereignty in these respects, two (Belgium and Holland) are kingdoms, one (Luxembourg) is a grand duchy, three (France, Italy and Western Germany) are republics, and one of these (Western Germany) is itself federal in form.

Another interesting, though unacceptable, illustration is the Union of Soviet Socialist Republics. This is nominally a federal union and indeed was able on that assumption to obtain separate membership for two of its constituent units (Byelorussia and Ukraine) in the United Nations. All Soviet republics, however, are subjected to a centralized, socialistic regimentation which in practice confines their autonomy to cultural matters and makes the claim to federal form extremely shadowy. Moreover, the first article of the Constitution of the U. S. S. R. defines this union as "a socialist state." Socialism and federalism are necessarily political opposites, because the former demands that centralized concentration of power which the latter by definition denies.[1]

The federal form of government has certain obvious deficiencies. The preservation of a multiplicity of relatively powerful local governments, within the union, creates a complicated and legalistic system. It makes the conduct of foreign policy, necessarily entrusted to the central government, unusually difficult for a true federation, since actions taken in regard to other sovereign powers are always likely to react on the domestic balance. In times of unusual strain, whether foreign or domestic, the central government is likely either to evade its constitutional limitations, or be frustrated by them. There is no question that a unitary state—where all significant governmental power is centered in the national capital—is in a better position to act promptly and decisively than is a federation. This explains the tendency of federations to alter their character, in the direction of strongly centralized government, during periods of stress. Once underway, that centralizing process is difficult to reverse, largely because of the vested interest in power which every governmental agency quickly establishes for itself unless continuously checked by those who pay for its support.

The great overriding advantage of the federal system is that it operates to avert the dangers inherent in government by remote control. The essence of federalism is reservation of control over local affairs to the localities themselves, the argument for which becomes stronger if the federation embraces a large area, with strong climatic or cultural differences among the various states therein. One justifying assumption for such a loose-knit system is that citizens as a body are both interested in, and for the most part competent to handle, local problems. When that assumption is valid there is little doubt that federalism, despite its disadvantages, serves admirably to foster freedom without the sacrifice of order.

What has been said applies to federations in general. That of the United States has certain special characteristics which make it the most interesting, as well as the most complicated, illustration of this type of political union. As De Tocqueville wrote: "In examining the Constitution of the United States, which is the most perfect federal constitution that ever existed, one is startled at the variety of information and the amount of discernment that it presupposes in the people whom it is meant to govern." And he further predicted that if this discernment should languish, as it certainly is languishing today, Americans would eventually "fall beneath the yoke of a centralized administration." [2]

The outstanding feature of the American form of federalism is that it carries the doctrine of the separation of powers a great deal farther than is required by the mere structure of federalism—a great deal farther than Canada, for instance, has attempted. In addition to the allocation as between Washington and each of the State capitals, such as Albany, Little Rock or Sacramento, there is a further specified division of power among the three branches of government within each of these capitals.

Both the Constitution of the Federal Union, and those of each of the 50 States that now together compose it, separate the legislative, executive and judicial powers, and balance the one against the others. This has been a uniform interpretation of that rather vague clause in the Federal Constitution which says (Art. 4, Sect. 4): "The United States shall guarantee to every State in this Union a Republican Form of Government." Republican, as contrasted with monarchical or democratic, meant to the founding fathers the division, as opposed to the concentration, of governmental power.[3] The Republic, while launched in revolt against the personal tyranny of a king, was most carefully designed to prevent any recurrence of monopolistic power, not merely by its federal form but also by establishing check and balance within the machinery of federalism.

The theory of check and balance, as superimposed on our federal structure, was derived from the writings of the French philosopher Montesquieu and has no relation whatever to the English political tradition. From the latter has evolved the wholly different, though widely adopted, system known as responsible parliamentary government. The Prime Minister, who is the leader of the party that controls the legislature, holds his executive office as long, but only as long, as he retains majority support in the House of Commons. By gradual steps, over a long period of political evolution, he has been made wholly responsible to this majority. If defeated in a "vote of confidence" this Premier must resign and is succeeded by the leader of the Opposition. In the United States there is no such device as a vote of confidence, neither in the national nor in any of the State legislatures. While President and Governors are customarily party leaders they hold office for fixed terms, during which they cannot be ousted, except by death, disability or successful impeachment.

This executive independence is but one of the extraordinary features of the American form of government, not the less worthy of clear understanding because its processes are as normal for us as they are baffling to many of our friends and allies. As a check to the guaranteed power of the executive the legislature may of course defeat bills which the former proposes, or adopt legislation which it opposes, though here the President has a qualified power of veto not possessed by prime ministers in parliamentary systems. While the Congress retains, at least nominally, the "power of the purse" it is further weakened, vis-a-vis the executive, by the fact that ministers or their deputies are not, as in England, present in the legislature to submit to questions from the elected representatives of the people. The vitally important substitute procedure, whereby Congressional committees may summon and interrogate executive officials or any other persons, is neither too well understood nor always too well handled, as the confused furor over what came to be called "McCarthyism" attested.

The Congress also appears to be at something of a disadvantage with respect to the Federal judiciary, which must decide the question of constitutionality whenever a test case to that end is brought. A huge amount of State legislation, and no small quantity of that enacted by the Congress, has been rendered invalid by this process of judicial review. In theory, the judiciary is as independent of the executive as of the legislative branch. And throughout our history the Supreme Court has often countermanded Presidential wishes, in addition to overriding the will of Congress. But in practice, whenever subservience on the part of the Court can be noted, it tends to be towards the President rather than towards Congress.

This is not primarily because the President appoints the Federal judges, on life tenure. Rather it is because the Congress can seldom exhibit the concentrated resolution of a single man, as it did in the extraordinary period right after the Civil War, and because the executive can more subtly ignore or circumvent judicial decisions than can the legislature. On the other hand, the judiciary is by its nature deprived from seeking that favorable publicity for its decisions which is always open to manipulation by spokesmen for the legislature and executive.

The Congress of the United States is undoubtedly a powerful body, especially because of the constitutional privileges of the Upper House, which must give consent to all treaties concluded by the executive, as well as to the appointment of diplomatic representatives, judges of the Supreme Court and all but "inferior officers" of the Administration.[4] The six-year tenure of Senatorial office, and the fact that Senators from the least populous State are in every respect peers of those from the greatest, gives them substantial individual importance. This is increased by the Senate rules, alterable only by that body itself, permitting blocking tactics, or outright "filibustering," which have time and again permitted a Senate minority successfully to frustrate the Presidential will. It is the Senate which represents par excellence the federal basis of American government. And the tradition that a Senator should not hesitate to place the welfare of his State, as he sees it, above that of the nation as seen by the President, is still very much alive.

There is, of course, nothing haphazard either about the federal structure of the United States, or about the careful balance of powers built into that structure. It may be said that the federal form was historically ordained, by the fact that the original thirteen colonies were separately established and had by the time of the Revolution developed widely differing political and social customs. Only a system which protected those diversities could combine these varying units in a general unity. But behind the determination to keep the rights of the several States inviolate was the even deeper determination to protect the citizens of these states from centralized governmental oppression. That is why the Republic was established not only as a federation of semisovereign States, but also as one of balanced authority, in which it would be extremely difficult to establish a nationwide monopoly power of any kind.

We could infer this hostility to monopoly power from the text of the Constitution, even without the abundant evidence available in the prolific writings of the founding fathers. Thus, Article I says flatly that: "No title of nobility shall be granted by the United States," insuring that no small group shall enjoy honorifics entitling its members to claim a social prestige—permitting them to "lord" it over others. Similarly the First Amendment says: "Congress shall make no law respecting an establishment of religion, or prohibiting the free exercise thereof." That is directed against any upper church, just as the denial of titles is directed against any upper class. This provision has insured that "disenter" or "heretic" carry no religious opprobrium for Americans, any more than the word "commoner" means socially declassé. As already noted, the opposition to concentration of political power runs through the entire content of the Organic Law, but is specifically emphasized in the Ninth and Tenth Amendments, which say:

> The enumeration in the Constitution, of certain rights, shall not be construed to deny or disparage others retained by the people.
>
> The powers not delegated to the United States by the Constitution, nor prohibited by it to the States, are reserved to the States respectively, or to the people.

The men who wrote the Constitution were personally familiar with the evil potential of social, religious and political monopoly, and therefore were for the most part insistent on these specific safeguards. There seems to have been no anticipation of economic monopoly, yet the spirit of the Constitution is clearly hostile to this also. Congress was given the power "to regulate commerce," in consequence of which the deep-rooted dislike of monopoly in time produced the Sherman, Clayton, and Taft-Hartley Acts. What is still lacking is an agency comparable with the Federal Trade Commission, designed to keep Big Unionism as well as Big Business within bounds.[5]

The fact that American trade unionism has been able to establish extraordinary legal immunities for itself is a matter of growing concern. But no aspect of this monopolistic phenomenon is more significant than its revelation of the tendency to disrupt a democratic social system in the name of democracy.

This desire to secure privileged position is by no means limited to labor leaders and is found in all strata of society. The "worth" of a man is habitually reckoned in dollars. In spite of the prohibition against titles of nobility there is scarcely a festival throughout the length and breadth of the land that does not crown its "queen." No American girl is more assured of publicity than one who manages to marry a foreign princeling. And the love for the trappings of distinction—Knight of Pythias, Blue Book listing or even a gaudy fin-tailed automobile if one can do no better—illustrates a most undemocratic trait in a nominally democratic society. One may even hazard that many Americans would be happy to see an established church in their Republic, if it could be the one of their own choosing.

In short, the mistrust of privilege among Americans has never been strong enough to dampen the individual desire to get ahead of others, even if that end involves the attainment of a monopoly position. Democracy, as the word is used in the United States, does not imply equality.

Probably the most remarkable characteristic of our governmental design is that it merely "holds the ring" for those who are endeavoring to get ahead of their competitors. Its basic purpose, not always successfully achieved, is to deny privilege to any so that opportunity may be kept open for all. This is very close to, if not identical with, the age-old ethical aim of Justice and it is no accident that to "establish Justice" is set forth as an objective second only to that of "a more perfect Union" in the Preamble to the Constitution. Since people, in a competitive or any other society, are by no means always just to each other, some regulation by the state in its capacity of umpire is unavoidable. What must be kept in mind is that the greatest injustice of all is done when the umpire forgets that he too is bound by the rules, and begins to make them as between contestants in behalf of his own prejudices.

The comparison with an athletic contest is valid to the extent that it emphasizes the strongly competitive nature of American society, and what originally seemed to Americans the true function of civil government in merely supervising competitive enterprise under definite constitutional rules. The merit of a supervisory, as opposed to a directive, state is that the former keeps "the power in the people," to use the phrase of William Penn. Our system encourages the individual to exertion for his own sake, instead of requiring exertion by an elite in behalf of the masses, which is the principle of communism and of national socialism put in the most favorable light. Our system further assumes that self-assertion will be for the good of all if balanced by self-discipline. To meet that proviso it relies heavily, as we shall see, on the services of organized religion.

Under the communist, or socialist, systems it is the function of the state and not the church to teach humility. For that reason the church is at best merely tolerated, and is likely to be actively suppressed, wherever totalitarian rule triumphs. To Lenin, religion was "the opiate of the people." [6] To Washington it was the "indispensable support" of "political prosperity." [7] From these polarized conceptions it follows that religious revival is a serious threat to the success of the Soviet system, just as the decay of religious observance is a serious threat to the success of our own.

This is by no means the only fundamental in

which meat for the one system is poison to the other. A strongly centralized government is aided by political ignorance and apathy among its subjects. But the docile acceptance of paternalism spells morbidity for a federal system, which can only prosper if its self-governing localities take politics seriously. So there is cause for concern in the fact that so many Americans have come to regard their Federal Republic as a centralized democracy. And this concern is not lessened by noting that the communists describe their system as "democratic centralism," operated through the medium of "People's Democracies."

This anomalous use of identical terms for political opposites demands a much more thorough examination than it habitually receives. We are proposing to demonstrate that it is incorrect, and therefore injurious, to call our Federal Union a political democracy. In so doing we shall also consider whether Soviet Russia has a better claim to that description.

TWO

Federalism and Democracy

Although representative government need not be democratic, a democracy, to deserve that name, must be representative.

Except where population is small the citizens cannot all get together in town meeting and make their decisions by direct vote. But the device of representation permits the majority will to function over wide and thickly populated areas, provided two conditions are fulfilled: the election of representatives must be completely uncoerced; and, when chosen, their power of decision must not be fettered by constitutional restraints. Soviet Russia does not meet the first of these essential criteria. The United States does not meet the second. It was never intended that it should.

The founding fathers certainly had a clear idea of the form of government they were establishing by the Constitution. And the most influential of them were strongly opposed to a democratic political system, meaning one that endeavors to facilitate the triumph of the majority will. In "a pure democracy," wrote Madison, "there is nothing to check the inducements to sacrifice the weaker party or an obnoxious individual. Hence it is that such democracies have ever been spectacles of turbulence and contention; have ever been found incompatible with personal security or the rights of property; and have in general been as short in their lives as they have been violent in their deaths." [1] John Adams, our second President, put it more sharply: "There never was a democracy that did not commit suicide." [2] That was certainly not the system these men were supporting for the United States.

Charles A. Beard, personally one of the most democratic of all our historians, thought it essential to emphasize the undemocratic nature of the American form of government. "At no time," he wrote, "at no place in solemn convention assembled, through no chosen agents, had the American people officially proclaimed the United States to be a democracy. The Constitution did not contain the word or any word lending countenance to it, except possibly the mention of 'we, the people,' in the preamble." [3] This phrase, incidentally, was one of the reasons why Patrick Henry, of Virginia, threw all his powerful influence against ratification of the Constitution. Its preamble, he argued, should have said not "We, the people" but "We, the States."

Actually, it is understatement to say that the Constitution gives no countenance to a democratic system of government. In many particulars this organic law sets up roadblocks calculated to frustrate the will of the majority. The most formidable of these are contained in the Bill of Rights, establishing for the individual a list of privileges which the Courts must uphold and which Congress cannot circumscribe. If the United States were a democracy the provision that: "No person . . . shall be compelled . . . to be a witness against himself" would by now probably have been qualified. Those who seek to hide a communistic, racketeering or otherwise unsavory background behind the Fifth Amendment are distinctly unpopular. But as the United States is not politically a democracy, readily responsive to strong majority opinions, this perhaps quixotic safeguard stands.

The Bill of Rights, as the first ten Amendments are collectively known, is an addition to the original Constitution. But we know that the Union would not have been formed as it was without advance understanding that these precise restrictions on democracy would be written into the organic law at the earliest opportunity. The ratification conventions in both Virginia and New York would certainly have rejected the federal plan except for the promise of specific checks to the majority will. Madison admitted as much, when, in the first session of the First Congress, he moved adoption of these amendments, all designed to protect individiuals against the ever potential tyranny of the majority. Indeed, both North Carolina and Rhode Island were still outside the Union when Madison, reviewing the many criticisms of the Constitution, said:

> the great mass of the people who oppose it, disliked it because it did not contain effectual provision against the encroachments on particular rights, and [for] those safeguards which they have long been accustomed to have *interposed* between them and the magistrate who exercised the sovereign power . . ."

The key word here, from the viewpoint of federalism, has been italicized because it was the first time that the doctrine of Interposition was foreshadowed as a proper and desirable constitutional practice for

the United States. Of course the Supreme Court itself, under the Bill of Rights, has on hundreds of
occasions "interposed" its power to protect minority
interests against both legislative and executive compulsion.

The original Constitution was not merely undemocratic in principle. It also established undemocratic political institutions which have functioned in
an undemocratic manner from the outset. In the
powerful Upper House of Congress the vote of a
Senator from Nevada still has exactly the same
weight as the vote of a Senator from New York,
with a population some seventy times greater. Similarly, Rhode Island, containing 1,058 square miles,
is in all the rights of statehood the exact equal
of Texas, of which sixty-four counties possess in
each case a greater area than all of Rhode Island.

The Supreme Court, as an institution, is even
more undemocratic than the Senate. Here are nine
appointed judges, intentionally safeguarded from
any popular control, who are vested with power
to nullify legislation approved by the elected representatives of the people. Some would even permit
this Court to declare "the law of the land" by
decree, though the Congress has taken no legislative
action in the matter at issue. The Supreme Court
may, as Mr. Dooley asserted, "follow the election
returns." But the only definite attribute of political
democracy found in that august body is that within
its own membership the majority opinion dominates.
The actual bearing of this arrangement, however,
is that in a five to four decision the judgment of
a single appointed magistrate may defeat the majority will of an elected Congress. Democratic is

about the last adjective that can be properly applied to such a process.

We find the same hostility to democratic theory in the executive, as well as in the judicial and legislative divisions of our government. The Presidential veto of legislation duly approved by both Houses of Congress has been practiced with increasing frequency in recent years. Since the seventeenth century the power of the purse has been regarded as the essential prerogative of the representative assembly. Yet under President Franklin D. Roosevelt the veto was for the first time used to nullify financial legislation. During the first session of the Eightieth Congress, President Truman twice vetoed tax legislation, although at the time he had not even been elected to the office carrying veto power. On the second of these occasions the most democratic organ of our central government—the House of Representatives—vainly voted by a more than two-thirds majority to override.

The current use of the veto power is a difficult hurdle for those who like to argue that our political institutions, though unquestionably undemocratic in origin and design, are gradually being adapted to an assumed craving for democracy. And the veto is by no means the only evidence to the contrary. The District of Columbia is as completely disfranchised today as it was half-a-century ago. The quasi-autocratic committee chairmen in both Houses of Congress continue to be chosen by the undemocratic seniority rule. In the allegedly "liberal" Eighty-sixth Congress the Senate again indorsed the fili-buster by overwhelming rejection of attempts to bring termination of debate by majority vote. All efforts to reform our highly undemocratic electoral college have been equally unsuccessful.

Adoption of the Seventeenth Amendment, providing for the direct election of Senators, is often cited as evidence of a democratic reform. It certainly made the process of choice within each State more democratic. But this procedure, advocated by James Wilson of Pennsylvania at the Constitutional Convention, did nothing to alter the federal principle whereby political power is divided without regard to population ratios. And that essentially undemocratic division is a basic characteristic of federalism.

The Nineteenth Amendment, ratified in 1920, extended the franchise to include women, much as the Fifteenth Amendment, shortly after the Civil War, had at least nominally extended it to Negro men throughout the United States. Enlargement of the electorate is widely regarded as a democratic measure. But the validity of that belief depends primarily on the character of the issues presented to the voters. To the extent that these issues are limited, the theory of democracy is also limited, because a larger number of votes means little or nothing if only inconsequential matters are decided thereby.

Universal suffrage is certainly a prerequisite of democratic government, but does not itself produce that result unless the *form* of government is also democratized. This is made clear by contrasting the relatively stable American form with the profound alterations in behalf of political democracy that have been made in Great Britain. There the franchise was progressively broadened by a series of Reform Acts—1832, 1867, 1884, 1918, 1928. These served to forward political democracy not so much because they enlarged the electorate to include practically all adult "subjects," but because they were accompanied by and heralded other measures reducing the political power of the throne and of the hereditary House of Lords, increasing that of the now truly representative House of Commons. This change of governmental form has simultaneously democratized the executive, since the Prime Minister, unlike an American President, cannot survive a defeat in the House of Commons and has no power of veto. Nominally, the veto is still a royal prerogative in Great Britain, but it has not been exercised as such since the reign of Queen Anne and would almost certainly cost the throne to any monarch who would now attempt to use it.

Finally, Great Britain has no judicial institution comparable to our basically undemocratic Supreme Court. Every Act passed by Parliament, which with substantial accuracy can now be called the House of Commons alone, has equal constitutional force. So in that nation there is no longer legislative, nor executive, nor even comprehensive judicial check to the triumph of the majority will,[4] as expressed by a fully enfranchised adult electorate which chooses and controls its representatives by secret ballot. This system is about as close to true political democracy as is in practice possible. But, for better or worse, it is a system wholly different from that of the United States.

How is it, we may now reasonably ask ourselves, that a form of government as politically undemocratic as that of the United States, should nevertheless be habitually referred to as a "democracy," even by officials sworn to defend and uphold a Constitution that originally so firmly blocked political democracy? It is a really important question, which every conscientious citizen should be willing and indeed anxious to face.

A part of the confusion, though only a part, is due to historical accident, to the illogical practice of referring to the central government as the "federal government."

Actually the federal government is a combination of the one centered in Washington and those located in the States, for it is this combination that constitutes the federal system. But in the early days of the Republic the fundamental political struggle was not to defend States' Rights against those of the central government, but rather to establish a central government which would have some real authority over the States. Consequently, those favoring centralization called themselves "Federalists," avoiding the more accurate title of "Nationalists" for fear of stimulating the already strong opposition to the formation of a firmly united nation. During the Civil War the soldiers fighting to preserve the Union were called "Federals," confirming the misusage.

The use of "federal" to denote the central government alone is not merely misleading, but also suggests that effort to keep the federal structure from being centralized is anti-federal, which is absurd. Nevertheless, the usage of "federal" when "national" is meant is now firmly established. In this study, however, wherever there is reference to the Washington government alone, as separate and distinct from those of the States, it is called either "national," "central," or in the phrase preferred by those who wrote the Constitution, "the general government." Also to avoid confusion, the word "state" is capitalized when, but only when, it refers to a State of our political Union.

Misleading use of "federal" has encouraged misuse of "democratic." Obviously, only the general government is able to promote political democracy, interpreted as the general will of the nation as a whole. Consequently, action by the misnamed federal government, in behalf of an alleged general will, is not merely called democratic, which it should be, but is also made to appear appropriate to the American system of government, which it frequently is not. Federal Aid to Education, for instance, is actually anti-federal, since it threatens to deprive the localities of one of their constitutional functions, vesting it in the central government. But it is argued that this should be done, regardless of constitutionality, if it can be demonstrated that a national majority wants the development. Because it is the so-called federal government that would take this action, its damaging effect on the federal structure is largely concealed. The same difficulty crops up, and is indeed increased, by giving the title of "Federal-State Relationships" to official studies of division of function between the national and State governments. The title implies that the States are somehow apart from, or even hostile to, the federal system, although without the States there would be no federalism.

But this, while important, is only a partial explanation of why "democracy" has become one of the "good" words; why it is fallaciously contrasted with dictatorship, and is habitually though inaccurately used by Americans to describe their form of government. A deeper reason, already suggested, is that the word "democracy" has a social as well as a political connotation, and somewhere along the line we lost the ability to discriminate between the two.

That which is undemocratic, socially speaking, is any generalized assumption that one man is not, fundamentally, "as good" as another. The affirmation of social equality in no way asserts that all men have equal intelligence; that they are uniform in health, wealth, strength, or manners; that all have the same gifts for leadership; or that all are equally competent either in abstract reasoning or in mechanical ingenuity. Social democracy merely means that in the sight of God, as the source of good, these differences are secondary. All men are subject to the same natural laws and therefore should be treated equally by man-made laws. All are brothers under the Fatherhood of God.

Social democracy is thus basically a religious conception, enormously strengthened by the precepts of Christianity. Its roots in the United States are deep and strong, both because of the dominant role that religion played in most of the early settlements and because of the levelling effect of pioneer life during the formative period of our institutions. In spite of the anomaly of slavery, most Americans in 1776 responded uncritically to the dogmatic assertions that "all men are created equal" and "endowed by their Creator with certain unalienable rights." Except for slaves, also excluded from the scope of both social and political democracy by the ancient Greeks, these claims really seemed to be "self-evident truths," justifying the Declaration of Independence and the establishment of a union of "Free and Independent States."

But between the drafting of the Declaration and the adoption of the Constitution there was a period of twelve very difficult years, both of war and peace, during all of which the social advantages and the political disadvantages of democracy were in continuous sharp contrast. It was crystal clear, when the Philadelphia Convention met in 1787, that no union would be established unless powers allotted to the general government were severely restrained in the interest of the several States. It was no less clear that democratic disorders would destroy the freedom that Americans prized, if the often ill-informed will of the majority were given free rein. "The general object" was stated by Edmund Randolph, of Virginia, at the opening of the Convention. It was "to provide a cure for the evils under which the United States labored; that in tracing these evils to their origin, every man had found it in the turbulence and follies of democracy." His more nationalistic colleague, James Madison, adroitly embroidered the point by emphasizing that the proposed "general government" must be given sufficient power to safeguard "the rights of the minority," continuously jeopardized "in all cases where a majority are united by a common interest or passion." [5]

The eventual accomplishment of this Convention was to evolve a form of government which would paradoxically fortify social democracy by blocking political democracy. The system established was hostile to monopolization of power, by any group, in any form. That, rather than anything distinctive in the nature of Americans, is what makes our Federal Republic socially democratic. But by the same token it is made politically undemocratic, because unless political power is centralized the popular will cannot be made nationally effective. Thus the dispersion of power simultaneously assists social, and hampers political, democracy.

This clever arrangement counteracts the fatal tendency of political democracy, through its requisite of centralized government, to destroy first social democracy and then itself. Centralization of power means, to begin with, that the seat of this power—the national capital—will tend to draw to this focus point the most talented and intelligent minds. There is nothing accidental in the fact that in the unitary nations of England and France all cities seem to be, and are called, "provincial" by comparison with London and Paris.

Unfortunately, this is not merely a matter of focussing literary and artistic, or commercial and financial, talent. The administrative skill necessary for government is similarly concentrated in the capital. It draws strength and encouragement from the general atmosphere of centralized culture and power. Soon the top echelons begin to regard themselves as a managerial elite, entitled to rule the rest of the country in the manner which the word "provincial" superciliously suggests. Such an attitude has nothing in common with democracy, either social or political. And it is well to recall that, in 1835, De Tocqueville had hope for the future of our "democratic republic" largely because "America has no great capital city, whose direct or indirect influ-

ence is felt over the whole extent of the country."
And "this I hold to be one of the first causes of the
maintenance of republican institutions in the United
States." [6]

Because it must be given close consideration later,
we have left to the end of this chapter mention of
the most legitimate reason for describing the American governmental system as a "democracy." As will
be demonstrated, two of the Constitutional Amendments—the Fourteenth and Sixteenth—have undeniably operated subtly to undermine the federal
structure of the United States as originally planned.
The Fourteenth Amendment in effect reversed the
emphasis of the first eight Amendments, all designed
to limit the powers of the central government, so
as to make these limitations applicable by the central government to the States. The Sixteenth Amendment supplemented this revolutionary change by
giving the central government virtually unlimited
power to tax the people without regard to State
needs or boundaries.

It is under the influence and judicial interpretation
of these two Amendments that the United States has
now moved far from the original concept of federalism, and ever closer towards that of a centralized,
unitary state which could actually become, temporarily, the political democracy which it is so often
loosely said to be. And, for causes now to be considered, there have from the outset been forces
working to destroy American federalism and to
substitute for it that type of political democracy
which springs from Rousseau's concept of the "general will."

THREE

The Concept of a General Will

The American system of government assumes that there are certain fundamental human rights, such as freedom of speech and association, of which the individual must not be casually deprived by other men. These natural rights are held to be gifts from the Creator. While the state should insure that as birthrights they are sustained, at least equal care must be taken to see that the state itself does not trespass upon them.

To accomplish this delicate objective the founding fathers devised a balanced political structure, designed to protect minorities against the majority, right down to that minority of one, the individual. This protection is justified by the belief that men as individuals, and in their voluntary social combinations, are in general moral persons, respectful of the rights of others and therefore worthy of freedom. But since this trust is by no means always justified, ample powers of coercion over the unruly are given to political government, both local and national. These coercive powers, however, are most carefully balanced against each other, to insure that they shall not be used arbitrarily.

The men who wrote the Constitution were fully aware that in thus trying to reconcile Order with Freedom they were steering between Scylla and

Charybdis. Madison posed the eternal problem in equally timeless words when he wrote: "In framing a government which is to be administered by men over men, the great difficulty lies in this: You must first enable the government to control the governed; and in the next place oblige it to control itself." And later in Number 51 of the *Federalist* he concludes that this "great difficulty" has been at least theoretically solved for the United States:

> In the compound republic of America, the power surrendered by the people is first divided between two distinct governments, and then the portion allotted to each [is] subdivided among distinct and separate departments.[1] Hence a double security arises to the rights of the people. The different governments will control each other, at the same time that each will be controlled by itself.

Those words were first printed on February 8, 1788, ten years after the death, in France, of a man whose political thinking was as brilliant, though far more erratic than that of James Madison, and whose influence throughout the world has been deplorably greater. Indeed it may be said that the struggle between the American and Russian ideologies today stems directly from the sharply antagonistic philosophies of James Madison, the Virginian, and Jean Jacques Rousseau, the uprooted Genevese. "Ideas have consequences," though it may take a long time for them to come to full fruition.

It was Rousseau's tremendous achievement to establish the conception of a "general will" for the triumph of which omnipotent government is the instrument. The conception is in theory thoroughly democratic, and indeed Rousseau deserves to be honored as the father of untrammeled political democracy. But the concept of the general will is also fundamentally, and in practice ruthlessly, opposed to that faith in the potential of the individual on which the government of the United States is founded.

Yet Rousseau's idea of a *volonté générale*, set forth with tremendous impact in the brief compass of his *Social Contract*, does not deny validity to individualism but on the contrary is based on the conviction that man is by nature good. The general will is not supposed to be capricious, passionate or instinctive. It is, rather, the whole of which all the individual wills in any community are parts. It is the composite, at any given moment, of the presumably rational judgment of all mature and competent members of the group. Without individuality as its basis, in other words, there could be no general will.

Conversely, it must be admitted, there can be no individuality worthy of the name without agreements in the nature of what Rousseau calls "the social contract." The unrestricted individualism of the savage in a state of nature is not enviable. What we really mean by individualism is the latitude of a person to choose for himself among the many fruits of a civilization in which he actually participates. It is not merely unfair but also impossible to cut oneself off from the disagreeable results of collective action, while continuing to benefit substantially from those regarded as pleasurable.

"Man is by nature a political animal," who for self-fulfillment needs contact with his fellows—in work, worship and play, in matters spiritual, intellectual, aesthetic and material. On that point Aristotle said the last word.[2] The prolonged helplessness of human infancy, man's unique ability to formulate and communicate abstract ideas, his habitual sociability as well as his need for cooperation—these and other distinctive human characteristics combine to demand that association which of itself creates society. And social contact implies some form of that social contract on which Rousseau placed deserved emphasis in his immortal essay under that title.

The social contract may, of course, be implicit rather than explicit. It may be as simple and elementary as the convention which allows the batter three strikes in a game of baseball. Or it may involve a constitutional division of power so complicated and refined that a supreme court must be established to interpret its bearing in any given case. The social contract, again, may be accepted willingly by citizens who have been given a continuing voice in its application; or it may be enforced by terrorism on unwilling subjects. But these diversities, whether of importance or of acceptability, are all secondary to the fact that there is some form of social contract behind every form of social organization, and that no member of any such organization can with impunity ignore the terms made applicable to him.

In England, which has no written constitution, some eminent political thinkers have since the French Revolution denied any validity to the theory of the social contract. Sir Frederick Pollock, for instance, called it a "plastic fiction," while admitting morosely that it "became one of the most successful and fatal of political impostures."[3] Of course it would be impossible to prove, as Rousseau intimates, that groups of prehistoric savages at some time

covenanted with each other to change the state of
nature into orderly political societies. But such evidence is not necessary to validate this part of his
argument. In our own history there are numerous
instances, such as the Mayflower Compact, where
men confronting primitive conditions individually
accepted generalized rules and regulations for cooperative ends. Hamilton, in the concluding issue of
the *Federalist* (No. 85), anticipates that the States
will form the Union by "compacts."

Up to and including the Constitution, however,
American social contracts have always been of limited scope. It has been generally believed, for instance, that man-made rules must not intervene
between the individual and his God. Thus the social
contract drawn up by Roger Williams in 1636, for
settlers in the then new town of Providence, specified
that it should apply "only in civil things." The
difference, and the danger, in Rousseau's *Contrat
Social* was in its all-inclusive, totalitarian nature. No
aspect of human life is excluded from the control
of that general will which Rousseau called "the
essence" of the social contract. In his own words:

> Chacun de nous met en commun sa personne et
> toute sa puissance sous la suprême direction de la
> volonté générale, et nous recevons en corps chaque
> membre comme partie indivisible du tout.[4]

Certain consequences follow inevitably from the
assumption that everybody "places in common his
person and all his power under the supreme direction of the general will." The thesis suggests, as
Rousseau himself proceeds to emphasize, that "whosoever refuses to obey the general will must in that

instance be restrained by the body politic, which actually means that he is forced to be free." [5] To most Americans this still seems an impossibly contradictory assumption—that one can be "forced to be free." But in the communist dogma it is a truism: one that traces directly to the above quotation.

The seductive argument of Rousseau is that a change in the character of individual self-determination is brought by the agency of the social contract. As and when it is adopted, whether actively or passively, man passes from the state of nature to the state of civilization. In so doing he exchanges his natural liberty for what Rousseau calls civil liberty. Or, as we may put it in English, under the social contract man exchanges Liberty—an individual attribute of varying intensity—for Freedom—an external condition created and controlled by social action.

It is politically significant that while the French use *liberté* extensively, their language has no word for "freedom." And while the Germans emphasize *Freiheit*, they have no word for "liberty." A good deal of the sharply differing history of these two great peoples might be deduced from these respective linguistic deficiencies. Since English is rich enough to possess the two words, at least the politically minded among us would do well to observe the subtle but very real distinction between them. Later we shall more closely consider the thesis that Liberty is an individual aspiration whereas Freedom is a generalized condition. As Rousseau says, the natural liberty of some must be restrained in order that the generality may enjoy civil liberty, or freedom. Conversely, however, the deprivation of freedom may well intensify the spiritual element in liberty.

There is no flaw in Rousseau's argument that society must have rules, and that those rules inevitably encroach on personality. If the warden permits me to play solitaire in my prison cell I am at liberty to cheat all I want; nobody else is affected thereby. But if my freedom is somewhat enlarged, to permit me to play bridge with three fellow-prisoners, I must observe the rules of the game, arbitrary though they may seem to me. For the freedom of a social game I have surrendered the liberty I had at solitaire. And if that simple illustration is acceptable, it goes a long way to prove that the social contract is a necessary consequence of social contact—is far from being mere "chaff and rags" as Edmund Burke so bitterly described it when the connection between the "general will" and the Reign of Terror in France became unmistakable.[6]

American political thinkers, instead of vainly denying validity to the doctrine of social contract, have concentrated on setting limits to its exploitation by political rulers. Where Rousseau is most open to criticism is for the conclusion logically drawn from his dogmatic assertion that a mystical general will is "the essence" of the social contract. Inevitably this means that the political sovereignty necessary to make the general will effective must be both indivisible and unquestionable. In both respects the American form of government is the living refutation of this argument. Sovereignty in this Republic is not merely divided, as it must be in any federation, but is also definitely limited in behalf of minorities as against majorities. It is perhaps too much to say that Madison's thinking denied any validity to the conception of a general will. But it was certainly careful to insure that if there is a general will it shall not at any time or place ride roughshod over the individual.

This is not only a matter of Constitutional guarantees. Protection is also afforded by the Common Law and by the clear distinction Americans make between society and state. Rousseau's refusal to admit any such distinction has been widely accepted in Europe, and is indeed a tenet of European socialistic as well as communistic thought. But American political thinking has preferred to follow the lead of John Locke, who in some respects anticipated Rousseau's idea of the social contract, but pointed out that it operates on both a private and a public level —a differentiation which Rousseau denied.

Locke's great influence on the founding fathers goes far to explain why the difference between society and state is generally recognized on this side of the Atlantic. Society is the voluntary collective action of individuals in areas where the state is not concerned. If the state is concerned whenever people gather for any purpose, as Rousseau implies, then of course the state absorbs society and the latter has no independent existence. Because the rules of society are voluntarily adopted they generally do not possess the coercive force of the laws that the state makes binding. And that is one reason why the state tends to encroach upon and diminish the areas controlled by society, which currently are becoming steadily less extensive everywhere.

On the moral scale, however, society is clearly a type of organization superior to the state, since its authority is based on individual agreement rather than on external coercion. Morally speaking, it is reactionary rather than progressive whenever the state expands its authority at the expense of society. Governmental handouts, subsidies and interventions of every kind, no matter how dressed up with a specious humanitarianism, are essentially coercive measures by the state, encroaching more and more on the voluntary action of society. The taxes paid by the individual, to support the expanding galaxy of governmental welfare measures, diminish by just that much what he might contribute under the promptings of his own conscience through associations and in directions of his own choosing.

Of course this truism does not imply that all voluntary associations are in themselves desirable; nor that they can be permitted to operate without any state control. A murderous teen-age gang is as much an expression of voluntary association as is a Sunday school. And we are all now familiar with the appalling corruption that has affected the leadership of a large portion of trade unionism in the United States. It is noteworthy, however, that juvenile delinquency has tended to increase with the extension of compulsory education, and that labor racketeering has developed with the legalization of compulsory trade unionism. There is a strong case for saying that the greater the degree of governmental intervention in the affairs of society, the greater will be the internal corruption of society, justifying—or being used to justify—ever more intervention and thereby an ever closer approach to totalitarianism. This regressive movement is certainly away from the course charted by the Constitution of the United States—and the fact that this tendency is commonly called "democratic" helps to explain why the founding fathers so hated and feared that seductive word.

The reason for their negative attitude is apparent from any close consideration of Rousseau's theory of the general will. If the general will is to become a reality all voluntary associations must be subject to rigorous governmental controls. The means by which this result is accomplished can properly be called democratic. The first adumbration of Rousseau's theory is in his early (1756) *Discourse on Inequality*, a social condition which he calls "the first source of all evils." Biologically absurd as this assertion is, it paves the way for the conception of the general will as set forth six years later in the *Social Contract*.

If all men are equal, not only before the law but in their physical, mental and spiritual composition, then any differences among individuals are wholly secondary, and the concept of a general will, binding them all in uniformity, ceases to be fantastic. By a reasonable development of the original fallacy Rousseau argues that every adult who subscribes to the general will thereby acquires citizenship. All being equal, all citizens must enjoy an equal voice in any elections that are permitted. The only exceptions are the wrong-headed individuals who deny validity to the concept of the general will.

The assumption that only the recalcitrant oppose the general will soon leads to the conclusion that it is always voiced by the majority and that dissenters therefrom are outlaws. They should, indeed, be regarded as worse than outlaws. By rejecting the fiction of the general will these "enemies of the people" may also be said to have rejected the fact of the social contract, of which the general will is "the essence." Dissenters are therefore self-defined traitors to the community based upon the social contract, and as such deserve extermination.

By the same token, however, adherence to the doctrine of the general will by somebody living under another political sovereignty makes him a *concitoyen,* who should if possible be liberated from bondage. Edmund Burke, who was one of the first to see the full implications of Rousseau's doctrine, estimated that in 1796 one-fifth of the influential people in England and Scotland were "pure Jacobins," eager to assist revolutionary France against their own country.[7]

This international aspect of Rousseau's democracy, developed in behalf of world revolution by the communists, has had a strong appeal for idealists who are properly appalled by the narrowness and bigotry of flamboyant nationalism. A system which simultaneously promises emancipation at home and brotherhood in foreign relations—*Liberté, Egalité, Fraternité*—could not fail to exert a strong emotional appeal, especially to youth. "Bliss was it in that dawn to be alive," declaimed the young Wordsworth at the outbreak of the French Revolution, "but to be young was very Heaven!" Much the same enthusiasm, in due course, was aroused in John Reed and other more modern Jacobins by the "Ten Days That Shook The World" from Russia.

If the concept of the general will had been voiced by itself, instead of being cleverly tied in with the valid theory of social contract, it would never have taken root and blossomed as is the case. The major fallacy is too obvious. In the last analysis some ruler must interpret and promulgate what is assumed to be the general will. The more sacrosanct the allegedly popular desire, the more authoritarian must be the power of those in a position to give it realization. A single, unified popular will obviously implies a single, unified governmental direction, to make the will effective. Moreover, in Rousseau's words: "La volonté générale est toujours droite et tend toujours à l'utilité publique." "The general will is always right, and always tends towards public utility." [8]

By "droit(e)" Rousseau very likely meant "straightforward" or "honorable." His revolutionary followers, however, for their own political purposes soon equated the word with "correct." With that translation the phrase has had momentous consequences. Since the general will must come to a precise conclusion in any particular issue, and if this single conclusion alone is "right," then there can be no justification for political opposition. The party that represents "the people" is the only one that speaks for democracy. It must not only dominate, but must extinguish all organized opposition to its program.

To see the implications of Rousseau's doctrine is to understand the bloody chaos of the French Revolution, the course of which was so profoundly influenced by his ideas. But Napoleon, when he successfully made himself the embodiment of the general will, did not attempt to eradicate a mystical concept so helpful to his ambitions. And under the strain of our times the concept has revived to give doctrinaire support to the ruthlessness of fascism, of nazism and of communism. In all these cases the theory of government has been essentially that inspired by Rousseau: the denial of local self-government in behalf of centralized power; the steady usurpation of the legislative and judicial functions by the executive; the elimination of any organized opposition to the *Fuehrer Prinzip;* the progressive encroachment on every form of free association by the state to the end that the latter alone directs, proclaims and rules—but always with ironic lip service to "the people."

If the concept of the general will brings dictatorship in its train at home, the result in foreign relations is no less certainly a continuous threat of war. The nearest approach to unanimity in the thinking of any community is always found when an enemy is present or effectively portrayed. Therefore any absolute ruler is likely to bolster his position by telling his subjects that their security, for which he takes all responsibility, is threatened. Beyond that, the spokesman of the general will can do much to promote a crusading and missionizing fervor—to bring the truth to those with less enlightened government.

The leaders of this messianic movement may, of course, renounce all conquest or imperial design, in keeping with their always humanitarian announcements. This was Robespierre's attitude early in the French Revolution, as it was Lenin's when communism gained control of Russia. But, even when sincere, such restraint is likely to give way before the more dynamic position of a successor—a Napoleon or Stalin—who must be aggressive in order to establish his own repute. Thus international stability is doubly disturbed, not only by the danger of aggression, but by the feeling that "preventive war" may be the best way to overcome a threat that is psychological as well as physical in nature.

The influence of Jean Jacques Rousseau has not been the less tremendous because many whose thinking has been affected by this warped genius are today unfamiliar even with his name.[9] To attribute the rise of the monolithic state entirely to the often inconsistent ideas of this one neurotic personality would of course be overdrawn. But what we do find in the doctrines of Rousseau is the evil seed from which, with cultivation, the brambles of modern totalitarianism have spread. Voltaire summed it up fairly, when he wrote to thank Rousseau for a presentation copy of the latter's *Discourse on Inequality*. "I have received your new book against the human race and thank you for it," said the great French cynic. "Never was such cleverness used in the design of making us all stupid! One longs, in reading your book, to walk on all fours."

And if in a large part of the world people no longer dare to walk upright, with their faces towards the heavens, it is in no small measure Rousseau's doing. "Man is born free," complained this enemy of the human race, "yet everywhere he is in chains." [10] After two centuries of experience with his remedial formula it is high time to bring the aphorism more in line with truth. Man is born in chains, yet under a government of limited and divided powers he may still be free.

FOUR

Marx Implements Rousseau

Without question, Rousseau's fiction of a general will has profoundly influenced, and continues profoundly to influence, American political thinking. It was joined with a theory of social contract which, in one form or another, had been implicit in the organization of every American frontier community. The almost pure democracy of a New England town meeting seemed in fact to illustrate the localized operation of a general will. During and immediately after the Revolution political democracy emphasized its central characteristic of intolerance by denying the minority rights of Tories who remained loyal to the British Crown. That consummate agitator, Tom Paine, was outstanding, rather than unique, as a skillful propagandist for Rousseau's ideas. These egalitarian seeds were scattered on American soil just as the socially democratic colonists were rising in revolt against British rule, and looking for a substitute form of government that would conform with their social customs as well as with their economic needs.

One might easily conclude, therefore, that the first of the "self-evident truths" proclaimed in the Declaration of Independence—"that all men are created equal"—was directly inspired by Rousseau. But of this there is no confirmatory evidence. Jefferson did not come under the influence of French egalitarianism until he went to Paris as Minister, after the American Revolution but prior to the much more profound upheaval there. Moreover, so far as the notes of Madison and others show, Rousseau was never once cited during the proceedings of the Constitutional Convention; nor is he ever mentioned in the *Federalist* papers.

This is not really surprising, since not even Tom Paine could speculate on the promulgation of a general will from a national capital before such a capital had been located. The entire hypothesis was academic, to say the least, when the immediate problem was the formation of a central government which could exercise some control over the independent and only loosely associated States. A Federal Republic was all that could be anticipated by the most convinced of the early American nationalists, like Alexander Hamilton and John Marshall. At the Philadelphia Convention the objective was not nationalism, but the preliminary stage of union. If anyone at that time had suggested even the possibility of a unified "general will," to be defined and exercised throughout the States from the seat of national government, he would have been denounced more roundly than was poor bumbling George III.

Nevertheless, it is a matter of record that the French apostles of Rousseau, if not the master himself, soon came into high favor in the fledgling United States. This was demonstrated by the adulation showered on Citizen Genêt, when he arrived here as Minister of the sanguinary French Republic, immediately after the execution of Louis XVI. It was Robespierre, the chief disciple of Rousseau, who had successfully engineered that tragic deed, approved by a bare majority of the Revolutionary Assembly in spite of all the pressures brought by "the man of virtue." But although the vote to guillotine the King was so close—387 against 334—it was nonetheless represented as "the general will" of France and as such found strong endorsement in the United States. With Genêt's arrival the underlying democratic surge burst forth, in many places and in many forms more dangerous than the poetic effusion with which cultured Boston heralded the act of regicide in Paris:

> See the bright flame arise,
> In yonder Eastern skies,
>   Spreading in veins.
> 'Tis pure Democracy
> Setting all nations free,
>   Melting their chains.

More worthy of recollection, in these days of communist cells, were the Jacobin Clubs which, with the open support of Genêt, sprang up in all our seacoast cities. They were named, of course, for the widespread organization through which Robespierre—until he himself was liquidated—directed the course of the French Revolution in line with Rousseau's concept of the general will, headquarters being the former chapel of the Jacobin monks in the rue Saint-Honoré. It was from these American Jacobin Clubs that Genêt organized what Foreign Minister Talleyrand called "the French party in America." The truly startling influence of Rousseau's adherents in the United States at this time is given careful consideration by Senator Albert J. Beveridge, in his famous biography of John Marshall, and can there be readily reviewed.[1]

American Jacobinism, however, ran contrary to the establishment of an American "general will." It worked against, not with, those, like John Marshall, who desired the strong central government necessary to give this faction effective expression. To their last member the Jacobin Clubs over here supported Jefferson and opposed the Federalists. These clubs, indeed, were the basis of Jefferson's Republican Party, which took that name to signify its sympathy with the revolutionary Republic of France. When Genêt was declared *persona non grata,* and the semi-treasonable activities of his Jacobin Clubs were exposed, they logically changed their names to Democratic Clubs. From these evolved the urban Democratic organizations like Tammany Hall, and in due course the Americans for Democratic Action of our own day, revealing its ancestry by its confidence in Rousseau's concept of the general will.

There is contemporary significance in the paradoxical fact that the Jacobin Clubs, which served in France to concentrate political power, were in this country organized by the followers of Rousseau to resist a similar concentration. As already pointed out, the general will in practice must become the personal or group will of those who have been able to seize power locally. After extending this concentrated power to the national confines there will be a halt, for purposes of consolidation. But if the concept of the general will is connected with a universal assumption, such as the equality of all men, or the exploitation of labor by capital, there is no reason to stop permanently at a political frontier. On the contrary, the establishment of a general will in a single powerful country then becomes a preliminary to its attempted establishment for all mankind. And if it is to be internationalized, those who have seized power nationally cannot look passively on the rise of another, possibly contradictory, general will in another country.

Consequently, the nation that gets a running start in this direction, as did France in 1792, or Russia in 1917, must work against nationalism in other lands, although of course it may as a tactical matter temporarily promote nationalism in colonial areas subject to its rivals. The vehicle for this subversive intrigue is the indigenous group which for various reasons is so discontented with the institutions of its own country that it will shift loyalty to the alien idea. And the fundamental task of this group, once organized, is to promote the general will for which it works, and to oppose the development of any other. Thus the Jacobin Clubs in the United States did their by no means trivial best to promote "the French interest" and to oppose the growth of American nationalism at the time of the French Revolution. And thus the essentially similar communist clubs, or "front" organizations, are today actively opposed to an American foreign policy antagonistic to that of Soviet Russia. Thomas Jefferson suffered from his "guilt by association" with Jacobins. And for the same reason contemporary Americans who merely seek a *modus vivendi* with Soviet Russia are liable to be labelled as "pro-communist."

This repetition of history would alone justify the emphasis placed on the role of Rousseau. But he is the more to be remembered because he was so unquestionably the progenitor of the modern totalitarian state, to the development of which the concept of the general will readily lends itself. That conclusion does not underestimate the influence of Karl Marx, generally and properly regarded as the prophet of communism. It is no discount of Marxism to point out that its powerful contribution has been to make Rousseau's more fundamental ideas effective. Practical accomplishment, as opposed to mere theorizing, was always the objective of this bitterly anti-Christian German Jew. As he himself wrote, shortly before the drafting of the famous *Communist Manifesto*: "The philosophers have only *interpreted* the world in various ways; the point is to *change* it." [2]

The leverage for change which Marx provided was his theory of class war. On the one side, as minutely analyzed in that turgid classic *Das Kapital*, are all the owners of property; on the other the propertyless, the "dispossessed" or "underprivileged," the proletariat. The effectiveness of this theory lay partly in its timing, coming when the industrial revolution was grouping large masses of unorganized workers in dingy factories, and partly in providing a channel for promoting Rousseau's conception of the general will. This channel, as Marx planned it, was to be labor organization. Through universal unionism, taking the direction of each factory unit out of the hands of the owners, the capitalistic exploiters would in their turn be expropriated, labor would come into its own and the general will fulfilled. Since this end was seen by Marx as wholly desirable, violent means to attain it were to him justifiable and indeed necessary because the propertied class, controlling the machinery of government, would itself use force to oppose the social revolution. Still another reason for communistic violence, Marx argued at great length, is the historic "inevitability" of the proletarian triumph. Since it *must* come, the sooner the better. "We are concerned with what the proletarian actually is; and what the proletariat will, in accordance with the nature of its own being, be historically compelled to do." [3]

The evolution of this thinking from that of the French Jacobins would be evident even if the early communists among them, like Morelli, Babeuf and Buonarroti, had not already laid down the lines Marx elaborated.[4] The doctrine of egalitarianism is useful for starting social revolution and during the transition to the new order the "dictatorship of the proletariat"—which is reasonably called democracy because the proletarians are the great majority—will prevail. But actually the dictatorship must be exercised by a dedicated elite, supported by the one authentic party that represents the general will.

Eventually, the Marxists surmised, the totalitarian state thus created will "wither away." When the workers of the world have united to cast off the chains of capitalism everywhere, there will no longer be any reason for national governments. The general will of mankind, not merely that of a particular locality, will have been fulfilled. It is difficult to conclude that Marx himself, who relied on passion and hatred to gain his ends, ever believed in this vision of a nationless world, held together by benevolent ties of human brotherhood. The idealistic picture, however, has been of great propaganda value to communism and has also served to distinguish it from the nationalist totalitarian systems of fascism, nazism and falangism.

Parliamentary socialism, strong in Western Europe and growing stronger in the United States under the deceptive alias of "liberalism," likewise is a direct offshoot from the theories of Rousseau and Marx, differing from communism not in basic theory but in application. The parliamentary socialist believes with Marx that capitalists should be dispossessed, and he believes with Rousseau that there should be no constitutional impediments to the attainment of the general will to this effect. In Great Britain the Labor Party, under predominantly socialist leadership, has now successfully eliminated most of these impediments to political democracy and—to Britain's cost—they are unlikely to be restored.[5] In the United States, as in Switzerland and the West German Federal Republic, the principle of federalism blocks all-out political democracy. This obstacle is particularly powerful in the United States because here federalism is supplemented by the careful separation of executive, judicial and legislative powers. Because the American system is so clearly and positively anti-socialist few Americans are willing to admit to that political affiliation, but prefer to seek the same end of centralized and unified governmental power under more euphonious labels.

The parliamentary socialist, whether or not masquerading as a "liberal," is less fanatical, more internationally minded, and therefore more humane, than the fascist or nazi, who puts the myths of national or racial grandeur above all else. Nevertheless, any type of socialism must tend towards national socialism, because of its complete reliance on an enlarged and empowered national government to attain its ends. Hitler, who was a thoroughgoing if highly disagreeable socialist, was at least constructive in shattering the fantastic belief that socialism is helpful and capitalism hostile to international amity —the exact opposite of which is more nearly the truth. The socialists, or "liberals," are also less logical than their more offensive communist cousins in thinking that socialism can eventually triumph peacefully everywhere, by using fabian, parliamentary tactics. If the concept of the general will is granted any validity it will follow that it cannot be localized by arbitrary frontiers. It must be promulgated from the directive center over as wide an area as fanaticism permits, whether that center be Paris, as it was after 1792, Moscow, as it has been since 1917, or Peiping, as it could be tomorrow.

Socialism in the United States, under whatever name, has been enormously helped by the Jeffersonian half-truth that "all men are created equal," which when quoted usually omits the immediately following and qualifying phrase "that they are endowed by their Creator with certain unalienable rights." It *is* self-evident that men are created equal in the sense that all have much the same basic needs and in the sense that all who are sound in body and mind are to be regarded as parties to whatever social contracts their communities may see fit to adopt. But at that point the line is, or should be, drawn, as it so clearly was in Jefferson's thinking.

To assert that men should have equal opportunity is to imply that with this opportunity they will become unequal. Some will push ahead and others will fall behind. "From the hour of their birth," to return to Aristotle, "some are marked out for subjection, others for rule." [6] That biological fact can be concealed by sophistries, but cannot be successfully denied. Moreover, as Calhoun so cogently pointed out, no system of government devised by man can prevent those who collect the taxes from dominating those who pay the taxes. What the "more perfect" system can do is to insure that those who have the taxing power possess it only provisionally, and within clear-cut limits. Under such a system human happiness can be pursued, if not effectively caught, in literally countless lines of competing endeavor.

Where political power is concentrated and unlimited, as it must be under the theory of the general will, the unscrupulous are always likely to rise to the top. The true liberal, who recognizes and cherishes the infinite variety of human nature, is by that fact alone estopped from issuing glib commands in the name of "the people." Here and there, for a brief period, a philosopher-king, a Marcus Aurelius, may fill the dictatorial role. But the odds are enormously in favor of the Neroes. It is of course bitterly ironical that, starting from the assumption of human equality, fake liberalism moves so easily to the conclusion of the one indispensable man. But that is merely another way of saying with Plato that the constant tendency of democracy is to slide into dictatorship.

For Americans the problem is especially poignant, since in their country and there alone was it carefully planned to keep political power diffused, in order to promote the individual as well as the general welfare. The validity of the social contract in Rousseau's political philosophy was admitted and indeed affirmed—by writing a Constitution in the name of the people which was eventually ratified, on the fulfilled understanding of a specific Bill of Rights, by all the States. His concept of the general will, however, was completely rejected, not only by establishing a central government of balanced powers, but also by withholding all but enumerated powers from the central government as such.

This system, though now more honored in the breach than the observance, would seem to mean that the fiction of the general will, and its Marxist realization in the form of totalitarian democracy, will never take root in the United States. The majority will is severely circumscribed, is binding only in the field of delegated powers, and even there is subject to many specific restrictions: "No bill of attainder or ex post facto law shall be passed." "No money shall be drawn from the Treasury, but in consequence of appropriations made by law." "Congress shall make no law respecting an establishment of religion, or prohibiting the free exercise thereof." "No person . . . shall be compelled in any criminal case to be a witness against himself . . . nor shall private property be taken for public use, without just compensation."

A political system in which the majority will is so carefully restricted cannot with any pretense of accuracy be called a "democracy." Those who wish to destroy the Federal Republic, and build a unified totalitarian dictatorship on the ruins, will understandably seek to spread confusion as to what the nature of our government is. Intentional subversion, however does not fully explain why so many of unquestionable patriotism so frequently assert that our political system is the socialistic democracy which it originally sought to avert. Nor is political ignorance so complete as to explain the mystery. For the full explanation, we must recall some American history.

FIVE

The Issue Disrupts the Union

The federal system of the United States is incompatible with political democracy, construed in terms of the nation-wide enforcement of Rousseau's general will. Yet federalism in no way discourages democratic government in any and all of the States considered separately. On the contrary, the principle of federalism serves to maintain all the many advantages of majority rule while preventing its degeneracy into dictatorship. Failure to realize that democracy functions best when localized, and worst when centralized, accounts for much of the confusion that surrounds the term. This is the more curious because, ever since colonial settlement, there have been great differences between the degrees of political democracy operative in, for instance, New Hampshire and South Carolina.

There is much more than political theory behind such differences between the States. But leaving factors such as climatic and cultural variation temporarily aside, it is still obvious that the essence of federalism lies in the reservation of a certain degree of sovereignty by the constituent parts. A federation is designed to prevent the full concentration of sovereignty in the central government. Therefore, at the risk of repetition, a federal system is by its very nature out of key with the domination of any "general will" expressed in terms of national majorities or centralized interpretation.

It does not follow, however, that federalism and democracy are necessarily antagonistic. While the United States as a whole is not a democracy, many of the States as units may lay claim to that description if it pleases them. Illustrations are found in the lead given by New York in abolishing imprisonment for debt; by Wisconsin when it established the first State income tax; by Nebraska when it eliminated its State Senate; by Georgia when it lowered the voting age to eighteen. Indeed, one of the great virtues of federalism is the power given to the constituent units to adopt experimental measures in accordance with the wishes of local majorities, without imposing such developments on sections not ready or willing to go along.

Political democracy is thus localized and qualified, but in no sense denied, under the American system. And, as already pointed out, democracy in the United States is actually saved from its suicidal characteristics by being limited. So there is some justification for loosely calling the Republic a "democracy," though it is much more accurate and discerning to prefer the adjective and call it "democratic."

Such discrimination is the more imperative because there is a point at which conciliation between the advocates of federalism and those of nationalistic democracy becomes impossible. That point was reached in 1861, and since the federal structure was not formally altered by the Civil War, the "irrepressible conflict" can always break forth again, though scarcely in the same sanguinary form. The local termination of services like public education, rather than any breakdown of government as such, is today threatened by disregard for the elements of division and balance in our political system. And such frustration can easily be produced by embittered antagonism between federalists and national democrats—between followers of Madison and followers of Rousseau, to clarify by over-simplification. To avert this frustration is clearly a primary duty of good citizenship, which is certainly assisted by at least some acquaintance with the major conflicts in American constitutional history.

As will now be emphasized, the two contrasting threads of federalism and democracy run through the entire skein of our national evolution. Indeed, their interweaving forms its major pattern, the general beauty of which itself suggests that the threads are by no means necessarily inharmonious. But whenever restraint is absent from our political leadership they tend to become so. This happens when federalists forget that no system which ignores the general welfare can long endure; and when democrats forget that the centralization which they espouse is much more likely to destroy than to advance democracy.

In the formation of our government, Alexander Hamilton was the great exponent of centralization. He attacked the whole idea of a federal republic, which he predicted with accuracy would at best divide loyalty between the "general government" and those of the States and could easily, as it did, produce civil war and national disruption. To avert this outcome he argued that power in the central government should be more fully concentrated in the executive branch, under a President with an absolute veto, holding office not for a set term but "during good behaviour." Failing in his effort to make the President comparable to an elected monarch, Hamilton was nevertheless influential in giving the Senate privileges which made it in some respects comparable to the British House of Lords of that period.[1]

Although opposed to federalism, there was certainly nothing even remotely democratic in Hamilton's thought. Whether or not he ever called the public "a great beast," he certainly regarded political democracy as a snare and delusion, roundly denouncing its "vices" on many occasions. Brilliantly and courageously cynical, Hamilton had no faith whatsoever in the ability of the common man to understand even his own immediate political interest. Precisely because of human stupidity, he reasoned, society must accept strong government by an entrenched elite, or else expect to succumb to anarchy. In his speech of June 18, 1787, to the Constitutional Convention, he said, in behalf of a life-term Senate, to be chosen by an electoral college of landowners: "All communities divide themselves into the few and the many. The first are the rich and well-born; the other the mass of the people . . . turbulent and changing, they seldom judge or determine right. Give therefore to the first class a distinct, permanent share in the Government. . . . Nothing but a permanent body can check the imprudence of democracy." [2]

To Alexander Hamilton, as this quotation illustrates, the concept of a general will was not merely utterly absurd, but also wholly pernicious. But while

his political thinking was poles apart from that of
Rousseau, it led to the same institutional conclusion
of strongly centralized government. Frequently, in
political philosophy, the wheel thus comes full circle,
so that extreme right and extreme left approve the
same ends, though with different slogans and from
opposite motives. The hallmark of authentic liberalism, of which Thomas Jefferson and James Madison
are the classic American exemplars, is its continuous
awareness of this double jeopardy to the condition
of freedom, and its continuous anxiety to steer the
narrow course between the two associated extremes
—called communism and fascism in modern political
parlance.

Jefferson favored federalism because a strongly
centralized government is always likely to deprive
men of the freedom which he thought, to that extent
with Rousseau, should be their birthright. This creed
made him democratic, and his mistrust of unpopular
government was at least as sharply voiced as Hamilton's confidence in the unfettered judgment of aris-
tocrats. But Jefferson drew sharp limits around the
doctrine of political democracy, as all who give it
any serious consideration must. He disregarded his
own "metaphysical subtleties"—as he himself defined
them—to ram the Louisiana Purchase down the
throat of a Congress which mistrusted both its constitutionality and desirability. In justifying his han-
dling of Aaron Burr's conspiracy Jefferson wrote
that "in an encampment expecting daily attack from
a powerful enemy, self-preservation is paramount to
all law. . . ." Despite his idealistic faith in human
nature Jefferson knew that in times of emergency
unqualified democracy simply does not work.

"Should we have ever gained our Revolution," he asked rhetorically, "if we had bound our hands by manacles of the law . . . ?" [3]

So Jefferson and Hamilton, the great protagonists of American political division, drew a clear issue between federalism and centralization, but not between federalism and democracy. These do not become opposites until the advocates of centralization demand it in the name of democracy, a non sequitur which Hamilton was far too intelligent ever to endorse. Democracy and centralization, however, began to be equated in popular thinking on the heels of the bitter Presidential election of 1824, which marked the breakup of the "Virginia dynasty." With the passing of the generation that had written, ratified and launched the Constitution a new issue came to the fore in American politics. This was the unnecessary but always easily possible antagonism between those who put federal structure above democratic desires, and vice versa.

In 1824, all of the four Presidential and six Vice-Presidential candidates significantly called themselves "Republican." This so divided the electoral vote that the election was thrown into the House of Representatives (under Article II and the Twelfth Amendment) for the second and as yet the last time in our history. Its election of John Quincy Adams was certainly most undemocratic, for Adams had trailed Andrew Jackson in both the electoral and popular vote, so far as the latter was then tabulated. Irritation over what seemed so unfair an outcome was instrumental in the decision of Jackson's supporters to call their party "Democratic," although the name did not become firmly established until

Van Buren ran under that label. For the first time a political party was then implicitly committed to that endorsement of outright majority rule which the founding fathers had so carefully avoided.

Another important political consequence of the 1824 election was the development of the Presidential nominating convention, replacing the Congressional caucus by which the candidates had earlier been selected. By 1840 the convention system was well established and has had the effective result of placing each party squarely behind one Presidential, and one Vice-Presidential, candidate. The degree of democracy in this method of nomination will be examined later. But the acute comment of Viscount Bryce may be quoted here. The invention of the nominating convention, he wrote:

> coincides with and represents the complete democratization of politics in Jackson's time. It suits both the professionals, for whom it finds occupation, and whose power it secures, and the ordinary citizen who, not having leisure to attend to politics, likes to think that his right of selecting candidates is recognized by committing the selection to delegates whom he is entitled to vote for.[4]

Jackson favored the idea of nominating conventions as democratic. His great antagonist, John C. Calhoun, opposed the institution as demagogic. That difference of opinion symbolizes the fundamental antagonism between the two. The opposition between these rival giants was just as sharp as that between Hamilton and Jefferson. It set the stage for the Civil War and established a cleavage in American politics which is clear, and of renewed importance, today.

The strong similarities in the background and character of Calhoun and Jackson make their rivalry the more interesting. Both were of the same Scotch-Irish, Calvinistic, recently immigrant ancestry. They were alike in physique, in energy, in high intelligence and indomitable courage. Both were born, though Calhoun was fifteen years the younger, in the Carolina foothills, under the shadow of the Blue Ridge. But it was the ironic destiny of the puritanical Calhoun to marry into and become the leader of the plantation aristocracy, while the more cavalier Jackson moved West, rising as the spokesman of pioneer democracy with the national reputation brought him by the battle of New Orleans.[5]

Their differences were sharpened by their likenesses. Jackson was preeminently the practical politician and Calhoun the brilliant political theorist, though the older man was by no means devoid of book learning, and though the Yale-trained scholar was certainly not of the cloistered type. Each had the ability and the personality to form and lead a political party. When the exigencies of politics made the younger man Jackson's Vice President, in 1828, the opportunity was also provided, by the sheer inability of these team-mates to agree on any issue—from the social acceptability of that "gorgeous hussy," Peggy Eaton, up to the basic character of American government.

In the Hamilton versus Jefferson alignment those favoring democracy had been, with Jefferson, opposed to centralization. Now the more ardent the democrat—with a small "d"—the more likely he was to discount federal theory in behalf of centralization. When Jackson raised the banner of nationalistic democracy, Calhoun turned against nationalism and became the sectional leader of strictly Constitutional federalism. It would have made the picture more clear if Calhoun had then formed a Southern Constitutionalist party, just as it would have clarified our recent politics if the Southern Democrats had made a clean break on essentially the same issue. But, in the eighteen-forties, this would have handicapped Calhoun's effort to unite the agricultural South and West against the industrial North, thereby offsetting the growing influence of Abolitionist New England in Washington. Then, as now, it was politically advantageous to conceal the fact that the Democratic Party was so deeply split. Then, as now, it would have been inopportune to admit that a large section of that party was not democratic in any national sense.

The work of John Marshall, meantime, had served to alarm all slave owners and develop a cleavage between the advocates of State's Rights and those of nationalistic democracy. As Chief Justice from 1801 to 1835—vitally formative years—Marshall most ably confirmed Alexander Hamilton's doctrine of "implied powers" and developed it to give the infant Republic a stronger central government. The opinions of this great jurist were certainly not democratic, but they encouraged that nationalism without which the democratic urge is localized and restricted.

The first and most famous of the Marshall decisions—in *Marbury v. Madison*—established that implied right of the Court to nullify an Act of Congress which is so clearly an undemocratic principle of our system. Subsequent decisions, built on this, were directed to enlargement of the national power at State expense. In *Fletcher v. Peck* (1810) Marshall annulled an act passed by the Legislature of Georgia, informing the State in prophetic words that it was only "a part of a large empire . . . a member of the American union . . . which opposes limits to the legislatures of the several states." This was followed by *McCullough v. Maryland* (1819) in which the Chief Justice demolished an attempt by that State to tax an agency of the central government. The same year witnessed the *Dartmouth College Case*, whereby Marshall struck down an Act of the New Hampshire Legislature infringing the charter granted to the college under British rule. The implication was that the central government, not those of the States, had inherited sovereignty over corporate charters from the British Crown. Marshall, however, stopped short of suggesting that the State governments were or ever might be superfluous. "No political dreamer," he said—perhaps pointing at Hamilton—"was ever wild enough to think of breaking down the lines which separate the States, and of compounding the American people into one common mass."

Divergent political philosophies do not of themselves stir passionate feelings in human breasts. But if the philosophy is directly associated with an economic interest, or with a racial prejudice, or possibly with both—then personal emotion is fortified and strengthened by use of the abstract idea. It makes individual self-interest collective and binds the parts firmly together with the mortar of honorable principle.

That was what happened, in both North and

South, when the seeds of civil war began to sprout. The centralizing decisions of John Marshall, the democratic tendencies of Andrew Jackson, the rapid industrialization of the North with the help of free immigrant labor—these were primary factors in uniting the agricultural South behind the doctrine of States' Rights and in defense of slavery. We shall not understand the inherited problems that the Union confronts today if we think that the slavery issue did more than exacerbate the constitutional issue. Slavery could have been ended peacefully, for it was actually neither essential to, nor dominant in, the Southern economy.[6] As fundamental as a cause of conflict were the opposing interpretations of our form of government, foreshadowed in the rivalry of Hamilton and Jefferson, crystallized by the antagonisms of Jackson and Calhoun.

The flame that was to spread like a forest fire—of which the embers are by no means extinct—was sparked by the high protective tariff of 1828. This law might have been written by Hamilton himself, so firmly was it based on the nationalistic principle, laid down in his famous *Report on Manufactures*, that trade barriers are desirable in order to foster domestic industry.

This "tariff of abominations," as the injured exporters of cotton called it, was actually passed by Congress towards the end of the John Quincy Adams Administration, under the promptings of his New England support. Its constitutionality, and indeed the constitutionality of any protective tariff law, was immediately questioned by all who had an interest in maintaining the supremacy of King Cotton. Jackson, fearful of losing the agrarian support which had brought him to power, vacillated; and Calhoun immediately pressed his advantage, although in 1816 he had seemed to endorse the principle of a protective tariff as "calculated to bind together more closely our widely-spread Republic." Now Calhoun was agreeing with that misanthropic genius, John Randolph of Roanoke, who observed that: "To ask a State to surrender part of her sovereignty is like asking a lady to surrender part of her chastity."

On November 4, 1832, the South Carolina Nullification Convention assembled in Columbia, most of the delegates wearing the blue cockades that defined them as outright secessionists. Calhoun himself opposed any such intent. But if a State can declare a national law inoperative in its territory, the further claim of a right to complete political independence is at least partially established. "The driveling old dotard in the White House," as South Carolinians called President Jackson, saw this clearly. His reply to the Nullification Resolution was a proclamation declaring that: "The Constitution . . . forms a government, not a league. . . . To say that any State may secede . . . is to say that the United States is not a nation." [7]

Calhoun, however, was not denying that the United States is a nation. He was denying that it is a centralized democracy; and he was arguing, with impressive logic, that the more democratic a government becomes, the closer to dictatorship it gets. "The government of the absolute majority," he told the Senate, "is but the government of the strongest interests; and when not effectively checked, is the most tyrannical and oppressive that can be devised."

To read the Constitution is to realize that "No free system was ever farther removed from the principle that the absolute majority, without check or limitation, ought to govern." And then, in a conclusion expanding the Jeffersonian doctrine of Interposition:

> To maintain the ascendancy of the Constitution over the law-making majority is the great and essential point on which the success of the [American] system must depend; unless that ascendancy can be preserved, the necessary consequence must be that the laws will supersede the Constitution; and, finally, the will of the Executive, by the influence of its patronage, will supersede the laws; indications of which are already perceptible. This ascendancy can only be preserved through the action of the States, as organized bodies, having their own separate governments, and possessed of the rights, under the structure of our system, of judging the extent of their separate powers, and of interposing their authority to arrest the enactments of the General Government within their respective limits.[8]

Thus the heretofore blended issues of federalism and democracy became sharply antagonistic. Even at the risk of civil war the rights of the States must be defended against the will of the absolute majority, for if they are not so defended the United States will in any case be destroyed, becoming first a united state and then an executive dictatorship, as have other democracies before it. Calhoun himself, however, argued that this emphasis on federal structure is not in fact opposed to the theory of democracy, but only to its suicidal aspects. What the federal system does is to refine democracy by requiring a *concurrent* majority. The majority will in the nation as a whole must be endorsed by the majority will in each of its constituent parts, whenever the degree of sovereignty assured those parts by the Constitution is called in question. To assert this is not to support secession, but merely the essential principle of federal union. For none can deny that the sovereign States of their own free will created this union. The union did not create the pre-existent States.

There is no question that Calhoun's argument was both historically sound and strongly reasoned. Its influence, and perhaps also the evidence that South Carolina was ready to fight for its beliefs, compelled Jackson to back down. "The tariff of abominations" was modified to be a revenue measure only, but was coupled with the passage of an act authorizing the national government to collect tariff revenues by force if necessary. The South Carolina convention accepted the concession but reaffirmed the doctrine of Nullification and indeed directed it against the Revenue Collection Act, which was never enforced, any more than Integration is likely to be enforced by national troops in South Carolina today.

And so the issue was tided over until, eleven years after Calhoun's death, its settlement moved from argument to arms.

SIX

The Fourteenth Amendment

The Civil War did not of itself affect the federal structure of the Republic. Except for the separation of West Virginia from its parent State, early in the struggle, no physical boundaries were in any way altered. When the always dubious right of secession was effectively denied, all the other, less contestable, rights of the States were inferentially reaffirmed. That the rebellious States had never actually left the Union was the magnanimous and farsighted thesis defended by both President Lincoln and by his ill-starred successor in the White House, President Andrew Johnson. This argument of course strengthened the constitutional case for the victorious side—the war was fought to preserve and not to destroy the Union—and was given explicit confirmation by the Supreme Court in the case of *Texas v. White,* in 1869. Nevertheless, during the political aftermath of the conflict, the cause of federalism was profoundly and permanently weakened.

The major cause of this weakening concentrates in one of the three Constitutional Amendments (Thirteenth, Fourteenth and Fifteenth) which were immediate results of the hostilities. The Thirteenth Amendment, with admirable brevity, merely abolishes slavery and "involuntary servitude, except as a punishment for crime, whereof the party shall have been duly convicted. . . ." The Fifteenth Amendment with equal succinctness prohibits limitation of the franchise "by the United States, or by any State, on account of race, color, or previous condition of servitude." If the word "sex" had been added to this list there would have been no occasion for the complementary Woman's Suffrage (Nineteenth) Amendment, adopted in 1920.

In both the Thirteenth and Fifteenth Amendments, however, as well as the Fourteenth and Nineteenth, there is a brief terminal section saying, in all four cases: "The Congress shall have power to enforce this article by appropriate legislation." No such provision is to be found in the original Constitution, nor in any of the first twelve Amendments. This seemingly insignificant innovation has served to advance the power of the Congress as contrasted with that of either the executive or judiciary.

Legislation written "to enforce" the Constitution appears itself to possess a certain constitutional sanction. If the executive vetoes such legislation he can be depicted as striking at the Constitution itself, an interpretation which in effect asserts that he has violated his oath of office and is therefore properly subject to impeachment. If the judiciary strikes down a law ostensibly designed to enforce the Constitution it too can be said to be acting *ultra vires*. All legislation passed by the Congress is presumed to be constitutional unless and until shown to be otherwise. All legislation that is constitutional necessarily "enforces" the Constitution. So there is really no place for a separate category of statutes which pretend to be especially essential to the operation of the organic law.

The balance of power among the three arms of central government was thus definitely, though unobtrusively, disturbed by this Congressional encroachment. And insofar as the Congress directly represents the people this important change was a definite step towards democratization of the American form of government. The permanence of this alternation of the traditional balance was reaffirmed when the same enforcement clause was, more than half a century later, attached to the Nineteenth Amendment.

There is little doubt that the major credit, or discredit, for this deft alteration of constitutional balance is attributable to one extremely able politician. And there is equally little doubt that this man—Thaddeus Stevens, of Pennsylvania—was much more of a political philosopher, in the direct tradition of Rousseau, than is generally realized. Whether or not Thad Stevens was an illegitimate son of Talleyrand, as legend has it, he certainly brought the leveling spirit of the French Revolution into American politics, and this at a time when the emotions stirred by the Civil War had made the country ripe for it. More than any other Congressional leader before or since, this Representative from Lancaster regarded himself as a personification of that "general will" which necessarily becomes merciless to all who oppose it. "Had he lived in France in the days of the Terror," says Claude G. Bowers, "he would have . . . risen rapidly to the top through his genius and audacity and will, and probably have died by the guillotine with a sardonic smile upon his face. Living in America when he did, he was to . . . impose his revolutionary theories upon the country by sheer determination." [1]

The Thirteenth Amendment, abolishing slavery, had finally received Congressional approval in January, 1865, of course without votes from Southern representation since the war was then still raging. There were thirty-six states, eleven of which were or had been in the tottering Confederacy. Lincoln's opinion, based on the thesis that these eleven had never really left the Union, was that a three-fourths majority of the entire thirty-six, meaning twenty-seven States, would be necessary for ratification. States that had seceded were being readmitted under variants of the generous "Ten Per Cent Plan," whereby that percentage of the electorate of 1860, having taken a prescribed loyalty oath, could reestablish a State government which would resume its place in the Union. After Lincoln's assassination the same procedure was followed by Andrew Johnson, who as its Military Governor had himself brought Tennessee back into the fold. On this basis, as the fighting ended, the Thirteenth Amendment rapidly secured the necessary number of State ratifications, in the South as well as the North, the twenty-seventh and culminating act being that of Georgia, on December 6, 1865.

But to close the chapter of civil war without taking revenge on the fallen foe, and without doing more for egalitarianism than merely freeing the slaves, was far from the intent of the Radical Republicans in Congress. The national legislature had convened two days before the ratification by Georgia and its first action was a refusal even to consider the admission of Southern members chosen under the formula satisfactory to the White House. The former Confederate States, said Thaddeus Stevens, "ought never to be recognized as capable of acting in the Union, or of being counted as valid States, until the Constitution shall have been so amended . . . as to secure perpetual ascendancy to the party of the Union." [2]

It was what is now the Fourteenth Amendment that Stevens had in mind. By it he and his associates proposed to secure full citizenship for the Negroes, together with unimpeded male suffrage and what were even then called "civil rights." The undertaking was necessarily revolutionary since most of the States, Northern as well as Southern, had long had laws in many ways discriminatory against even free Negroes and there was certainly no strictly constitutional way in which Congress could override these various aspects of segregation. The Thirteenth Amendment having been ratified, the initial step, indicative of tactics still to come, was to validate its Southern ratifications, but then to exclude Southern representation from consideration of the forthcoming civil rights amendment.[3] And the stated objective of "perpetual ascendancy" for the Republican Party helps to reveal Stevens' remarkable affinity for the single dominant party demanded by Rousseau's concept of the general will.

The mechanism through which this consummate politician operated was, in the first instance, the Joint Committee on Reconstruction. Here he was far too astute to tie himself down with the chairmanship, leaving that post, with mock deference, to one of his Senate henchmen. Never since Stevens' time has a majority leader of the House of Repre-

sentatives been able so skillfully to control the
Senate. His chief deputy there was Senator Sumner
of Massachusetts, who at least rates high in the an-
nals of political vilification for his description of
President Johnson as "an insolent, drunken brute, in
comparison with which [*sic*] Caligula's horse was
respectable." [4] The case of the Radicals against
much maligned Andrew Johnson, however, was not
his pathetic lapse from sobriety at his inauguration,
but his resolute refusal to take any unconstitutional
shortcuts along the thorny path of reconstruction.

The memory of Andrew Johnson, soon to be im-
peached and all but convicted of criminal conduct
in the Presidential office, is still unfairly tainted by
the vitriolic attacks of the Radical Republicans.
But his strongest defenders admit that he played
into the hands of the coldly calculating Congressional leadership. Johnson's effort to check this 39th
Congress was by profuse use of the veto, which was
sustained in the first bill (Freedmen's Bureau) endeavoring to eliminate racial discrimination. But that
temporary check to Congress only increased the
pressure to attain the Radical objectives by the constitutional amendment which Stevens and his colleagues really wanted. In May and June of 1866,
after a most stormy session, the Fourteenth Amendment was approved by both Houses with well over
the requisite two-thirds majorities in each. Because
of the size of these majorities the President had no
option other than to let it be submitted to the States
for ratification or rejection. And the timing of
the Radical strategy was perfect, with the elections
to the 40th Congress coming up at a moment when

every critic of the Amendment could be stigmatized as "pro-Rebel."

This political motive explains the extraordinary drafting of the Fourteenth Amendment, which not only pulls together unrelated subjects but also unhappily enshrines in the Constitution transitory issues which could have been handled far better by ordinary, easily revisable legislation. Thus, Section 2 was designed to pressure the South to grant Negro suffrage by reducing the Congressional and Electoral College representation of any State in proportion to its abridgement of the right to vote. As seen in restrospect this was a wholly unworkable formula. The admitted purpose of this section was to make people think that the election of Radical Congressmen would assure full citizenship to the emancipated slaves.[5] Its one constructive result was the elimination of that sorry compromise in Article I of the original Constitution which counted slaves and indentured servants as three-fifths of "the whole number of free persons" for purposes of national representation.

Section 3 of the Fourteenth Amendment, denying civil rights and military office to the leaders of the Confederacy, until removal of the disability by two-thirds vote of Congress, was also temporary legislation wholly out of place in the organic law. It is only of melancholy historic interest today, but in 1866 was undeniably effective election propaganda of the "Hang-the-Kaiser" type. Much the same must be said of Section 4, which voided all debts of the Confederacy while affirming those of the United States in language which has no current meaning. These three vindictive sections, however, had the desired and anticipated effect of diverting contemporary attention from the permanently significant first Section of the Amendment, which has had and continues to have profound effect on the federal structure of the Republic. Section 1 of the Fourteenth Amendment says:

All persons born or naturalized in the United States, and subject to the jurisdiction thereof, are citizens of the United States and of the State wherein they reside. No State shall make or enforce any law which shall abridge the privileges or immunities of citizens of the United States; nor shall any State deprive any person of life, liberty, or property without due process of law; nor deny to any person within its jurisdiction the equal protection of the laws.

The first sentence of this was designed to establish, beyond any question, the full citizenship of all American Negroes in perpetuity, those who were free before the Emancipation Proclamation as well as those whose freedom was then established and confirmed by the Thirteenth Amendment. It further confirms the federal principle of dual citizenship, though now for the first time that of the nation was given constitutional primacy over citizenship in any of the States. This disarming approach, however, served largely to conceal the anti-federal, pro-national import of what follows.

The Philadelphia Convention of course confronted the question of which government—general or State—should be responsible for the protection of life, liberty and property. And with little debate it was decided that this should be a local function.

This is evidenced by the fact that internal police power, except for the F.B.I., is still out of the hands of the central government, but there is also abundant contemporary proof. Thus, in No. 45 of the *Federalist*, Madison examines the assertion that powers delegated by the States to the Union "will be dangerous to the portion of authority left in the several States." He notes first that "The State governments may be regarded as constituents and essential parts of the federal government; whilst the latter is nowise essential to the operation or organization of the former." Soon thereafter he concludes: "The powers reserved to the several States will extend to all the objects which, in the ordinary course of affairs, concern the lives, liberties and properties of the people; and the internal order, improvement and prosperity of the State."

This assurance, however, was not deemed sufficient by those who with good reason feared future encroachment by the central government. So in the Fifth Amendment, as part of the Bill of Rights, it was specified that "No person shall be . . . deprived of life, liberty or property without due process of law; nor shall private property be taken for public use without just compensation." This, as well as all the other articles in the Bill of Rights, were designed and adopted as limitations on the central government, in behalf of the States and the citizens thereof, as so clearly put in the Tenth and crowning Amendment: "The powers not delegated to the United States by the Constitution or prohibited by it to the States, are reserved to the States respectively, or to the people."

Building on the Dartmouth College case, the first

section of the Fourteenth Amendment upset this balance, giving Congress for the first time power to enforce, in all the States, rights as to which it had previously possessed no power to legislate. This was frankly and openly stated at the time. Representative John A. Bingham, an Ohio lawyer and a very able lieutenant of Thaddeus Stevens, was primarily responsible for phrasing this ominous section and made its purport clear on the floor of the House on May 19, 1866, just before that body approved the whole Fourteenth Amendment by a vote of 128 to 37, the Senate approving 33 to 11 on June 8. There was a "want" in the Constitution, said Mr. Bingham, which explained "the necessity for the first section of this Amendment." That want "is the power in the people, the whole people of the United States, by express authority of the Constitution, to do that by Congressional enactment which hitherto they have not had the power to do, and have never even attempted to do; that is, to protect by national law the privileges and immunities of all the citizens of the Republic, and the inborn rights of every person within its jurisdiction, whenever the same shall be abridged or denied by the unconstitutional acts of any State."

In some of these, Mr. Bingham continued, "Contrary to the express letters of your Constitution, 'cruel and unusual punishments' have been inflicted under State laws within this Union upon citizens, not only for crimes committed, but for sacred duty done, for which and against which the Government of the United States had provided no remedy and could provide none." [6]

Alleged violation of the Eighth Amendment, pro-

In promoting the Fourteenth Amendment, however, the Congress usurped power in a manner explicable only by the Radical exploitation of post-war emotionalism and excusable from no viewpoint. What happened was that the Southern States, with the single exception of Tennessee, within eight months flatly rejected the Amendment as certified to them in June, 1866. In several cases these rejections were by unanimous vote of both Houses; in all, by heavy majorities. Faced with this seeming impasse, and the collapse of all their plotting, the Stevens junta quickly prepared the infamous Reconstruction Act, adopted March 2, 1867. Although it was then almost two years since the complete collapse of the Confederacy, this Act defined its States as "rebel," declared that "no legal State government" existed in that area, placed these States under military rule, and added the blackmailing provision that this tyranny would continue until new and compliant legislatures "shall have adopted the Fourteenth Amendment." Only thereafter would any recalcitrant Southern State "be declared entitled to representation in Congress."

President Johnson promptly vetoed this "Reconstruction Act" as completely and obviously unconstitutional and many suits against it were brought in the courts. But the Radicals overrode the veto, brought impeachment proceedings against the President "for high crimes and misdemeanors" and further threatened impeachment of the Supreme Court justices, who thereupon supinely bowed themselves out of the picture on the curious reasoning (*Georgia v. Stanton*) that the issues aroused by the Act were political and not justiciable. They surely were political. The clear objective of Stevens was to change the form of government into that of a parliamentary democracy with the President—Senator Ben Wade was tapped to succeed Johnson—wholly subordinate to a Congress in which the Radicals would be a permanently dominant party. But if that revolutionary design was not justiciable then there is no such thing as constitutional law.

Under military occupation the South perforce caved in. Compliant legislatures, composed for the most part of Negroes and Northern carpetbaggers, were installed and promptly adopted the previously rejected Fourteenth Amendment, though even then with opposition which under the circumstances was remarkable. The procedure was almost too preposterous for Secretary of State Seward, who on July 20, 1868, issued a very tentative proclamation of ratification. This pointed out that the legislatures of Ohio and New Jersey had, on sober second thought, repudiated their earlier ratifications, and that in Arkansas, Florida, North Carolina, Louisiana, South Carolina and Alabama, in that order, alleged ratifications had been given "by newly constituted and newly established bodies avowing themselves to be, and acting as legislatures. . . ."

Such back talk was not acceptable to the free-wheeling Radicals. The following day they jammed through a concurrent resolution asserting that the Amendment had been ratified by twenty-nine States, including those questioned by Seward, and ordering him to promulgate it as a part of the Constitution. On July 28, the Secretary of State did so, in a statement which made clear he was acting by command of Congress. And as a highly dubious part of the

Constitution the Fourteenth Amendment has remained there ever since.[11]

Ironically, the triumph was too late to bring pleasure to its architect. Old Thaddeus Stevens died on August 12, at the age of 76, in the modest apartment close to the Capitol which he had dominated the past three years. Probably only his adamant will had kept him alive that long, for he had been sinking since the Senate, three months earlier, had by the margin of a single vote declared President Johnson "not guilty" of the impeachment charges which Stevens had framed. To the last he echoed the doctrines of Rousseau, urging the House in his final major address to "fling away ambition and realize that every human being, however lowly or degraded by fortune, is your equal." Although a Republican by party, democracy was to Thaddeus Stevens far more important than the Constitution. Had he been twenty years younger when his hour came, with Lincoln's untimely death, the Federal Republic might never have survived his assault on its foundations.

On the momentum of the Fourteenth Amendment, which was really the momentum of Thaddeus Stevens, its postscript in the Fifteenth was carried through Congress in the immediately ensuing months. This too was approved by the puppet Southern legislatures and was added to the Constitution early in 1870. Another seven years were to pass, however, before the last of the army of occupation was withdrawn and self-government restored to the South.

SEVEN

Commerce and Nationalization

By the adoption of the Fourteenth Amendment
the State governments were not only made definitely
subordinate to that of the nation as a whole. They
were also, North and South alike, defined as untrust-
worthy guardians of the rights of their own citizens.
They were pilloried as well as subjected, insult being
added to injury. Thus the stage seemed to be set
for a complete centralization of power in the hands
of the central government, the necessary prerequisite
for establishment of real political democracy on a
nation-wide basis.

But the strong foundations of federalism could
not be destroyed. Radical Republicanism, which
under Thaddeus Stevens had been dedicated to this
end, began to crumble with the death of its brilliant
leader. For this there were two major reasons, apart
from the lack of any Radical lieutenant of equal
competence. In the first place the element of passion,
always necessary for a strong egalitarian movement,
was subsiding. The war was over; the South was
crushed; the Negroes were free. Abolitionists could
no longer rattle the chains of slavery. On the contrary, they were thrown on the defensive by the
all too abundant evidence that the freedmen were
morally and mentally unable immediately to asso-
ciate with the whites on equal terms. Along with the

unconcealable and all but inconceivable scandals of the carpetbagger period came realization that Emancipation had not solved, had merely posed, the problem of merging the two races peacefully in a common society.

Equally important, attention was focused and energies absorbed by the enormous material opportunities which were opening for the reunited country. For this economic development not more but less governmental intervention was wanted. With the election of President Grant the Republican leadership passed to men willing to bend a knee as well as an ear to the wishes of those industrial tycoons who now began to finance and direct that party. There is no doubt that this era of laissez-faire contributed enormously to the rapid growth and sharing of wealth. Unfortunately, unethical practices increasingly stained the amazing record of free enterprise. And the political consequences of this Gilded Age were much more in the long-range interest of socialism than of federalism.

Big business wanted freedom from all governmental controls—from those of the States as well as from that of Washington. Indeed, with the winning of the West and the rapid expansion of commerce across State lines, interference from local government could be more frustrating—to railroads, for instance—than any controls now likely to be attempted by compliant Republicanism in Congress and the White House. This situation worked against centralization of power. But it also worked at least as vigorously against federal theory. The issue was no longer between federalism and democracy, because of the reaction against the extremes to which the latter had been carried. The issue now was between federalism and plutocracy, sure to swing the pendulum towards democracy again as the "Robber Barons" in their turn established monopoly power. "The will of the people" was temporarily out. This did not mean that "the public be damned" would remain in.

With this new phase the Supreme Court was placed in an extraordinarily difficult situation, not less so because it had temporarily bowed out as a determining factor by refusing to pass on the constitutionality of the Fourteenth Amendment. Soon or late, however, the Court would have to decide whether or not that first section, plus the final clause giving power "to enforce," did or did not fundamentally alter the American form of government. Were the "privileges" and "immunities" of citizens matters with which the central government alone should henceforth concern itself, or did the States still have some say in a vital domain which prior to the Fourteenth Amendment had belonged to them exclusively? The political ambitions of Chief Justice Salmon P. Chase had helped to keep this knotty problem in an abeyancy which ended with the foundering of his Presidential hopes.

In 1873, by the famous Slaughterhouse cases, the erosion of States' Rights was temporarily checked, though by an ominously close (5 to 4) decision. The Supreme Court then decided, rightly or wrongly, that the Fourteenth Amendment was not intended "to destroy the main features of the general system" of federal government. The "great source of power in this country," said Justice Samuel F. Miller for the Court, continues to vest in "the people of the

States." For Congress to seize this power, in a manner violative of the original Constitution and the Bill of Rights, would be to "fetter and degrade" the States. "Undoubtedly," said Chief Justice Hughes years later, this decision "gave much less effect to the Fourteenth Amendment than some of the public men in framing it had intended, and disappointed many others." [1]

That decision, again fragmenting the "general will" into State compartments, was indeed calculated to make both Thaddeus Stevens, and Rousseau before him, turn in their graves. But as expanding business found State legislatures inimical to its plans, the Court's interpretation shifted, though not at all in a manner calculated to assist political democracy, from either the State or national viewpoint. In this hostility to any local regulation of free enterprise the leading spirit on the Court was Justice Stephen J. Field, whose tenure there for almost thirty-five years was to exceed the record of even John Marshall, if only in regard to length. Field had been with the minority in the Slaughterhouse decision, but it was well said that his early rejected dissents "gradually established themselves as the view of the Court." [2]

During the decade following the adoption of the Fourteenth Amendment only three cases were decided by the Supreme Court under all its clauses. The numbers then rapidly increased. Following 1896, to quote Professor Edward S. Corwin, "the flood burst":

Between that date and the end of the 1905 term of court, 297 cases were passed upon under the Amendment—substantially all under the "due process" and "equal protection" clauses. What was the cause of this inundation? In the main it is to be found in the Court's ratification of the idea, following a period of vacillation, that the term *liberty* of the "due process" clause was intended to annex the principals of *laissez faire* capitalism to the Constitution and put them beyond reach of State legislative power.[3]

Corporation lawyers, in other words, had discovered that the Fourteenth Amendment could be as amenable to the safeguarding of commercial interests as its designers had expected it to be for the protection of individual, especially Negro, civil rights. And the frontal attack on the States had thereby been diverted into a more subtle undermining of their original authority. Here was the origin of the three-cornered ideological division which would in time come to characterize American politics: (1) Southern Democrats regarding States' Rights as more important than civil rights; (2) Northern and Western Republicans giving their primary allegiance to laissez-faire capitalism; (3) socialistic dissenters from both camps making the promotion of civil rights by the central government their main objective. With the confusion produced by the Fourteenth Amendment each faction could claim constitutional sanction for its position.

The Fifth Amendment had stipulated that "no person" shall be deprived of property "without due process of law." The Fourteenth Amendment repeated this, but with the provision directed specifically against "any State." Now the ingeniously simple formula was to define a corporation as a "person," whose property under the Fourteenth Amendment was then not subject to deprivation by any State without due process of law. In practice this meant that any regulatory action by the States could be appealed to the Supreme Court, which thus gradually replaced them as guarantors of property rights. As described by Charles A. Beard: "before the end of the nineteenth century the once almost sovereign powers of the States over property and business within their borders were reduced to mere shadows of their former greatness." [4]

By a logical extension of the corporate person argument the railroads, again for instance, soon found it expedient to apply to national instead of State courts, under the interstate commerce clause. That procedure brought the granting of injunctions against strike action, the violation of which in turn resulted in summary imprisonment of labor leaders, without jury trial, for contempt of court. Thus the national development of industry on the one hand, and of trade unionism on the other, led through the channel of the Fourteenth Amendment to the nationalization of governmental power and the resumed weakening of federal structure. Business leadership, too "practical" to theorize on politics, welcomed this centralization of power as long as it seemed to favor laissez-faire at the expense of labor organization. There was all too little anticipation that, in the name of democracy, this favoritism would eventually be reversed.

Yet there were elements of totalitarian democracy in all this judicial interpretation. Whether it was coercing the States in behalf of individual or corporate persons, the Supreme Court was impelled by the Fourteenth Amendment to act in autocratic manner. Emotionally, however, sharp distinction was made between Court intervention in behalf of "human" and of "property" rights. The former was "democratic"; the latter "plutocratic." In the field of human rights the Court could be regarded as forwarding "the will of the people," even when it was striking down local democratic processes to do so. In the field of property rights, on the other hand, the Court could be accused of favoring capitalism at the expense of the proletariat, as Marxists said it would continue to do until the triumph of communism. Long before Lenin's day the flood of European immigration, exhibiting on the whole far more sympathy for socialism than for the American form of government, was obscuring the issue of centralization versus federalism. To many this was displaced by the class-war concept, depicted as democracy versus plutocracy. Because it leads directly to their goal none preach democracy more ardently than do the socialists.

The position of the Supreme Court itself, called upon to determine cases under the first section of the Fourteenth Amendment, was, as it continues to be, unhappy. Even before this Amendment the Court had gone far to weaken the authority of State governments. Now powers, which to Hamilton and Marshall were only implied, had been specifically given to the central government as against the States. So the Court was compelled to fall in line, the more so because the social tide in the rapidly industrializing nation was setting in the direction of centralization anyway. It was not, however, necessary for the Court to go as far as it has gone in recent years in altering judicial review into a sociological interpretation of Rousseau's general will.[5] As we shall see, this served to revive "interposition" of the authority of a State, between its citizens and Court decree, as an effective defense of federal doctrine.

In any government, but especially in one with a structure as delicate as that of federalism, it is far easier to initiate a major reform than to conclude it. The box of troubles opened by the Civil War Amendments helps to explain why forty-three years elapsed between certification of the Fifteenth Amendment, in 1870, and of the Sixteenth, on February 25, 1913. It took some two-score years of judicial interpretation to confine the centralizing work of the Radical Republicans within bounds generally consistent with original constitutional intent.[6] And by then the forces of democracy had gathered sufficient strength to take what Professor Burgess called "a very long step towards governmental despotism and the extinction of the original constitutional immunity of the individual against governmental power in the realm not only of his property, but also of his culture." [7] The reference of this famous teacher of constitutional law was to the Sixteenth Amendment, the text of which is short as well as sweeping: "The Congress shall have power to lay and collect taxes on income, from whatever source derived, without apportionment among the several States, and without regard to any census or enumeration."

Passed by the Congress early in the Republican Administration of William Howard Taft, this momentous Amendment went into effect just before Woodrow Wilson's first inauguration. Its complete disregard of State lines showed how far the judicial interpretations of the Fourteenth Amendment had gone in weakening the federal system. Hailed as "a

direct attack on concentrated wealth," the Income
Tax Amendment was much more directly and effectively an attack on the remnants of State sovereignty.
For it openly bypassed the entire structure of the
States to bring the full coercive power of central
government to bear continuously on their citizens.
The Sixteenth Amendment has not only given the
central government access to virtually unlimited
funds, with all the power, prestige and extravagance
resulting therefrom. It has also served to make the
financing of State and local government more on-
erous, and therefore to encourage the acceptance of
"federal" aid for all sorts of services which in both
theory and practice were formerly regarded as the
clear and full responsibility of local government.
It is supremely ironical that this agency of centralization, invidious in every respect to the health of
federalism, should nevertheless be known as the
"federal" income tax.

The Fourteenth Amendment had rather subtly
undermined federalism. The Sixteenth, in the name
of democracy, made a much more frontal attack on
the American system. The causes for this subversive
development were complex, but certainly the peculiar vulnerability of federalism to modern war
was one of the most influential. And the Civil War,
while the last of the chivalrous struggles in some
aspects, was more outstandingly the first truly totalitarian combat. What it lacked in this respect because
of relatively primitive governmental techniques, it
gained from the fact that two national governments
mobilized all available strength at the expense of a
single federal creed. In a sense the advocates of
federalism, whether uniformed in blue or gray, were

on the losing side in every battle. In form the federal structure was, thanks largely to Lincoln, maintained intact. But the aftermath showed it substantially weakened in spirit.

Indeed, any war that requires centralized mobilization of power is necessarily helpful to the national and injurious to the federal principle. Consolidation of power is the essence of the national system, as diffusion of power is the essence of the federal. It follows that the more bitter and enduring the hostilities between governments, the stronger will be the nationalistic trend among all the belligerents— up to the point where the governmental structure of the defeated power collapses. If the victorious power demands the "unconditional surrender" of its adversary, the nationalistic emphasis will be the greater, for in that case the people of the defeated adversary will have to be governed, and to some extent supported, by proconsuls from the victorious capital.

A second political characteristic of modern war is the lip service that must be paid to democracy. Precisely because both civil and military operations in wartime are necessarily arbitrary, and affect everyone, it is vital to rally the people with glittering assurances. Woodrow Wilson's slogan in 1917, a war "to make the world safe for democracy," is a classic example. And such propaganda does serve to advance, though not to consolidate, the cause of democracy. Veterans' organizations, to illustrate, employ democratic processes to give their members undemocratic advantages in return for the wartime sacrifices of their members.

Both in the enlargement of centralized power and

in the encouragement to democratic theory, the Civil War had profound effects upon our form of government. For years the Southern States were ruled as conquered provinces. The silencing of their separatist viewpoint combined with Northern industrial expansion and the opening of the West to encourage a stimulus to national democracy well pictured in Walt Whitman's extravagant panegyrics. At the outset of his *Democratic Vistas* (1871) the "good gray poet" announced expansively that "I shall use the words America and democracy as convertible terms." They were beginning to become so.

Democratic action is always competent to tear down an established hierarchy, and therefore to open opportunities for those whose abilities are restricted by the rules and customs of a stratified society. But the more liquid the society becomes, and the greater the opportunity of the alert individual to act without restraint, the more certain it is that the shrewd, the dynamic and the ruthless will forge ahead of the mass. Having established economic, social and political preeminence, they will seek to confirm it.

Thus a new stratification sets in and we find that the characters in the drama have been altered, but not the lines they speak. The nobility created by Napoleon was very different from that of the *ancien régime*, but took its privileges just as seriously and arrogantly. The same was true of the Nazis in Hitler's Germany. The unvarying rule applies to the communist hierarchy in Soviet Russia. It applied to the privileged business leadership in the United States after the Civil War, as it applies to the privileged labor union leadership in the United States today. Society as a whole gains nothing—though it may lose much—when privilege is merely shifted from one group to another. The problem is the control of privilege as such.

This sociological truth, which weighed so heavily on Lincoln's overburdened mind, was all but forgotten by Americans following his assassination. Economic power passed quickly from agriculture to industry and finance, with the sharp political shift that always accompanies a change in the economic balance. The Republican Party, gradually accepting the role of puppet for the newly dominant elements, governed unbrokenly from 1861 to 1913, except for the two divided terms of that very moderate Democrat, Grover Cleveland.

During this half-century, Republicanism was certainly not interested in the promotion of democracy, either social or political. Unfortunately, it was equally little interested in the maintenance of the federal system. Expanding industry was hampered by the often narrowly obstructionist and divergent attitudes of the State governments. The same irritations annoyed Wall Street, as the essential and always faithful financial partner of Big Business. When the people of the agricultural States resisted the march of what was undoubtedly industrial progress, the "ploy" of the corporation lawyers was to influence —and even corrupt—the State legislatures. If that proved impossible, the Fourteenth Amendment, forcing a very rigorous exercise of "judicial review," could be relied on to nullify State laws offensive to business interests. Thus the strength of federalism was steadily undermined. In the South it had been crushed by military defeat. In the rest of the country it was either seduced or overborne by the philosophy of "Get Rich Quick." It was not a noble period, that Gilded Age of the "Robber Barons," and the Republican Party still suffers from its memory.[8]

This lack of statesmanship in the Republican Party was certainly in part responsible for channeling the social democracy which is truly American into a swelling demand for that nationalized political democracy which conforms so poorly to the federal structure of our government. But for several reasons this development was slow. Indeed, in spite of the stimulus from the Civil War, political democracy as a national objective did not become really potent in the United States until the rise of William Jennings Bryan.[9] Democratic leaders today, seeking to establish an authentic American tradition for their party, claim Andrew Jackson and even Thomas Jefferson as lineal political ancestors. But both of these men actually called themselves Republicans and neither was the accomplished demagogue—as Bryan certainly was—needed to head a Democratic Party appealing to a General Will which recognizes no State boundaries.

Why was Bryan, or somebody like him, so slow in coming to the fore? In the first place, the old Democratic Party was tainted with the stigmas of slavery and secession and could not be reformed and re-established overnight. In the postwar climate it was impossible to take political advantage of the contemptuous Republican attitude towards States' Rights. To raise that banner would have been tantamount to flying the Stars and Bars again. To quote

Calhoun would have invited castigation for treason. So the South kept silent, biding its time.

In the second place, there was for at least a generation after the Civil War too much free land, too much opportunity for the industrious, and too much unassimilated immigration, to encourage effective opposition to well-entrenched Republicanism. The scandals of the Great Administration, the very doubtful election of Rutherford Hayes, the colorless passivity of Chester A. Arthur—such political assets had to be reinforced by serious economic discontent before a rival party could hope for more than Congressional success. In the House of Representatives the Democratic Party, during these lean years, did well. But that was largely due to the representation from the Southern States, unreconstructed rather than socialistic Democrats, inclined to oppose rather than to support any Presidential candidate standing to the left of Grover Cleveland.

The campaign of 1896 marked the first irreversible turn towards national democracy in American political thinking. There had been a portent four years earlier when the Populists polled sixteen percent of the total vote and captured four Western states. Then, during Cleveland's second Administration, several events combined to set the parched undergrowth ablaze. The march of "Coxey's army" dramatized the plight of the unemployed. Over the protest of Governor Altgeld, of Illinois, President Cleveland sent national troops to Chicago, threw Eugene V. Debs in jail and broke the Pullman strike. On May 20, 1895, the Supreme Court, in a five to four opinion, threw fuel on the flames by declaring the one remaining part of the contemporary income tax law unconstitutional. And agrarian unrest found the formula of free silver, to be coined in the ratio of 16 to 1, as its panacea.

At the Democratic Convention of 1896, in Chicago, William Jennings Bryan proved himself a highly effective demagogue—meaning that his fervent oratory was also politically shrewd. By straight emotional appeal he sought to accomplish that fusion of West and South, against the industrial East, which Calhoun had vainly attempted to achieve by reason alone. And Bryan hammed it so cleverly that he allied both agriculture and labor in his cause. The designing speech which brought him nomination is well worth study by all who are concerned with democratic theory. He saw the farmers "rearing their children near to nature's heart, where they can mingle their voices with the voices of the birds." And for the factory workers, deprived of such pastoral delights, he saved his thundering metrical climax:

> You shall not press this crown of thorns
>> On labor's brow.
> You shall not crucify mankind
>> Upon a cross of gold.

But the United States was not yet ready for political democracy. Even a section of the Democratic Party refused to accept Bryan's socialistic leadership and in a rump convention nominated a rival "National Democratic" candidate. This forgotten man— John M. Palmer—asserted: "Every true Democrat . . . profoundly disbelieves in the ability of the government, through paternal legislation or supervision, to increase the happiness of the nation."

That was not accurate then, is not so now and never will be. For the "true Democrat"—as soon as his thinking becomes national rather than parochial —is drawn inexorably towards paternalism. The majority of people can always be said to need assistance of some kind and there is no question that a powerful central government can for a time do much to furnish those needs. And since majority opinion— by democratic definition—is all that counts, it follows that it is proper as well as expedient to increase the power of the central government so that it can meet the real or fancied wants of the majority. The fact that such centralization must undermine the federal structure of this Republic is secondary to the fiction of the general will. So there is little doubt that William Jennings Bryan rather than John M. Palmer was both the "true" and the "national" democrat in 1896.

But Bryan did not win, and would not have won if he had obtained all of Palmer's relative handful of votes. Nor did Bryan win in 1900, nor in his third and final effort in 1908. Whether he would have won had the tools of radio and television then been available is an interesting speculation. Bryan was unquestionably a silver-tongued orator, and his speeches, like those of Franklin D. Roosevelt after him, were much more impressive to hear and witness than to read.

It seems probable, however, that even with the aid of broadcasting Bryan would never have reached the White House. For in his day the country did not yet regard itself as a democracy. In spite of, and also partly because of, resentment against plutocracy, most Americans continued to believe in the separation rather than the concentration of governmental powers. Prior to World War I the average American was not conditioned to the supremacy of Washington, as he is today. The federal faith still stood, and indeed grew stronger as the South regained its economic health. And with this Southern restoration the fissure between the States' Rights Democrats and the Socialist Democrats began to form.

The accomplishment of Bryan, however, is not to be minimized. His constant threat shook the Republicans to the marrow of their being and forced them to make concessions to democratic demands which came more easily because Republican political philosophy was on the whole so cynical, untheoretical and narrowly materialistic. It was largely due to the influence of "The Great Commoner" that both the Sixteenth and Seventeenth Amendments received the necessary Congressional majorities during the Taft Administration. It was William Jennings Bryan, much more clearly than Andrew Jackson before, or Woodrow Wilson after, who had the vision of the Service State.[10]

EIGHT

Democracy and Empire

Centralization of power is of course the essential prerequisite of any dictatorship. When a governmental system already centralizes power, as did that of Czarist Russia, it is not necessary to go through democratic preliminaries in order to establish tyranny. Successful revolutionists need only adapt existing institutions to their particular purpose, as Lenin did. In his words, "bureaucrats . . . work today, obeying the capitalists; they will work even better tomorrow, obeying the armed proletariat." [1]

But when governmental institutions hamper centralization, as they must in a federal republic from its very nature, then it is clearly necessary to reform those institutions before dictatorship can be established. And if those institutions are well designed, and have popular esteem, then a political tour de force becomes necessary. Somehow or other people must be made to believe that their traditional governmental machinery is out of date, incompetent to cope with new problems, a block to "Manifest Destiny," or perhaps manipulated for evil by unscrupulous men who distort the operation to the general disadvantage.

This accusation of distortion has always been the first attack of those who would reform our government, and unquestionably it has often been a jus-

99

tified attack. Unfortunately, those who denounce "entrenched minorities" in their zeal often give the impression that a minority is objectionable as such, whether it be composed of slave-owners or of Philadelphia Quakers. Thus deeply sincere reformers have helped to spread the wholly un-American belief that a minority is disreputable just because it is a minority, regardless of whether its concern is to protect "the interests" or to defend conscientious objectors. In this manner, reformist zeal has been of incalculable assistance to the concept of a dictatorial general will.

The initial objective of the reformer is not so much to centralize power as to prevent the abuse of power where already centralized. Yet the most admirable reformers all but invariably argue that there "oughta be a law." To prevent abuse of power, superior power should be concentrated in some government agency—an argument which strangely assumes that men become more moral when they serve the unmoral instrumentality of the state. This absurdity is compounded, but also made more difficult to discern, by calling the concentration of power "democratic." The average reformer, however, does not usually invoke the word with the intention of making the bureaucracy all-powerful. He merely equates the general will with his own particular opinion. But the easiest way to make the particularist viewpoint dominant is to call upon the power of government, especially centralized government, in its behalf.

In the case of war, which is the perfect device for replacing federalism with centralization, the motive of the centralizers is not always innocent. There is good reason to think that Hitler wanted war, or at least was willing to risk it, precisely because the condition of war furthered his expressed objective of centralizing all power in the Nazi Party with himself as Fuehrer. In the manner of Rousseau's *Confessions*, Hitler was also a very honest man, and put his inmost thoughts, offensive though they often were, on paper. Other dictators have been as ruthless —Stalin was posthumously so revealed—but very few have been equally outspoken. Some, undoubtedly, have been merely as naïve as is the small reformer when he assumes that power centralized in the state will be used more beneficially than power distributed in private hands.

Anyway, it is evident that power is most easily centralized by war, or by the expectation of war. And it is further evident that to obtain this centralization of power in a political federation, the national government must prevail on people to surrender their individual and State rights, on the plea of national necessity. Since there will always be a minority of skeptics, perhaps even fortified by actual sympathizers with the real or alleged enemy, the theory that the majority will should prevail becomes imperative in times of emergency. That is the theory of democracy, and that is the essential reason for the anomaly whereby the greater the centralized regimentation, the more feverish the claim of the regimenters that this is true democracy. To quote Lenin again: "Communism alone is capable of giving a really complete democracy." [2]

It is at least a curious coincidence that every war in which the United States has been engaged was both immediately preceded by a political flowering of democratic theory and immediately productive of centralization. That applies even to the War of 1812, which was really a continuation and affirmation of the Revolution against Great Britain. Even so, the opposition to it was strongest among the very undemocratic Federalists and as a direct result of what they called "Mr. Madison's war" we got a national debt, a national bank, a high protective tariff and certainly a great impetus for the strongly centralizing Supreme Court decisions of Chief Justice Marshall.

Desire to extend the area of slavery was unquestionably a factor in the Mexican War. There were, of course, other, and weighty, considerations in all these cases. Nevertheless, we must note the coincidence that faith in democracy surged up in the Jacksonian era, and that war with Mexico followed soon after. Centralization was of course encouraged, by government of the conquered areas as dependent territories pending their development into Statehood.

This centralization was in turn a factor in bringing the Civil War, also forwarded by the democratic belief that because the majority deemed slavery an intolerable practice, it thereby became a duty of the central government to abolish it. And while the Civil War did not seem to do more than shake the federal structure severely, this political earthquake did greatly increase the subordination of the individual States to Washington, not only those ruled for years as conquered provinces, but all of them. Bureaucracy was greatly expanded to handle the problems of the emancipated slaves—through the Freedmen's Bureau and other agencies.

For a generation, after the Civil War, the American people were occupied in winning the West and filling their continental domain. The final conquest of the Indian tribal organizations can scarcely merit the name of war, as now understood, but it did provide reason for the maintenance of a national army and gave the central government experience in the direct rule of conquered and primitive subjects.

During this peaceful generation, indeed, the dynamic forces of imperial expansion were gathering strength all along the line. Secretary of State Seward was an avowed imperialist and his annexation of the Midway Islands paved the way for that of Hawaii. Soon the itch for world power was being constantly stimulated by big-Navy advocates like Admiral Mahan, by vigorous politicians like Theodore Roosevelt, and by sensational journalists like William Randolph Hearst. None of these were above using the clichés of democracy to justify a war which would place the growing strength of the nation more firmly under the control of Washington. "Teddy" Roosevelt, indeed, was "convinced . . . that the country needs a war" and "rather hoped" it would come with Great Britain over the Venezuela dispute.[3] But a much less costly conflict, with decadent Spain, served the imperial purpose just as well.

Again there was the coincidence between the flowering of democratic sentiment, under the leadership of William Jennings Bryan, and the reluctant move to war by President McKinley, who to Theodore Roosevelt seemed to have "the backbone of a chocolate eclair." [4] Neither Bryan nor any of his

principal supporters can possibly be accused of
wanting war with Spain, any more than he or
Woodrow Wilson wanted it with Germany twenty
years later. But Bryan, like Wilson, did desire the
triumph of the general will. Theodore Roosevelt,
in 1896 and in 1916, could argue plausibly that this
general will demanded freedom for poor little Cuba,
or poor little Belgium as the case might be. Certainly
the war with Spain was generally accepted as an
altruistic undertaking—merely the liberation of Cuba
from the cruelties of Spanish domination, which in
retrospect seem to have been no worse than those
of Batista, or of Fidel Castro. In the illuminating
words of the latter: "Those who want to know
what democracy is, let them come to Cuba!"

But the outcome of the war with Spain was not
quite altruistic. The outcome was the annexation
of Puerto Rico, Hawaii, the Philippines and lesser
Pacific islands. It was the establishment of the United
States as a colonial power, compelled to justify the
suppression of the Filipinos which followed immediately on the liberation of the Cubans. And the
deeper result was to make Washington for the first
time classifiable as a world capital, governing mil-
lions of people overseas as subjects rather than as
citizens. The private enslavement of Negroes was
ended. The public control of alien populations had
begun.

Only twelve years separated the suppression of the
Philippine Insurrection and the outbreak of World
War I in Europe. They were years in which the
country moved simultaneously towards democracy
and towards imperialism. The Income Tax Amend-

ment provided the means whereby the central government could finance colonial operations, or any other undertaking deemed desirable for the general welfare. The Amendment for the direct election of Senators was expected to break down the recalcitrance of the undemocratic Upper House, which in its old unregenerate condition had rejected the attempted acquisition of Santo Domingo in Grant's Administration[5] and almost repudiated the annexation of other Spanish colonies after the war of 1898.

Simultaneously, what had traditionally been known as the "Administration" in Washington began to act as though it were what it is now inaccurately but habitually called—i.e., the "Government." A revolt was provoked in Colombia, to facilitate the building of the Panama Canal.[6] The Monroe Doctrine was interpreted by President Theodore Roosevelt to mean that the United States should use force to stop any Latin-American disorders. His successor, President Taft, applied this policy to establish a "protectorate" in Nicaragua. Woodrow Wilson then made the policy bi-partisan by extending the protectorate device to Santo Domingo and Haiti, and by ordering two punitive invasions of Mexico. He also reversed the traditional American policy of extending diplomatic recognition to any de facto government, regardless of its morality by our standards. This change was initiated by Wilson's refusal to recognize the Huerta regime in Mexico and one need scarcely comment on the extraordinary inconsistencies to which it has led. It is doubtful that our foreign policy was ever really assisted by withholding recognition from other governments because we deem them unreliable. But in the fledgling stages of imperialism this not too subtle form of pressure seems to have advantages.

It was "to make the world safe for democracy" that the American people were at last pushed, prodded and precipitated, with the aid of German aggressiveness, into World War I. The phrase has been greatly ridiculed, but if we use our political terms correctly it must be said that the aim was very largely achieved. Political democracy is actually a form of government in which the executive can successfully assert that its direction is in accord with the general will, and World War I certainly gave enormous impetus to that claim. Old forms of constitutional government were everywhere overthrown or sharply modified, in the victorious as well as in the defeated nations. Most of the new forms, like that of Soviet Russia, could be called democratic, in the sense of representing what was alleged to be the majority will, and except where counter-revolutions broke out and were sustained it was impossible to prove that more than a minority were in opposition. The great utility of Rousseau's mystical *volonté générale* to dictators is that the more recalcitrant the minority, the stronger the case for suppressing it.

In the United States, World War I brought no written Constitutional Amendment. But the enlargement of centralized power, and the new national agencies deemed necessary to win the war, were here to stay. The machinery for centralized action to cope with subsequent domestic difficulties was either already designed or foreshadowed. We shall consider later how the New Deal made use of this disposition to centralize power. But one should be careful about giving Franklin D. Roosevelt too much credit, or discredit, for exploiting a situation already made ready for him. World War I had helped to make the world safe for democracy, and in the process had done a lot to make constitutional government unsafe in the United States.

On Armistice Day of 1918 Woodrow Wilson wrote out in longhand his announcement to the American people: "Everything for which America fought has been accomplished." In a sense that also was true. Our participation in World War I took us out of the bush league and made us a great imperial power, a molder of world destiny. It was for this, historically speaking, that America fought. The trouble is that the great majority of Americans did not contemporaneously realize for what they were fighting. And one cannot say with assurance that Woodrow Wilson ever did either. For his was the tragedy of a man of peace, an idealistic reformer, a scholar and a close student of American institutions, who in this crisis could not uphold the traditions which he revered.

Every war in which the United States has engaged since 1815 was waged in the name of democracy. Each has contributed to that centralization of power which tends to destroy that local self-government which is what most Americans have in mind when they acclaim democracy. But every war has also been followed by a reaction, in which Americans have thought soberly about the implications of the drums and trumpets and have sought, almost instinctively, to restore the upset constitutional balance. After World War I this reaction was immediate.

It undermined the League of Nations, for which
Woodrow Wilson had worked the more valiantly
because of his passionate desire to validate the
hope that good might come out of the evil he had
reluctantly endorsed.[7] The reaction also cut expenditures by the central government severely, curtailed its swollen functions, and by the time of
Herbert Hoover had done much to re-establish the
federal form, modified, of course, but nevertheless
true to its original principles of divided powers
and maximum home rule.

Then, out of stricken Europe, came the depression,
with all its tremendous stimulus to what some call
democratic action and to what others can as properly
term demagoguery. There is no iron curtain between
the two.

The great depression unquestionably helped to
promote World War II, in any case a not unnatural
consequence of the injustices and stupidities committed in the name of democracy after World War
I. And an unusually authentic "general will" for
relief from depression hardships brought that same
perennial flowering of democratic theory that seems
to be a constant element in American belligerency.
Consequent to World War II we certainly see a
permanently increased centralization of power and
a further weakening of federal theory.

World War II was, historically speaking, a ghastly
aftermath of World War I. The Korean War, on
the other hand, stands out separately, as something
which might easily have been a prelude, and was
assuredly a portent, in regard to World War III.
There is still much about World War II, the Korean "episode" and lesser "brush fires," on which

only partial information is available. But the consequences of these events in the promotion of American imperial practice are not at all obscure.

As with all political terms in this study, the adjective "imperial" is not to be taken in any invidious sense, but merely descriptively. An empire is a far-flung political organization, of which all the territorial parts are not necessarily contiguous, but are subject to a centralized administration of which the head was originally called an emperor, from Latin *imperator*. The essential feature of an empire, however, is not the title of its executive, but whether the executive rules overseas or alien territories without the freely given sanction of their inhabitants, as the Romans ruled Britain, as Russia now rules Hungary, as the French rule Algeria or as we rule Okinawa.

The alien domain incorporated into an empire is almost always in the first instance seized by force and is retained either for reason of military strategy or of economic advantage, real or imaginary. The adjective "imperial" is properly used to describe practices that resemble, or point towards, those of an established empire, even if these are temporary improvisations rather than settled policy. The United States cannot as yet be correctly described as an empire. But it cannot be denied that the central government of the United States has for more than half a century been engaged in imperial practices.

There are several definite characteristics of empire, all more or less connected with the fact that empires get their start from military conquest. This conquest leads to territorial aggrandizement, which is followed by the establishment of military alliances to secure or protect the conquered territory. Alliances, as a device of imperial policy, are as old as recorded history but they are by nature impermanent, and the ally of one empire today may always be the ally of its enemy tomorrow—an elementary political practice on which Marshal Tito has done something to inform us.

From the uncertain nature of military alliances springs a second characteristic of empire. Allies must be continuously subsidized from the imperial treasury, both with military and economic aid. Once undertaken, these subsidies can never be stopped and are more likely to require increasing outlay in order to keep the ally bought. As there is no morality in the state as such, so there is no such moral factor as loyalty in the relations between states. An English statesman summed it up neatly when he said: "Great Britain has no permanent friends and no permanent enemies, but only permanent interests."

The need of alliances explains a third characteristic of empire, which is hostility to the theory of neutrality. Thucydides tells how, during the Peloponnesian War, the Athenians demanded a "we or they" decision from the little island of Melos, then seeking to preserve neutrality as between Athens and Sparta.[8] That was in 420 B.C., but twenty-four centuries later it is still a characteristic of empire to dislike neutrality. One strong indication of the American shift to imperial thinking is the way India has been criticized for upholding a neutrality which was a cardinal point in our own foreign policy less than half a century ago. On October 10, 1955, Secretary of State Dulles told an American

Legion Convention: "The United States does not believe in practicing neutrality." [9]

A fourth characteristic of empire is the argument that there should be no political debate over foreign policy. Politics it is said, should stop at the water's edge, because the intricacies of imperial policy demand the most expert direction and it is dangerous to have them criticized and impeded by those without inside knowledge. This theory of nonpartisanship depreciates what we call democratic procedures, by suggesting that these work only in issues of secondary importance. It thereby emphasizes again that once democracy has served to centralize government, the executive will assume the right to interpret "the general will."

Still a fifth characteristic of empire is to dilate in grandiose terms about its blessings for mankind. *Pax Romana* is the classical version of this trait. After World War II the phrase was: *The American Century*. There has never been an empire, from that of the Hittites to that of Hitler, that could not and did not justify itself in terms of Manifest Destiny—more manifest to the Imperator than to anyone else.

Now all these five characteristics of empire— alliances, subsidies, dislike of neutralism, impatience with domestic criticism and extreme self-righteousness—are actively promoted from Washington today. But almost equally apparent throughout the entire country is an undercurrent of popular opposition which suspects every one of these imperial characteristics and makes a stubborn fight against them.

There has been, and is, a great deal of American support for the political objectives of the United

Nations, so far as they can be understood. But, excepting State Department propaganda, it is difficult to detect any great enthusiasm for NATO and still less for that jerrybuilt structure known as SEATO. If NATO were popular there would have been more support for the British and French efforts to hold together what is left of their crumbling empires, for the essence of an imperialist alliance is mutual respect for the colonial positions of the allies. So far as one can judge, American sympathies were as much with the Greek Cypriots as with the British, and with the Algerian rebels as much as with the French. In neither case, at any rate, did the usually vociferous State Department attempt to defend the imperial viewpoint of its allies. Nor has there been any denunciation, official or otherwise, of the indigenous efforts, from Iceland to Japan, to secure evacuation of the American garrisons overseas. At Suez, in 1957, the United States actually thwarted an entirely natural imperial action by our Franco-British allies.

In spite of the turn towards empire, Americans are paradoxically highly critical of colonialism. Alliance with colonial powers is officially defended on the negative grounds that Soviet oppression is much the worse of two evils and that the colonialism of Western Europe is in any case on the way out. NATO is explained and excused on grounds of immediate necessity, and seldom defended by assertions that it has any permanent intrinsic merit. This attitude makes the organization seem particularly impermanent, and likely to weaken further if a *modus vivendi* with Soviet Russia can be found. Indeed, NATO's chief asset for us is perhaps discernible in the economic importance of defense spending to the American economy.

Even so, there is growing opposition to the cost and waste of the subsidies necessary to maintain our imperial alliances. The historic pattern is that such subsidies continuously grow larger, yet analysis of Congressional voting indicates that opposition to them continuously grows stronger. Much semantic ingenuity has been used to gloss these military subsidies as "economic cooperation," "technical assistance" or "mutual security." This propaganda has not been very successful. In the minds of most Americans it is all classified as "foreign aid" and is all unpopular as such. That is one reason why effort to obtain bi-partisan foreign policy has failed. It is too obvious that politics should stop at the water's edge only if policies stop there also. When policy becomes imperial, involved in every quarter of the globe, the American tradition demands its continuous critical scrutiny by Congress. It is only the theory of democracy which revealingly maintains that matters of supreme importance to the people should not be investigated by the elected spokesmen of the people.

The attempt to condemn all governments that would be neutral between our alliances and those of Soviet Russia has also failed. When Secretary of State Dulles attacked the concept of neutrality as "immoral" he was disowned by President Eisenhower. Not even our NATO allies, still less the neutrals, could be coerced into the effort to blockade Red China. A full reacceptance for others of our own traditional doctrine of neutrality, however, has not come, partly because many former isolationists, confused and bitter, have swung to the opposite pole of collective counter-attack wherever communist conquest seems to threaten.

But, in spite of xenophobia, talk about Manifest Destiny and The American Century has now almost completely evaporated. There is widespread recognition that the national talent is not imperial and that an extremely large number of people all over the globe are more disposed to dislike than to admire our much-vaunted "American Way." As problems of every sort increase at home we realize that what happens to Israel or Ethiopia is not our first concern. And this is not to be called a rebirth of "isolationism," but rather a recognition that federalism, even if we misname it democracy, is not adapted or adaptable to the path of empire.

Acting on this recognition, we have freed the Philippines and given dominion status to Puerto Rico. The Hawaiian Islands, however, were after long hesitation finally admitted, by the Eighty-sixth Congress, as an integral part of the Federal Union. This favorable resolution of the issue of Hawaiian Statehood may seem to indicate willingness to transform a relatively homogeneous Federal Republic into a racially heterogeneous empire. It could be compared with the unhappy French experience in making Algeria—nominally—a part of "metropolitan" France. On the other hand, if federalism is to be a factor for international political stabilization, it must demonstrate capacity to incorporate racially alien peoples into its structure. When this is done with the evident approval of the foreign stock, as in the case of Hawaii, the extension of the federal idea cannot be called imperialism. None would so characterize Switzerland because its government incorporated the purely Italian canton of Ticino into the Swiss Confederation, even though in this case the original annexation was by force.

So the set of the tide towards an American empire, though strong and sustained, may actually have reached highwater mark. At least there are many who hope this is the case. Librarians report a lively interest in Roman history, stimulated by desire to avoid the mistakes that led Rome from republic, to empire, to ruin. And the rather surprising popularity of Professor Arnold Toynbee's tortuous writings may be due to an American disposition to heed his warnings on the broad and beckoning path of empire, perhaps especially this one:

> Whatever the human faculty, or the sphere of its exercise, may be, the presumption that because a faculty has proved equal to the accomplishment of a limited task within its proper field it may therefore be counted upon to produce some inordinate effort in a different set of circumstances, is never anything but an intellectual and a moral aberration and never leads to anything but certain disaster.[10]

The fiction of a general will has not yet beguiled our Federal Republic into the "intellectual and moral aberration" of an American empire. But the imperial trend has nevertheless played no small part in the demoralization of federalism.

NINE

Nationalization Through Foreign Policy

The real character of a man is seldom fully revealed by what he says, or even likes to think, about himself. It is much more clearly defined in his relations with other men. Similarly, the real character of a government, composed of and directed by men, must be analyzed not merely from official declarations of lofty national purpose but also from its actual dealings with other governments—in other words, by foreign policy. At any given period foreign policy tells us much about the course a nation is following through the stormy seas of history.

Indeed, external relations are an even better test of governmental than of individual character. The dealings of a man with other men are controlled both by enforceable law and, at least to some extent, by implanted moral principles. As yet, there is no really effective law of nations and it is questionable that morality is ever strongly instrumental in the dealings of governments one with another. "My country right or wrong" is a sentiment generally condoned, and seldom openly challenged. So that if a nation can be said to have a collective psyche, its development and quality will be reflected in foreign policy.

Furthermore, a written constitution is more effective in controlling the domestic than the foreign policy of a government. It can be intolerably disadvantageous to hamper your own sovereign in its dealings with others not subject to what Jefferson called "the manacles" of your own law. Ways to circumvent the spirit, if not the letter, of the organic law are the easier to find when dealing with other nations. Thus, while our Constitution gives Congress alone the power "to declare war," it is demonstrably possible for the United States to engage in "police action," undistinguishable from war, without Congressional approval. Foreign policy can therefore be strongly at variance both with the formal pretensions of those who conduct it and with the Constitution which these officials are sworn to uphold.

For instance, in a statement on "Back Door Spending," issued from his office on March 9, 1959, Senator Harry F. Byrd cited, as one of several instances, the fact that

> there never was an appropriation for the $3,750,-000,000 British loan. Under this loan expenditures totalling $2,050,000,000 were made in fiscal year 1947 and $1,700,000,000 in 1948, at the convenience and desire of the British Government, and charged directly into the American federal debt. I am not quarreling with the purposes of the British loan. I cite it at this late date only as an example of one type of federal spending outside the appropriation process.

Therefore, some examination of the actual trend of American foreign policy is very important for consideration of the permanence of this Federal Republic.[1] If the United States is now the democracy that we so frequently call it, then it will be clear that our foreign policy is really controlled by the majority will of the American people. The truth of that conclusion is so debatable as to cast doubt on the hypothesis.

There is no question that the original policy of the United States was strongly isolationist. Even before the Union was formed, the Congress of the Confederation, on June 12, 1783, adopted a resolution saying: "The true interest of the States requires that they should be as little as possible entangled in the politics and controversies of European nations." Four years later, at the Constitutional Convention, Charles Pinckney, of South Carolina, sought to prove that an active foreign policy would be incompatible with the federal system then being formulated. In his words: "We mistake the object of our Government if we hope that it is to make us respectable abroad. Conquest or superiority among other powers is not, or ought not ever to be, the object of republican systems." [2]

Isolationism was further recommended as a permanent policy by President Washington in the famous Farewell Address (1796), still somewhat disconcertingly read aloud to the House of Representatives on each anniversary of his birth. "The great rule of conduct for us in regard to foreign nations," said Washington, "is in extending our commercial relations to have with them as little political connection as possible. . . . 'Tis our true policy to steer clear of permanent alliances with any portion of the foreign world. . . ."

A quarter of a century later isolationism was again confirmed and strengthened by the Monroe Doctrine, which served as the cornerstone of our foreign policy for the remainder of the nineteenth century.[3] It is too little realized that this was no mere "hands off" warning to Europe, but a well-balanced program drawn up with the advice and guidance of Jefferson and Madison. In the first part of his message to Congress (December 2, 1823) Monroe asserted that "the American continents, by the free and independent condition which they have assumed and maintained, are henceforth not to be considered as subjects for future colonization by any European powers." But he promptly added: "In the wars of the European powers in matters relating to themselves we have never taken any part, nor does it comport with our policy so to do."

Then Monroe emphasized:

> Our policy in regard to Europe . . . nevertheless remains the same, which is, not to interfere in the internal concerns of any of its powers; to consider the government de facto as the legitimate government for us; to cultivate friendly relations with it, and to preserve those relations by a frank, firm and manly policy, meeting, in all instances, the just claims of every power, submitting to injuries from none.

The warning to Europe—not to intervene in the *New* World—was thus logically and properly balanced by a reciprocal pledge to Europe—not to intervene in the *Old* World. It was this judicious bilateral proposal that gave the Monroe Doctrine validity and prestige in international affairs, wholly independent of the physical power of the United States. When isolationism gave way to interventionism the admonitory part of the Monroe Doctrine of course lost all its moral strength and became entirely dependent on the physical power of the United States for its enforcement. This was itself an incentive to national, at the expense of federal, development. For the power of our government in external affairs is mobilized by and directed through Washington, not through the State capitals.

Isolationism, as an overall policy, demanded two specific applications to be enduring. It meant, first, that diplomatic recognition must be promptly extended to any stable government, regardless of the means by which it had acquired control. This was emphasized by President Monroe in the passage just quoted—"to consider the government de facto as the legitimate government for us." The same thought had been earlier voiced by President Jefferson, when he said: "We surely cannot deny to any nation that right whereon our own government is founded, that every one may govern itself according to whatever form it pleases, and change those forms at its own will." [4]

The second corollary of isolationism was strict neutrality in the wars of other nations. This, too, was emphasized in the quoted passage of the Monroe Doctrine, with the more pride because neutrality had been successfully observed throughout the upheaval of the French Revolution. For a country with a population as heterogeneous in national origins as is that of the United States, neutrality was also intrinsically a desirable policy, the more so because of the commercial importance of "Freedom of the Seas," to recall a once popular American slogan.

There was no part of their well-reasoned creed which American isolationists yielded more reluctantly than neutrality. After being drawn into

World War I we were still an "associated" and not
an "allied" power. On that definition the Senate refused to ratify the Treaty of Versailles and thereby
stayed out of the League of Nations. Even today
one finds doubts as to whether membership in the
United Nations is really in the American interest.
There are skeptics who still maintain that neutrality
served this country better than the diametrically opposite policy of collective security, which starts
from the premise that all "peace-loving" nations
should combine to resist aggression by any government, anywhere. This leads on to the somewhat arbitrary division of "We or They," under which we
attempt to deny others the right of neutrality which
we once claimed so vigorously for ourselves. It gets
even more kaleidoscopic when the *we*'s of one decade become the *they*'s of the next, and we find ourselves making allies of former war-loving nations
to prevent aggression from peace-loving Soviet
Russia, permanently but naively defined as such in
the U.N. Charter.

Another very present difficulty springs from the
complete abandonment of isolationsm that came with
participation in World War II. Under the old practice of automatic recognition we quickly approved
the establishment of all the Latin-American republics and were indeed more inclined to encourage
than to discourage the nationalistic aspirations of
subject peoples, from Ireland to Korea. Anti-coloni-
alism can be quite a useful card in the diplomatic
deck, as the Russians have disagreeably demonstrated
by playing it with a good deal of skill themselves.
But our diplomats can no longer denounce colonialism, not only because we have practiced it a bit

ourselves but even more because we have made allies of the remaining colonial powers. Yet a belief that there is something un-American in the denial of political freedom to subject peoples still lingers in this country. It was demonstrated when we split with our French and British allies over the Suez Canal issue.

This dilemma of colonialism, like that arising from the reversal of position on neutrality, has consequences that bear directly on the subject of governmental form. When the people of a country are confused, or doubtful, about the rectitude of their government's foreign policy, it does not mean that this policy will be changed. To the extent that the country is really a political democracy its foreign policy will eventually conform to public opinion. In this manner British democracy is liquidating the British Empire. But if a country is only a pseudo-democracy, its foreign policy may for a long time be something very different from what most of its people really want. It will then be expedient for those in charge of foreign policy to conceal the objectionable manifestations from those whose taxes pay the cost. Democratic pretense, therefore, tends to encourage a dishonest and increasingly dictatorial foreign policy, as Soviet Russia has consistently demonstrated.

Nobody is likely to deny that the foreign policy of the United States is now, in theory and practice, completely at variance with its original isolationist character. What is not so clear is whether this change reflects or presages an equally fundamental alteration in the character of our political system. Offhand, one would say that such a change has not yet come, because, even with due allowance for the Fourteenth and Sixteenth Amendments, the Constitution is still clearly that of a federal republic. But any review of constitutional development will also strongly indicate that a changing political philosophy is stretching the organic law to the very limits of its elasticity. One is again reminded of De Tocqueville, who anticipated that the Constitution would in time become a dead-letter document. "The government of the Union," he said, "depends almost entirely upon legal fictions." And only the naive "imagine that it is possible by the aid of legal fictions to prevent men from finding out and employing those means of gratifying their passions which have been left open to them." [5]

The very large authority granted to the President in the field of foreign policy is undoubtedly the easiest means of "gratifying passions" in a seemingly constitutional manner. This authority is greatly reinforced by the provision which makes him commander-in-chief of the armed forces. As the Roman Republic deteriorated, the position of Senator was frequently sought by military men as a good springboard for the leap to dictatorial power. To block any such development here, the founding fathers decided to make the chief executive the supreme military commander. The purpose was to insure that the army would always be under civilian control.

While a military man could by civilian election become commander-in-chief he would thereby become a civilian rather than a military commander. That was the clever idea, fortified by a number of precise constitutional checks, such as the limitation of military appropriations to the two-year term of each successive Congress. Further controls in the field of foreign policy were given to the Senate. With the President thus hemmed in, and chosen by the States acting separately through the Electoral College, there was no anxiety about the natural choice of General Washington as the first President. It is to be noted, however, that since the time of Jackson, when political democracy began to make headway, there has been a recurrent tendency to nominate generals for the Presidency. Coincident with this is an increasing disregard of Washington's warning that "overgrown military establishments . . . under any form of government are inauspicious to liberty, and . . . are to be regarded as particularly hostile to Republican Liberty." [6]

"Overgrown military establishments" became inevitable for the United States as soon as it accepted the role of world leadership, whether gladly or sadly. An active foreign policy without armed force to sustain it is a contradiction in terms. Men can influence other men by moral means alone. But governments, being amoral instrumentalities, can never be sure of influencing other governments without the latent coercion of military strength.[7] Bribery is not an adequate substitute, for the government that can be bought is for that very reason unlikely to stay bought when a higher bidder appears. So it follows that the magnitude of the American foreign-policy shift, from isolationism to whatever it should be called today, is accurately plotted by the consistently upward curve of our peacetime military expenditure.

Since defense is unquestionably a function of the

national government this enormous outlay, continued year after year, is of itself a centralizing influence of the first magnitude. The economic and political importance of defense spending on the current scale will be given close consideration in a subsequent chapter. Here only one rather obvious result need be mentioned. The defense planning necessary to implement a global foreign policy cannot be effective if the responsible military officers must come cap in hand to Congress, requesting the financial wherewithal as the Constitution demands. These technical officers alone are in a position to say what flow of funds is "adequate," and to fulfill their responsibilities they must demand that the flow be both continuous and assured for years in advance. Intercontinental ballistic missiles, with atomic warheads, cannot move from drawing board to operational perfection within the span of a single Congress.

The real determinant of defense spending is therefore the whole body of overseas commitments as made by the executive branch of the national government, of which the "democracy" as a whole knows little or nothing. Its legislative representatives may be partially informed, but are impotent to make any real cuts in the military estimates. If Congress does so it will not only be accused of endangering national security, but will also shortly be confronted with "deficiency" appropriations which must be voted because the money is already obligated. Therefore in fact, if not in theory, the constitutional control of Congress over military expenditure has been reduced to what is at best a pressure for economical management. Both federalism and representative government have been undermined, the first by draining power from the States to the national government, the second by concentrating the power thus drained in the executive at the expense of the legislative branch. It is small consolation to call this dual degeneracy "democracy."

All this may well be an inevitable result of two world wars and their aftermath. Many are inclined to say with a shrug that it is the fault of the Kaiser, or of Hitler, Tojo, Stalin, Khrushchev or some other personal devil. But the issue we seek to confront is not where the blame lies, but what the development portends. And there is much evidence, far too little considered, that the trend has been advanced from internal as much as from external compulsion. Undoubtedly "overgrown military establishments" are currently forced upon us by Soviet policy. But it is highly doubtful that this is the whole truth. If the objective is to save the Federal Republic, we must look deeper than the external threat.

There is one modern political writer who saw very clearly that military centralization is helpful in undermining a federal republic. His name was Adolf Hitler. Chapter 10 of Volume II of *Mein Kampf*, which is devoted to an indictment of German federalism as an obstacle to the triumph of national socialism, is well worthy of current attention by those who do not realize that a concentration of political power can be used for evil as well as for good—and is perhaps much more likely to be used for evil than for good.

Germany in 1924 was a federal republic, and almost the only feature of its government that pleased Hitler was the fact that the small professional army was a national instrument and not under the divided control of the various States—Prussia, Bavaria, Saxony and so forth—as had been the case until World War I. "The army," wrote Hitler in 1924, "must definitely be kept away from all influences of the individual States." From this he logically proceeded to the assertion that "we cannot permit any single State within the nation to enjoy political sovereignty." And then:

> National Socialism must claim the right to force its principles upon the entire German nation, and to educate Germany to its ideas and thoughts, without consideration of the former boundaries of the federated States. . . . National Socialist doctrine . . . has the life of a people to regulate anew, and therefore it must claim the positive right to ignore [internal] boundaries, which we reject.

In the United States, as in Germany, World War I led to the unification of all State military contingents under centralized direction and command. The Second Amendment, however, prevents complete absorption of the State militia in the national establishment, as Governor Faubus of Arkansas dramatically reminded those who had forgotten this part of the Constitution. In the United States, moreover, there is still a great deal of latent opposition to conscription by the central government as a settled and permanent policy. Here it is not so much our variant of national socialism but rather the constant drain of our "overgrown military establishment" that makes it, in the words of George Washington, "particularly hostile to Republican Liberty." The taxes necessary, or deemed necessary, for defense cut down the financial resources of the States and make it all but impossible for most people to provide for their own security. Then more centralized taxation is imposed to return to the States and people, under controls, a part of what has been taken from them! Hitler, who had plenty of political shrewdness, cleverly exploited a similar situation in Germany. In the chapter already cited, he wrote:

> For reasons of self-preservation the Reich is forced today to curtail more and more the sovereign rights of the component States. . . . Since it drains the last drop of blood out of its citizens by tactics of financial extortion, it is bound to take away from them even the last of their rights, unless prepared to witness the general discontent some day turn into open revolution.

Then comes the punch-line:

> a powerful national government may encroach considerably upon the liberty of individuals as well as of the different States, and assume the responsibility for it, without weakening the Empire Idea, if only every citizen recognizes such measures as means for making his nation greater.

What this suggests, in a manner difficult to refute, is that political democracy provides the ideal formula for converting a federal republic into a centralized empire. Encroachment on States' Rights and individual liberty, Hitler reasoned, will not be resisted "*if only every citizen* recognizes such measures as means for making his nation *greater.*"

In other words, the problem of empire-building is essentially mystical. It must somehow foster the impression that a man is great in the degree that his nation is great; that a German as such is superior to a Belgian as such; an Englishman, to an Irishman; an American, to a Mexican: merely because the first-named countries are in each case more powerful physically than their comparatives. And people who have no individual stature whatsoever are willing to accept this poisonous nonsense because it gives them a sense of importance without the trouble of any personal effort. Empire-building is fundamentally an application of mob psychology to the sphere of world politics, and how well it works is seen by considering the emotional satisfaction many English long derived from referring to "the Empire on which the sun never sets." Some Americans now get the same sort of lift from the fact that the Stars and Stripes now floats over detachments of "our boys" in forty foreign countries.

But, as Hitler emphasized, "every citizen" must *himself* "recognize" that he is mysteriously transformed into a bigger person when his nation becomes imperial. He must *himself* say "ja" to the proposals of his government. That implies political democracy, under which the emotionalized majority "ja" is taken as binding on the minority of clear-thinking people who will be disposed to say "nein." For what he called "racial Germans" Hitler was not opposed to the *processes* of democracy, and indeed achieved control through their wholly normal operation. Once in power, however, he immediately sought to portray himself as the single embodiment of a German general will, using the concentration camps for all dissenters.

Stalin, we are told by those who knew him best, attempted the same personal embodiment of the general will for Soviet Russia. The communists never condemned Hitler more bitterly than Khrushchev pilloried Stalin in his speech to the Twentieth Party

Congress, in Moscow, on February 25, 1956. There
the once all-highest was portrayed as one "who practiced brutal violence . . . toward that which to his
capricious and despotic character seemed contrary
to his concepts." In that speech the "cult of the individual" was attacked for its tendency to establish
a ruler who "supposedly knows everything, sees
everything, thinks for everyone, can do anything, is
infallible in his behavior." This cult, alleged Khrushchev, runs directly counter to the basic concepts of
Marxism-Leninism. But it is certainly not counter
to the even more basic concept of Rousseau's general will. It is not counter to the theory of political
democracy. It did not even prevent Khrushchev from
soon making himself another Stalin.

Our natural tendency is to say that the later leaders of Russia belatedly discovered in Stalin characteristics which we always knew were his. But, if we
knew it, our own leaders were singularly blind to
the defects of "Good Old Joe." When he was our
ally, neither President Roosevelt nor Prime Minister
Churchill ever described Stalin as "a capricious
despot." Possibly we were then ourselves victims of
"the cult of the individual." One recalls the general
approval given to Roosevelt's edict that Germany
must be "completely and permanently disarmed,"
and to Churchill's proud statement that he did not
become Prime Minister "in order to preside over
the liquidation of the British Empire." All this was
only yesterday, historically speaking, yet already the
British Empire is largely liquidated and a chief
anxiety of our State Department has been West German reluctance to build another army.

So Hitler, Stalin, Roosevelt and Churchill were

curiously alike in completely misjudging the shape of things to come, though certainly none of them was deprived of the information necessary for good judgment. Furthermore, for all their differences one from another, each of these powerful national leaders regarded himself as qualified to speak for his nation as a whole, and to direct its destiny. Such similarities, between such very different characters, strongly suggests some common denominator operating to obscure the vision of these chiefs of state. And it would seem that this common denominator, in each of the four cases, was the undoubtedly sincere conviction that the particular chief of state was because of that office the authorized and responsible spokesman of a mystical national will—the *volonté générale* of Rousseau.

If there were some common factor operating in all of these four diverse cases, political scientists should be profoundly concerned to identify and analyze it, for surely anyone who calls himself a scientist will not be content to view the problem in the light of nationalistic prejudice. And there is a tremendous problem in this seemingly strong tendency to let one man assume control of the political direction of an entire nation.

There is clearly one way in which such a tendency would be encouraged—anywhere. Suppose it were argued that the majority will should control, and that minority opinions, in either groups or localities, are contrary to the public welfare. Then, when the majority will has been expressed, those empowered to make it effective may properly feel a solemn responsibility to do so. These officials might even conclude that it is a positive *duty*, rather than a tyrannical act, to suppress obstructive minority opinions.[8] They would in consequence urge and welcome repressive action by their chief administrator, be he called Fuehrer, Duce, President, Prime Minister, Commissar or Generalissimo. And so in complete— perhaps inevitable—accord with the theory of democracy would come dictatorship.

TEN

New Deal Democracy

Franklin Delano Roosevelt assumed the Presidency on March 4, 1933, and died in that office early in his fourth term, on April 12, 1945. The only visible change in the Constitution during these twelve years was the adoption of the Twenty-first Amendment, which had been submitted to the States for ratification before Mr. Roosevelt took office. As this merely repealed the Eighteenth (Prohibition) Amendment one might conclude that there was no further centralization of government during the era of the New Deal.

Such a conclusion would be correct only as far as outward structure is concerned. In spirit, American political philosophy altered enormously between 1933 and 1945. The conception of government as a service agency then for the first time took firm hold on American thinking. As a necessary corollary, the principles of federalism were severly subordinated to those of a centralized Service State. This strong movement towards socialism, however, was never defined as such. It was all done in the name of democracy, a word which Mr. Roosevelt did much to popularize.

But while he employed the word thousands of times, in hundreds of speeches and state papers, this President never used it with any precision. Lincoln, on the other hand, rarely spoke of democracy, but always with clarity when he did so. In 1858 he wrote: "As I would not be a slave, so I would not be a master. This expresses my idea of democracy." And on July 4, 1861, after civil war had begun, Lincoln supplied the positive political side of this description by calling democracy "a government of the people, by the same people"—a definition which did not in any way conflict with Calhoun's plea for "concurrent" majorities.[1]

Probably the nearest approach to a definition of democracy by Franklin D. Roosevelt was in his Chicago campaign speech of October 28, 1944:

> The creed of our democracy is that liberty is acquired and kept by men and women who are strong and self-reliant, and possessed of such wisdom as God gives to mankind—men and women who are just, and understanding, and generous to others—men and women who are capable of disciplining themselves. For they are the rulers and they must rule themselves.

This seems to say that in a political democracy an elite of the strong and self-reliant become the rulers and then are subject to no external rules. The same, of course, could be said of a dictatorship. But the meaning is very cloudy, perhaps intentionally so. It is not the words but the actions of F.D.R. that give us a true understanding of his conception of the American system of government.

If there is doubt as to what President Roosevelt meant by "democracy" there is no question about the one unvarying objective of his protracted Administration. It was the centralization of power in the executive arm of the national government. The power thus vested in the White House and its subordinate agencies was of all sorts—political, economic and social. And it was taken from a great variety of other agencies, public and private, both by direct and by indirect action. Political power was drained both from the State governments and from the Congress of the United States. Economic power was drained from business and banking, while social power, in the broad sense of the word, was taken from the localities and concentrated in the new network of alphabetical agencies.

The one notable exception to this capture of power was in the case of the labor unions, which were strengthened by governmental action without being subjected, in any significant manner, to governmental control. Critics of Mr. Roosevelt charged that this exception was made to guarantee the support of organized labor for the Democratic Party. However that may be, it seems probable that the trade unions also would have been brought to heel if Mr. Roosevelt had continued much longer in office. When the general policy is comprehensive centralization no single element in the community can long be favored at the expense of others—unless the aim is to turn political domination over to that element.

Mr. Roosevelt's statements on his political objectives were as precise as his use of the word "democracy," to describe procedures, was vague and intangible. The following quotation, out of the hundreds available, shows that this four-term President had a reasoned philosophy of government, and was by no means the mere political juggler, the apostle of expediency, that is sometimes charged. It is from the foreword to his compilation entitled *On Our Way*, describing the first year of the New Deal:

> In spite of the necessary complexity of the group of organizations whose abbreviated titles have caused some amusement, and through what has seemed to some a mere reaching out for centralized power by the Federal Government, there has run a very definite, deep and permanent objective.

The President then proceeded to define this objective, as "a measured control of the economic structure," justifying his program by the scope of the "emergency" when he took office. That emergency, he asserted,

> covered the whole economic and therefore the whole social structure of the country. It was an emergency that went to the roots of our agriculture, our commerce and our industry. . . . It could be cured only by a complete reorganization and a measured control of the economic structure. . . . It called for a long series of new laws, new administrative agencies. It required separate measures affecting different subjects; but all of them component parts of a fairly definite broad plan. . . . We could never go back to the old order.

What was not emphasized was the fact that "a complete reorganization" of the economic structure necessarily involved profound modification of the political structure within which the free economy had developed. Whether or not that economic reorganization was actually as necessary and desirable as President Roosevelt claimed is a separate issue. We are here concerned with the effect of the policy on the federal system. But it should be emphasized that the New Deal policy of centralization was evolved without the stimulus of war. Roosevelt and Hitler took office on the same day and the statement of objective quoted above was published early in 1934—nearly eight years before Pearl Harbor.

At first there was nothing sharply invidious to established constitutional procedures. Before his inauguration President Roosevelt had invited the Governors of all the States to meet with him in Washington immediately after the ceremony, and all of them came or sent representatives. At this meeting, on March 6, 1933, Mr. Roosevelt spoke of his familiarity "with the duties of Governors and also with the rights and duties of States." He said that in a number of respects, which were mentioned, policies should be coordinated along national lines, but there was no threat of interference with traditional State functions. On unemployment relief, for instance, Mr. Roosevelt said:

> The Federal Government, of course, does have to keep anybody from starving, but the Federal Government should not be called upon to exercise that duty until other agencies fail. The primary duty is that of the locality, the city, county, town —if they fail and cannot raise enough to meet the needs, the next responsibility is on the States.

But in his first Inaugural Address, two days earlier, President Roosevelt had said: "Our Constitution is so simple and practical that it is possible always to meet extraordinary needs by changes in emphasis and arrangement, without loss of essential form." There was a disturbing note in this observation—how does a President change the "arrangement" of the Constitution? And Mr. Roosevelt underlined this by warning that, if necessary, he would ask the Congress for "broad Executive power to wage a war against the emergency, as great as the power that would be given to me if we were in fact invaded by a foreign foe."

These hints of what Mr. Roosevelt liked to call "positive leadership" soon acquired more substance, as people responded to his invigorating personality and read personally helpful meanings into his references to "essential democracy." The fist broke through the velvet glove when, on July 24, 1933, the President told the nation that "this is no time to cavil or to question" the NRA, which was soon to be declared unconstitutional by the Supreme Court. And with that check Mr. Roosevelt revealed that his interpretation of democracy was executive domination.

The National Recovery Act was a very significant step in the totalitarian development of American thinking. The wholly logical reasoning behind it was that since the Fourteenth Amendment had already nationalized civil rights, nobody should "cavil" at the nationalization of that political power necessary to enforce those rights.[2] The Act was clearly designed to promote the cartelization of American industry. Its price- and wage-fixing provisions were of course in direct contradiction to the anti-trust laws, as Mr. Roosevelt himself was compelled to admit. He ignored the salient factor of the free economy by posing the issue as between price-fixing by market operation and price-fixing by government authority. The latter would be more "democratic," even though it would need "a rigorous licensing power" to force all employers into line. Many business leaders, however, were wholly willing to be so coerced. They pinned blue eagles in their coat lapels, to signify their acquiescence, and meekly awaited orders from Washington.

But the Supreme Court, as then constituted, saw a great difference between the earlier protection of property rights against State encroachment and the currently demanded surrender of industry to guidance by centralized government. On May 27, 1935, the Court unanimously declared the NRA unconstitutional. The President, four days later, said this decision had returned the United States to the "horse and buggy age." He predicted, bitterly, that the Court would also invalidate the AAA, which it promptly did. With his whole program of centralized power jeopardized, the President fought back. On July 5, 1935, he sent his notorious letter to Representative Samuel B. Hill, chairman of the subcommittee then considering the Guffey-Vinson bill for regulation of the coal industry. To Mr. Hill the President wrote: "I hope your committee will not permit doubts as to constitutionality, however reasonable, to block the suggested legislation." The legislation was enacted, but since the purpose was to re-establish for the coal industry the monopoly system already outlawed for industry as a whole, its elimination by Supreme Court action, on May 18, 1936, was all but automatic.

This was the final straw that determined the President to strike directly at the Supreme Court as an undemocratic block to executive authority. A Presidential election was coming up, and with his faith in political democracy one would have thought that Mr. Roosevelt would have raised the Court-packing plan as a campaign issue. Prior to the 1936 election there were unconfirmable rumors of what he had in mind. But Mr. Roosevelt did not reveal his design until his Republican opponent, Governor Landon of Kansas, was snowed under and a Congress with only sixteen Republican Senators and eighty-nine Republican Representatives had been returned.

Then he struck. "The deeper purpose of democratic government," the President told the new Congress on January 6, 1937, "is to assist as many of its citizens as possible . . . to improve their conditions of life." But, "adequate pay for labor and just return for agriculture" cannot be obtained "by State action alone." The Legislative branch of the national government, said the President, must "continue to meet the demands of democracy" and "the Judicial branch also is asked by the people to do its part in making democracy successful. We do not ask the Courts to call non-existent powers into being, but we have a right to expect that conceded powers, or those legitimately implied, shall be made effective instruments for the common good."

Never was sophistry used more effectively by a great political leader than in this Annual Message of 1937. Of course State legislation cannot secure "*adequate* pay for labor and *just* return for agriculture." No legislation can achieve and none should even attempt such imponderable and undefinable objectives. But by the half-truth of pinning inability to do the impossible on the States alone, Mr. Roosevelt neatly impugned the whole theory of federal government and strongly suggested that he personally would provide these benefits—described as "making democracy successful"—provided the Congress and the Courts were acquiescent. And there didn't seem to be much doubt about the Congress, with the House nearly four to one, and the Senate five to one, of the President's own party.

The scheme for controlling the recalcitrant judiciary was unveiled a month later, in the special message of February 5, 1937. It was both simple and ingenious. If a Federal judge failed to retire voluntarily at age seventy, the President was to be empowered to appoint a duplicate judge, with equal authority. The proposal was obviously aimed directly at the existing Supreme Court, to which it would have added six new judges immediately. The prompt confirmation of Mr. Roosevelt's personal selections, by a Senate composed of eighty Democrats and sixteen Republicans, was scarcely improbable.

Yet the whole scheme blew up in the President's face.[3] It was just too smart. On March 9, 1937, worried by the dim reception given the Court-packing plan, the President explained in a "fireside chat" that his only purpose was "to make democracy succeed." If the personal note is excusable, this radio speech for the first time brought home to me, as the then editor of the Washington *Post*, the demonstrable fact that uncritical praise and practice of political democracy can readily be the highway to dictatorship, even in the United States. The collection of material for this book was begun that evening.

The Senate, with characteristic indifference to democratic theory, simply refused to act on the Court-packing bill. It was condemned, in a scathing report from the Judiciary Committee, as calculated to "subjugate the courts to the will of Congress and the President and thereby destroy the independence of the judiciary, the only certain shield of individual rights." Then a motion to recommit was adopted by a vote of 70 to 25, in spite of the President's assertion, at the Democratic Victory Dinner of March 4, 1937, that "If we would keep faith with those who had faith in us, if we would make democracy succeed, I say we must act—NOW!"

In the 1938 primaries Mr. Roosevelt personally intervened to defeat the Democratic Senators who had been most instrumental in scuttling his Court-packing plan. In not one case was this attempted purge successful. The attempt has generally been attributed to the vindictive streak which many detractors of Franklin D. Roosevelt believe to have been an important part of his nature. It is more impartial to conclude that Roosevelt, like Robespierre before him, was really imbued with the *mystique* of that "democracy" which he so incessantly praised. This able President unquestionably realized that the federal principle is an insurmountable barrier to the triumph of that *volonté générale* which he felt fully competent to interpret and indeed personify. His popularity, however, led him to underestimate State pride and to commit the egregious political blunder of interfering in State primaries.

If it had not been for World War II, and the complete demoralization of the Republican Party after the crushing defeat of 1936, Mr. Roosevelt might well have been retired at the end of his second term. Under the more democratic British political system the no-confidence vote in the Court-packing issue would alone have brought him down. Although the "off-year" Congressional elections of 1938 could not achieve this, they did reveal Mr.

Roosevelt's prestige at a low ebb. The Republicans then gained eleven governorships, eighty-one more House seats, and eight more Senators, aside from the re-election of all the Democratic Senators whom the President had sought to purge.

But just at this time the storm clouds were growing unmistakably ominous over Europe. Sage Jim Farley was skeptical when Roosevelt told him: "Of course I will not run for a third term." [4] At the Chicago Convention, on July 19, 1940, his party "drafted" the President for that third term, and he immediately went on the air from the White House with a speech prepared in anticipation of this "draft." It would be most improper, he said, to expect others to answer calls "into the service of the nation" and at the same time decline to serve himself.

So F.D.R. served, until his death in the closing stages of America's biggest war—as yet. Whatever the other results of this war there can be no argument as to its twofold effect on the economic and political structure of the United States. The economy of the country was tremendously stimulated by the war effort, and far-reaching governmental controls were imposed, to direct both production and consumption in accordance with centralized planning. Every type of power was simultaneously concentrated and nationalized, to the point where it was able to shatter the similarly focused strength of the Axis nations.[5]

On our side this process was carried on in the name of democracy, and on the other side we called it dictatorship. But the political scientist must conclude that there was an extraordinary parallelism of method on both sides. This was symbolized by the equal ease with which Hitler and Roosevelt, at different moments, accepted Soviet Russia as an ally. Undoubtedly there were vitally important differences in the various national objectives and procedures. It is not for a moment suggested that the outcome of the war was a matter for indifference. But it is indisputable that World War II, even more than World War I as curtain-raiser, required in every belligerent country an enormous proliferation and strengthening of central government. As a result of this essentially socialistic process the stimulated and mobilized power was in every case concentrated in an enlarged and increasingly omnipotent bureaucracy.

It is often pointed out that the United States was the only one of the major belligerents which did not experience physical ravishment in either chapter of World War. In Europe this is often emphasized as a reason why our Allies, at least, could accept financial aid for reconstruction without the embarrassment of gratitude. What is never emphasized, in England or France, is that the damage done to the governmental structure was far greater in the United States than in the case of any other victorious power.

In the latest great war the United States was the only major belligerent with a federal system of government. All the others were unitary states. The necessary concentration of authority in the national executive was therefore far more injurious to our system of check and balance, than to their systems of continuously concentrated power. A damaged city is much more easily restored than a damaged political system, and can much more easily be improved by reconstruction. Even so, we have given far more help to the physical reconstruction of other countries than any of them have given to the governmental reconstruction of the United States.

Sometimes, indeed, one is given to feel that European socialists actually dislike the Constitution of the United States, precisely because it makes the flowering of socialist theory more difficult. After his Premiership in Great Britain, Mr. Clement Attlee made a truthful if tactless observation to that effect. So it might be well to recall the more tactful though no longer wholly true opinion expressed by Daniel Webster, when the cornerstone of the Bunker Hill Monument was laid, in 1825: "We are not propagandists," said Webster:

> Wherever other systems are preferred, either as being thought better in themselves, or as better suited to existing condition, we leave the preference to be enjoyed. Our history proves . . . that with wisdom and knowledge men may govern themselves; and the duty incumbent on us is, to preserve the consistency of the cheering example, and take care that nothing weakens its authority with the world. If, in our case, the Representative system ultimately fails, popular governments must be pronounced impossible. No combination of circumstances more favorable to the experiment can ever be expected to occur. The last hopes of mankind therefore rest with us. . . .

If Americans now prefer to be governed from Washington, rather than to govern themselves, there will certainly be no objection to that choice from other countries. There is a great deal of foreign propaganda, not all of it communist by any means, which continuously urges us to carry political democracy to its logical conclusion of complete centralization. There is no foreign influence, at least of any consequence, that urges us to strengthen representative federalism. Yet if lost here, as Webster warned, that system very likely goes forever.

ELEVEN

The Service State

President Roosevelt, the record shows, demonstrated long before 1940 that he had scant interest in the doctrines of federalism. And there can be no doubt that the centralization brought by the war permitted him greatly to advance the cause of a unitary American state. More and more, as the fighting progressed towards a victorious conclusion, this objective was publicly revealed. In spite of his defeat on the bill for reorganization of the judiciary, mere tenure of office soon enabled the President to appoint a Court of his choosing. During the war period he had nothing to fear from Congress. The now enormous executive branch of government, stiffened by many patriotic businessmen with administrative know-how, began to shake down into a competent managerial regime. Most people thought of this centralized power as a temporary evil, to be ended with the ending of the war. That was by no means the President's idea.

The first indisputable evidence of New Deal intent to undermine the federal system actually came eleven months before Pearl Harbor. In his "fireside chat" of December 29, 1940, the President had told the American people that although "we must be the great arsenal of democracy," nevertheless "you can . . . nail any talk about sending armies to

Europe as deliberate untruth." This assurance was immediately followed, on January 6, 1941, by the annual "State of the Union" message, in which Mr. Roosevelt outlined what he called the "four essential human freedoms."

These four freedoms, he said, provide "a definite basis for a kind of world attainable in our own time and generation." And, at least so far as the United States was concerned, these freedoms were going to be compulsory. "Freedom," said the President, "means the supremacy of human rights." "A free nation has the right to expect full cooperation from all groups." "We must especially beware of that small group of selfish men who would clip the wings of the American eagle in order to feather their own nests." And "the best way of dealing with the few slackers or trouble makers in our midst is, first, to shame them by patriotic example, and, if that fails, to use the sovereignty of government to save government."

There is no injustice to Mr. Roosevelt's thought in thus taking exact quotations from this historic message out of their somewhat rambling context. It was said of President Van Buren that he "rowed towards every objective with muffled oars." The same was equally true of F.D.R. He was far too able an orator to present his thought in an orderly but plodding progression. This does not mean, however, that President Roosevelt was lacking in a systematic and intelligent political philosophy. He stands out imposingly from the massive ranks of the disciples of Rousseau.

As was the case with Robespierre, so also this modern advocate of the *volonté générale* preferred quick action to consistent thought, and the easily spoken to the painfully written word. This justifies us in cutting through the maze of his oratorical by-play, concerned only with the incidental, in order to focus the major objective that he had in mind. That goal was unquestionably totalitarian democracy, which has long been a part, though never long the dominant part, of the American political tradition. It is certainly not a hostile criticism of Mr. Roosevelt, but rather a tribute to his dynamic courage, to say that he fought so valiantly and successfully for socialism in spite of the general American prejudice against it, and in spite of the formidable constitutional obstacles to its attainment.

The "Four Freedoms" speech is an excellent illustration of the subtle manner in which—with the aid of war psychology—this strong American President waged an uphill fight. The inharmonious quartette was billed as "Freedom *of* Speech"; "Freedom *of* Worship"; "Freedom *from* Want"; "Freedom *from* Fear." As indicated by the necessarily different propositions—"of" and "from"—the first two are of a wholly different nature from the second pair. But few, if any political scientists have ever closely examined the monstrosity produced by this clever amalgamation of contradictory concepts.

The first two "freedoms"—of speech and of worship—are of course written into our Constitution, in the first article of the Bill of Rights. But there they are set forth as natural rights on which the government of the United States shall never commit trespass: "Congress shall make no law respecting" them. In Mr. Roosevelt's presentation, however, it became the province of government to *provide* rather than to *respect* these rights—"everywhere in the world."

The second pair of "freedoms," cited without any distinction from the first pair, are not by any possible stretch of the imagination definable as natural rights. No priest, no prophet, no spiritual, ethical or moral leader of any era or any creed, has ever had the temerity to assert that men have a natural right to freedom from want or from fear. On the contrary, nearly all religions have sedulously inculcated a healthy fear of God, and Christianity in particular teaches the definite danger in placing material satisfactions ahead of the fulfillment of spiritual wants. Therefore, as Lenin argued, it is necessary first to weaken faith in God in order later to establish faith in government as the authentic source of freedom.[1]

Moreover, though this does not bother the communists, there is an obvious tendency which makes freedom from want and freedom from fear mutually contradictory, as soon as they are regarded as dominant governmental responsibilities. As Robespierre soon discovered, dissenters must be terrorized if egalitarianism is to be enforced. Evidences of this are not lacking in the United States today. One illustration can be found in the enforced collection of social security taxes, designed to provide the elderly with "freedom from want."

The sect of the Amish, excellent farmers and peaceful citizens, are forbidden by their old-fashioned religion to accept money they have not earned. So, when democratically blanketed into the social security program, many of these Amish simply failed to pay the tax involved, quite in the tradition of 1776. The riposte of Washington (not George) has been to seize the livestock of these trouble makers and sell it at public auction. One of these outrages, in Wayne County, Ohio, was graphically reported under the heading "Twilight for the Dissenter" by Walter Leckrone, editor of the Indianapolis *Times* in its issue of November 2, 1958. An excerpt is very much to the point:

> As the sale began, a young Oberlin College student turned up wearing on his back a crudely hand-lettered sign that read, "If Government can take these horses today it could take yours tomorrow—Don't Bid!"
> He had hardly walked a dozen steps before two burly sheriff's deputies grabbed him and hustled him off to their car. The Gestapo couldn't have done it more efficiently. The sale went on.

But the deputy sheriffs were only doing their duty. The real blame rests with those who fail to see that political government cannot assure freedom of any kind, to anybody, without regimentation of those who would prefer to fend for themselves. It was to emphasize the importance of these individual immunities that the Bill of Rights was immediately added to the original Constitution and that the powers reserved to the States were intended to include, in Madison's words, "all the objects which, in the ordinary course of affairs, concern the lives, liberties and properties of the people." Under the original theory of American government it would have been flagrantly unconstitutional to force "freedom from want" on the Amish farmers by the extraordinary device of seizing the farm horses essential to their independent way of life. But the Fourteenth and

Sixteenth Amendments have brought great changes.

Still greater changes are foreshadowed by the theory that it is the role of centralized government actually to provide freedom, for all but "trouble makers." The implications of this we shall examine later, but at this stage it is appropriate to ask whether freedom *from* something is really freedom? The word originally denoted a positive condition. To be free was to be at liberty *for* a self-decided course of action. Freedom *from* implies paternal protection, rather than individual choice, making the condition negative and reversing its traditional meaning. *Security* from want and *security* from fear were more accurately the last two desiderata of Mr. Roosevelt's "Four Freedoms." But it was supremely adroit to equate "freedom" with "security" because any government must have some responsibility to its citizens in the latter field though, under our Federal Constitution, as President Roosevelt himself had emphasized in 1933, the responsibility is much more clearly local than national. So, merely by calling security "freedom" there was an assertion of the "right" of centralized government to play the role traditionally assigned to God.

There would be no justification for taking the Four Freedoms speech so seriously, if the Presidential Message of January 6, 1941, had been a mere flash in the pan. But throughout the war Mr. Roosevelt kept referring to the Four Freedoms and, as victory began to be assured, in his Message to Congress of January 11, 1944, the President proposed an "Economic Bill of Rights" squarely based on the earlier theorizing. Under this "second Bill of Rights," said the President, "a new basis of security and prosperity can be established for all." He then named eight of these "rights," making clear that this was an incomplete list, as follows:

1) The right to a useful and remunerative job in the industries or shops or farms or mines of the nation.

2) The right to earn enough to provide adequate food and clothing and recreation.

3) The right of every farmer to raise and sell his products at a return which will give him and his family a decent living.

4) The right of every business man, large and small, to trade in an atmosphere of freedom from unfair competition and domination by monopolies at home or abroad.

5) The right of every family to a decent home.

6) The right to adequate medical care and the opportunity to achieve and enjoy good health.

7) The right to adequate protection from the economic fears of old age, sickness, accident and unemployment.

8) The right to a good education.

"All of these rights," continued the President, "spell security. And after this war is won we must be prepared to move forward, in the implementation of these rights, to new goals of human happiness and well-being." Mr. Roosevelt then asserted that "it is definitely the responsibility of Congress" to legislate "this economic Bill of Rights" and concluded:

Our fighting men abroad—and their families at home—expect such a program and have the right to insist upon it. It is to their demands that this government should pay heed, rather than to the whining demands of selfish pressure groups, who seek to feather their nests while young Americans are dying.

Throughout 1944, despite his rapidly developing mental incapacity, Franklin Delano Roosevelt continued to emphasize his "Economic Bill of Rights," and to endeavor to bind the Democratic Party to its realization. In the Presidential campaign of 1944, running for his fourth term, he several times repeated the eight points quoted and in his Chicago campaign address, October 28, 1944, he added federal crop insurance to them. "I know," he then asserted, that the American people "agree with those objectives—that they demand them—that they are determined to get them—and that they are going to get them."

Much water has flowed down the Potomac since the "Economic Bill of Rights" was drafted on its banks. None can determine the extent to which it has been implemented because none can define such iridescent generalities as "adequate recreation," "decent living" or "good education." All these phrases have different meanings for different people, and what little definable meaning they have is constantly changing. What seemed decent living to Abraham Lincoln—without TV, without a car or telephone, without even any comics in the newspapers—would seem horrible to many Americans today. Conversely, what seems a good education to some modern pedagogues would certainly not have been so regarded by Woodrow Wilson.

But in the case of the asserted "right to a useful and remunerative job," attainment is measurable. In the first Truman Administration an effort to make centralized government responsible in the matter was made by the introduction of a "full employment" bill. This proposed to step up "Federal in-

vestment and expenditure" whenever free enterprise
fails to maintain "the level required to assure a full
employment volume of production." This unperspi-
cacious proposal was greatly modified in the eventual "Employment Act of 1946" which nevertheless,
though with many qualifying clauses, does declare
that "the continuing policy and responsibility of the
Federal Government" is "to promote maximum employment, production and purchasing power." It
was this legislation which created the Council of
Economic Advisers to the President, and also the
Joint Congressional Committee on the Economic
Report (now Joint Economic Committee) of seven
members each from Senate and House.[2]

The philosophy behind the Employment Act of
1946 has often encouraged Congress to appropriate
more for defense spending than the military departments themselves have recommended. But the unemployment relief statistics show that it has done little
to secure that "full employment" which is an attainable policy only in a completely socialized state.
Nor is there any very convincing evidence that
Americans are willing to pay this price in order to
establish "the right to a useful and remunerative
job." Indeed, there is little evidence to suggest that
there was ever any strong popular demand for any
part of Mr. Roosevelt's "Economic Bill of Rights."
The "demand" which this President visualized did
not well up from below, but was sedulously and
artificially stimulated from above.

During the depression there was certainly widespread anxiety and distress. The great majority of
people welcomed the relief measures of the early
New Deal. No President has ever received a stronger

popular endorsement than did Franklin D. Roosevelt when he ran for his second term. But this does not mean that farmers were demanding permanent price supports, that organized labor expected guaranteed employment or that people in general were insisting on government housing, socialized medicine, and so forth. There is much more evidence to indicate that the demand for governmental subsidies developed *after* the "right" to them had been proclaimed. That did not happen until the war had centralized power to the extent that made permanent "federal" subsidization seem practical. Naturally, the general will to receive regular bonus checks from Washington acquired reality, once people had been assured by the highest authority that this was no more than their democratic right.

What is beyond question and above controversy in this matter is that the program enormously strengthened the power and prestige of the general government at the expense of the constituent States. Only the central government could assert an "Economic Bill of Rights" and only the central government could do anything to make these alleged rights real for all. Coupled with the centralization inevitably resulting from the war effort, this "Roosevelt revolution" turned the political thinking of the American people away from that of Jefferson and Madison, towards that of Rousseau and Marx. One may gauge the extent of the change by comparing the social science courses offered in our colleges today with those of 1931. Emphasis on the demands of the "general will" has increased enormously, while consideration of federal theory and structure has greatly diminished. As recently as 1956 those popular historians, Morison and Commager, were telling undergraduate readers that "State rights are now an historical exhibit maintained by the Republican party." [3]

Obviously the trend back to Rousseau did not stop with Mr. Roosevelt's death, and is continuing independently of what party is in power. In farming, housing, health, education, road construction, old-age pensions and unemployment insurance, to mention only the more important services, centralized "aid," always with centralized control in the background, is now an established principle. It emphasizes the trees at the expense of the wood to make a detailed catalog of what is involved in the proliferation of nationalized service agencies. But one other development must be specifically noted as part of the transformation of our Federal Republic into a democratic Service State. Its starting point is also those very dubious "Four Freedoms," which President Roosevelt sought to see established "everywhere in the world."

An attempt to implement these, on the international level, is made by Chapters IX and X of the United Nations Charter.[4] The Charter is, of course, a treaty and was ratified as such by the United States Senate on July 28, 1945, with only two dissenting votes. Treaty provisions rank as "the supreme Law of the Land," to quote the wording in Paragraph 2, Article VI of the Constitution. Therefore, prior to 1945, great care was taken to insure that treaties ratified by the United States did not run counter to basic constitutional provisions. This doubt as to consistency was a major reason for the refusal of the Senate to ratify the Treaty of Versailles, con-

taining the Covenant of the League of Nations, after
World War I.

Such doubts were not raised, at least not in effective form, when the Senate debated the U.N.
Charter, although this went a good deal farther to
infringe national sovereignty than did the old League
Covenant. That contained nothing like Articles 55
and 56 of the Charter:

> Article Fifty-five—With a view to the creation
> of conditions of stability and well-being which are
> necessary for peaceful and friendly relations
> among nations based on respect for the principle
> of equal rights and self-determination of peoples,
> the United Nations shall promote:
> a. higher standards of living, full employment,
> and conditions of economic and social progress
> and development;
> b. solutions of international economic, social,
> health and related problems; and international cul-
> tural and educational cooperation; and
> c. universal respect for, and observance of, hu-
> man rights and fundamental freedoms for all with-
> out distinction as to race, sex, language or religion.
> Article Fifty-six—All members pledge them-
> selves to take joint and separate action in coopera-
> tion with the Organization for the achievement of
> the purposes set forth in Article 55.[5]

The above language is so fuzzy that for the most
part it can be taken to mean almost anything. And
nowhere in the Charter is there any attempt to
define such highly generalized terms as "conditions
of social progress," "solutions of related problems"
or "respect for fundamental freedoms." What is
certain is that in many of these matters, such as
cultural and educational issues, our central government has only dubious constitutional prerogative in

the domestic sphere. So its agreement to promote throughout the world what it lacks clear-cut authority to promote at home was startling, to say the least. And the pledge to take "separate action," to achieve ends of very doubtful constitutionality, was bound to raise serious trouble, assuming that any significant number of Americans retain loyalty to the principles of their Federal Republic.

We shall shortly consider the lingering vitality of the American political tradition, which so clearly runs counter to the unlimited duties accepted by the central government in these, and other, articles of the U.N. Charter. But it is not premature to point now to the counter-revolution which is obviously building up against the conception of the all-powerful, centralized Service State.

After adopting the Charter of the United Nations the logical sequal would have been a Constitutional Amendment abolishing the forty-eight States as partially sovereign entities. They no longer have any real excuse for being if all the functions so sweepingly adumbrated in Article 55 are the prerogative of the central government. Yet, the only Amendment actually adopted since 1945 is the one that limits a President to two terms, which certainly does nothing to forward centralized executive power. Other proposed amendments, definitely designed to re-establish the system of checks and balances, have received considerable popular support, especially the one sponsored by former Senator Bricker to limit the scope of "treaty law." [6]

As we have gone through a revolution without amending the Constitution, so we could also accomplish a counter-revolution without amendment. The

Supreme Court alone could do a great deal by adopting a policy of strict rather than loose interpretation. And Congress is in a position to force the hand of the Supreme Court in this matter. That is the significance of the Byrd-Smith bill, in which these two Virginia legislators seek to inform the Court that when Congress intends a federal law to invalidate all State laws in the same field it will say so, and otherwise the Court is not to presume such intention. In the legal profession the pressure is stronger. In August, 1958, the Conference of State Chief Justices adopted, by a vote of 36 to 8, a report asserting that "at times the Supreme Court manifests, or seems to manifest, an impatience with the slow workings of our federal system." This report questioned whether the United States still has "a government of laws and not of men." And it warned that "The value of our system of federalism and of local self-government in local matters . . . should be kept firmly in mind." [7] Further sharp criticism of the trend in Supreme Court decisions came from the February, 1959, meeting of the American Bar Association's House of Delegates. There are many other indications of a growing movement towards the restoration of State sovereignty, a movement which tends to reverse the trend towards centralization, and thereby to hamper the progress of unbridled democratic theory.

This totalitarian concept of democracy originated with Rousseau. His theory of the social contract hinges on the mystical conception of a "general will," which may be mistaken but can never be wrong. Such a will, of course, must be formulated into concrete terms by somebody, regardless of how extended and perfected the machinery of democratic elections. The legislature may do its conscientious best to reflect and interpret the general will, but still that will must be defined by the executive. There lies the tremendous danger. For the executive, though a mere finite man, is always under pressure, and is by democratic theory indeed compelled, to formulate the general will as he sees best.

Of one thing the executive may be sure: that the majority want more of the good things of life, and if they can get them without undue personal effort, so much the better. So the executive naturally tends to promise material gain, contingent of course on his remaining in power. The impetus to personal rule is obvious. Inevitably the theory of the general will leads towards dictatorship.

Against these implications of the *social* contract the spirit, and for the most part the letter, of our *political* contract—the Constitution—stand four-square. It so divides and circumscribes the concept of the general will that its embodiment in a single person is extremely difficult. Franklin Delano Roosevelt, a man of highly unusual political ability and ambition, did under war conditions succeed in this embodiment—temporarily. We do not yet know the permanence of his work.

It could be that the Federal Republic is now undermined beyond hope of restoration. It could also be that the American people have had more than they want of totalitarian democracy and are turning against it as they earlier turned against Jacobinism. But the problem is more complicated now than in the days of Citizen Genêt.

TWELVE

The Need for an Enemy

In the relations of individuals "a friend in need is a friend indeed." But in the relationships of governments, which lack the moral qualities of men, the opposite is often true. Occasions arise when, from the viewpoint of those in power, it is as important for the state to have external enemies as to have friends.

History shows many such instances. In the third century B.C. it was necessary for Rome, if that city-state were to unite all Italy under its sway, to emphasize and even promote the hostility of Carthage: *Carthago delenda est*—"must be destroyed." To build a colonial empire it was important for England, after the discovery of America, to "singe the beard" of Spanish kings. In his work for the unification of Germany, under Prussian hegemony, Bismarck was greatly helped by, and certainly welcomed, the aggressive tactics of France under Napoleon III.

From the viewpoint of political science, as distinct from politics, it is fruitless to apportion blame, when the emotions of one people are for reasons of state channeled into enmity against another. To defend the course taken by one's own government, "right or wrong," is of course the natural reaction. But it contributes nothing to any solution of the international anarchy. To improve that situation it must

first be admitted that no state as such has ever voluntarily recognized any law superior to that of its own
self-preservation, and that the government of every
state—including our own—always interprets that law
in terms of its own necessities. This is what the
Apostle Paul evidently had in mind when he
voiced his warning "against the rulers of the dark-
ness of this world, against spiritual wickedness in
high places." [1] The amorality of the state is as pronounced today as it was then, or as it was early in
the sixteenth century, when Machiavelli wrote:

> Where the very safety of the country depends
> upon the resolution to be taken, no considerations
> of justice or injustice, humanity or cruelty, nor of
> glory or of shame, should be allowed to prevail.
> But putting all other considerations aside, the
> only question should be: What course will save
> the life and liberty of the country? [2]

The "safety" of a country, however, is no longer
merely a matter of its immunity from armed aggression. Economic, as well as physical, security has now
come to be regarded as a right of citizenship. And
in the United States the provision of employment is
regarded by many as a settled responsibility of the
national government, which neither of the major
political parties is likely to deny. There are differences of opinion as to the procedures necessary to
prevent any serious unemployment. But there is general political agreement that Washington has an
underlying duty to provide jobs, if, as and when
private employers are unable to make them available.
Since the great depression, governmental function in
this field has been enlarged from the relief of unemployment to the provision of employment, a change

of emphasis with very far-reaching consequences.

One measurement of this change is the coincident rapid expansion of labor union demands, mounting from work relief and unemployment compensation to the ambition of a guaranteed annual wage. If employment, regardless of productivity, is a "right," then there is good reason for making it permanent. And there is no reason whatsoever for thinking that the effort of organized labor in behalf of contractual employment will slacken. On the contrary, every achievement in this direction is likely to lead to further demands which will be supported by political as well as industrial pressures. The inflationary effects can be offset, for the well-organized, by obtaining "escalator" clauses which automatically increase wages in proportion to any increase in the monthly cost-of-living index. Thus, with the cooperation of business management, inflation can be made less of an anxiety for a large and especially favored portion of the electorate.

It does not follow, however, that the trade cycle has been, or can be, stabilized under a system of free enterprise. Regardless of the provisions for "social security," and despite a flexible monetary policy, any lessening of consumer demand will still result in heavy inventories and force a cutting of production schedules in order to reduce unsalable surplus. This curtailment of production, with consequent idleness, is the more inevitable when costs have been made rigid by factors beyond the employer's control.

Then, through a process of chain reaction, any "soft spot" in a major industry will tend to spread— backwards to the producers of raw materials, forwards to the distributive occupations. If automobile sales fall off, whether in spite or because of fantastic design and gadgetry, the slow-down soon threatens the employment both of steel workers and of sales-men. Further effects then come into play. Clothing stores in Pittsburgh don't need so many clerks and advertising agencies in New York dispense with copy writers. Grocery sales go down and oil com-panies stop hiring geologists. There is no end to it—until the demand again becomes effective.

Reflection on this basic characteristic of the free enterprise system is necessary because of the wide-spread belief that governmental intervention has somehow solved the problem posed by downward fluctuations of effective demand. Many assert there is no longer any need for the economy to "go through the wringer" of periodic depressions, with all their by-products of anxiety and distress. Now, it is argued, we have "built-in" safeguards against any such periodic deterioration as has been described. There is a very real question as to the efficacy of these safeguards, but to explore that is not the pur-pose of this study. Our concern is an assessment of their general effect on the constitutional structure of this Federal Republic.

So far as agriculture is concerned a temporarily effective, though highly dubious, safeguard against depression has been set up. Its basis is the Com-modity Credit Corporation, through which the cen-tral government pays a guaranteed price for the un-disposable surplus in certain crops, from peanuts through butter to wheat, storing it up as a "built-in" headache for the Secretary of Agriculture. When this naive device for maintaining prices increased the farm surplus to colossal proportions it was supplemented by adjuncts like the euphemistically named "soil bank," the central purpose of which is to pay farmers not to produce.[3] This even-handed policy of subsidizing both to increase and to curtail production has done little for the small farmers but has at least been successful in maintaining thousands of Department of Agriculture employees at the taxpayers' expense. An ever-mounting government payroll, civilian and military, is certainly one route towards the goal of full employment.

From the viewpoint of consistency Congress might properly apply the same remedy to a saturated automobile market. The Ford Company could as reasonably be paid a subsidy for every Edsel it can produce, but doesn't. And simultaneously a parity price might be set on Buicks and Plymouths, taking over those unsold at that price and storing them, for possible later presentation to our allies, in the holds of moth-balled Victory ships. While that may sound absurd it would be precisely as sensible as the present policy for excess agricultural production. So the reason why such procedure goes unadvocated for industry would seem to be the alternative which is available in the case of industrial capacity to produce.

That alternative is what we call "defense production." So long as the country is menaced, or thinks itself menaced, Congress will readily vote almost unlimited funds for its protection. Such armament is for the most part "hardware"—metal vehicles and weapons which, together with the requisite fuels, are directly stimulative to the extractive and fabricating industries. It is these which absorb the greater part of investment capital and provide the bulk of employment. If business is good in these basic industries it will be good throughout the nation as a whole, and vice versa. For while the retarding effects of curtailed spending spread quickly through a capitalistic economy, so do the stimulative consequences of "easy" money.

Congress, which nominally controls the purse strings, never cuts the military estimates by any substantial amount. They are presented as essential for the national security, and it is all but impossible for the most conscientious legislator to prove that this is not the case. It is, of course, easy to find evidence of almost incredible military waste. Many instances of this have been detected and publicized, especially by the Hoover Commission on Organization of the Executive Branch of the Government. But the defense budget cannot be substantially reduced by effecting relatively minor economies. Moreover, there is reason to believe that these estimates are not infrequently padded to an extent necessary to offset cuts that may be insisted upon by the Budget Bureau and the Congress. And even when the military estimates are conscientiously held down it is always possible for "defense-minded" Congressmen, with an eye on military production in their own communities, to combine to push appropriations higher.

To outline this situation involves no substantial criticism of the Department of Defense, either under present or previous managements. This department does not direct the foreign policy of the United States, but is saddled with the responsibility of providing the physical power without which that foreign policy could not even pretend to be effective. Consequently, the more far-flung and grandiose our overseas commitments, the more extravagant must be the defense estimates necessary to give them substance. And the net result is military spending which, since the close of the Korean War, has never fallen below thirty-five billion dollars annually and in most of these years has been close to or even over forty billions.

The mind finds it difficult to grasp the significance of such astronomical figures. They acquire more reality by saying that the military expenditure of our central government now runs continuously at a rate well above one hundred million dollars a *day*. Another way of looking at it is to point out that only about eight days of defense expenditure, during 1958, were covered by the federal income taxes levied that year on the enormous Bell telephone system, though these taxes were then more than 13 per cent of the system's total revenue.

Marshal Göring was much ridiculed by Americans, in the early days of the Nazi regime, for saying that Germany could not afford both guns and butter. But exactly the same thought was expressed by President Eisenhower in his report to the American people immediately after the Russians got their second *Sputnik* aloft. "We cannot," the President then said, "have both what we must have and what we would like to have." That is because: "Defense today is expensive and growing more so."

Indeed it is. The cost of intercontinental missiles and nuclear explosives is fantastic, and to produce these and scarcely less intricate weapons a tremendous expansion and integration of scientific industry has been necessary. It is consolingly pointed out that the total defense cost can still be held to just under 10 per cent of the gross national product, whereas in Soviet Russia the percentage spent on armament undoubtedly runs higher. But this slim consolation overlooks two vital points. It is wholly consistent with the communist system, but not at all with ours, to have a handful of officials planning and managing the economy. The second point is that even a 10 per cent armament leverage on a free-market economy is more than enough to spell the difference between boom and bust.

The gigantic infusion of public funds goes far to explain why the United States has had a fairly continuous inflationary "prosperity" since the close of World War II, instead of the contraction that should be expected to afflict a capitalistic economy when war spending is terminated. We have avoided the depression that normally follows war by the unusual expedient of avoiding peace, a course necessitated by the obvious enmity of the wartime ally which our own government built up as a formidable threat to our security. The story is told in the annual budget figures. In only one year since the close of World War II has the military expenditure of the United States been less than double what it was at the peak of World War I, and in that single year —fiscal 1950—this outlay was almost double. To minimize these figures by considering dollar depreciation is also to emphasize that military spending on this scale is a cause of that depreciation.

Along with the spurious prosperity produced by cold-war spending has come increasing acceptance of the theory that it is a duty of the national government to guarantee full employment for all. The affirmation of socialism at this time is no mere coincidence. Once the White House has announced that everyone has the right to full employment, and has seemingly shown the ability to provide it, people naturally and properly expect all pledges in this respect to be fulfilled. They do not ask, any more than does a child, how the accepted paternalistic responsibility will be met. That is the business of those who have assumed the parental role, not less so if temporarily they refrain from the parental discipline without which any household soon becomes anarchic. This sharply qualified individualism is of course far less logical than the thoroughgoing socialism of Soviet Russia, which assuredly can provide employment of a kind for every adult, but only by applying an iron regimentation which none may question.

It would seem that a very large number of Americans now actually believe not merely in "the right to a useful and remunerative job," but also in all the other "Economic Rights," such as "adequate recreation," "adequate medical care" and "good education," as promised them by President Roosevelt in 1944. The primary responsibility for providing most of these "rights," in the form of fringe benefits additional to wages and salaries, is currently placed upon employers, either by legislation, by labor union pressure, or by both. So far private enterprise has been able to carry this additional load of pensions, medical care, paid recreation, free meals, etc., etc., though the cost of such extras rose from one cent an hour per employee in 1929 to 25 cents an hour in 1955, and is projected by the United States Chamber of

Commerce at approximately $1.00 per hour per employee for 1975. But if private enterprise should now for any reason be unable to provide all these subsidies it is apparently the "general will" that Washington should do so, in accordance with the assurance that these are "Economic Rights," based on "the Four Freedoms," which the central government has a positive duty to provide.

Thus there has arisen an inexorable pressure to maintain that full employment which is unfortunately incompatible with the free market. This pressure bears on the trade unions, the leadership of which—whether or not honestly elected—must ever strive to make each contract with management more favorable to organized labor than its predecessor. It bears heavily on management, which to make any profit over and above arbitrarily fixed expenses must press for government contracts, either direct or indirect. And most heavily of all the pressure to maintain full employment bears down on the Administration in office, which knows that it will become a target of popular criticism, subject to overthrow at the next election, if it fails to do so. Of course there is no solution to the problem in the use of automation to cut costs since, if only temporarily, this increases unemployment.

It is this complex of pressures, the direct if generally unforeseen consequence of Mr. Roosevelt's "Economic Bill of Rights," which makes it virtually impossible to keep both the national and the State budgets from rising, year after year, no matter how grievous the tax burden necessary to keep them even nominally balanced. And, more especially, it is this situation which has now made the American economy very largely dependent on a huge and continuous expenditure for defense.

If that type of spending were cut from a rate of well over one hundred million dollars a day to a rate of one million a day, which in a rational world would still seem a sizable amount for any nation to spend on armament, the economic dislocation in the United States would be profound. Indeed, it would be so disastrous that such reduction—or anything approaching it—is simply not a matter of practical politics and therefore cannot possibly be expected. A part of the evidence is found in the comments of the financial writers who, whenever the stock market slips, assure their readers that this is a "secondary adjustment" and that the constant outpouring of defense expenditure insures a fundamentally "sound" economy. Only a real prospect of disarmament would be—to use the word actually employed—a "threat."

There are, certainly, alternative forms of government spending which theoretically might be expanded to offset a serious curtailment of defense expenditure. Foreign aid might be boosted even higher. Very substantial additional amounts could be channeled into roadbuilding, housing, school construction, irrigation, flood control and numerous other public undertakings. We may overlook the fact that this would still be "government spending." That aside, it is more difficult to obtain Congressional authorization for any of these projects than in the case of armament. Only in that one form of gigantic outlay is it possible to assume the need, to ignore the cost completely, and to provide a spillway of money from the Treasury into the economy on the mere assertion of national necessity. Also, defense is the clear prerogative of the central government whereas the domestic improvements are not. It is suggested that more commodious public school facilities, for instance, might in a general way be regarded as contributory to "defense," and financed by Washington as such. But this is one of the issues in which the tradition of federalism dies hard, and is related to the burden of taxation with a critical scrutiny seldom directed against armament expenditure.

Nevertheless, the Congress will continue to appropriate upwards of $100,000,000 a day for defense only so long as people believe that the national security is actively menaced by an aggressive foreign power. And since this rate of expenditure must now be continuous, an equally constant official propaganda must be exercised to make it appear that the potential foe is the personification of evil, a dire threat to a way of life which we are ourselves undermining by the way we confront that threat.

The communist regimes have certainly done much to make such a portrayal of Russia and China wholly plausible, but other factors are involved. They were suggested when the Moscow Government, on May 14, 1956, announced a decision to carry out substantial unilateral disarmament. Whether or not sincere, an immediate result was a definite downward turn in the New York stock market. In the words of the Associated Press: "The declines were attributed by brokers to a fear that defense spending in America might be curtailed." Secretary of Defense Wilson thereupon promptly let it be known that the Administration would cancel no military contracts merely because Russia proposed to do so. Some months later, when economy pressures began to cut a little fat from the military establishment, there was a real stock market break, and a quite perceptible business recession. The coming of the *Sputniks*, defined in the United States as an enemy accomplishment, served to re-stimulate the cold-war economy.

There is also a powerful, though intermittent, political leverage operating to maintain defense spending at a very high level. This becomes especially effective as a Presidential election approaches. The great industrial States are those with the highest number of electoral votes, and therefore those in which the political struggle for the Presidency is keenest. Percisely because the leadership of organized labor tends to favor the Democratic Party, "modern" Republicanism must seek to offset this by espousing a policy of "full employment" for which huge and continuous defense contracts are essential. In behalf of defense spending, if not for foreign policy as a whole, the bi-partisan attitude is well established. Thus there is little or no political criticism of the uncompetitive channeling of defense contracts to areas in which the Department of Labor certifies unemployment as "substantial." The practice violates both the principles of free enterprise and the spirit of the anti-trust laws, and thereby illustrates the triumph of socialist planning.

Although economic and political considerations now make it difficult for the Administration to curtail defense spending, it is equally impossible for anyone in authority to admit the fact. No official can openly suggest that the Kremlin may conceivably be sincere in seeking a relaxation of the now completely fantastic armament race. One might as well expect the Secretary of the Treasury to say publicly that during an inflationary period Savings Bonds are a bad buy. And because it is in practice impossible for our officials to tell the whole truth they are gradually forced into overt deception. In spite of the cost-of-living indices the steadily depreciating "E" Bonds are advertised as "the safest investment in the world." In spite of the logic and good reasoning often found in Russian overtures it is consistently maintained that because communists are congenital liars, no conciliation of any kind is possible.

Such an attitude is of course barren of any promise for improvement in the international situation unless one can assume either that communism will collapse from incompetence, or that the Russian people will rebel against its centralized tyranny. Since the *Sputniks* the former hope seems untenable. And when Americans are themselves so disposed to accept governmental dictation there is small reason to anticipate that people with no tradition of individual freedom will dare oppose the "general will."

Unfortunately, there is no longer room for doubt as to the official desire to keep the American people ignorant as to the actual motives and forces directing national policy. This anxiety is suggested by the proliferating network of information and public relations officers with which the policy makers in every government agency are now surrounded. These are not yet coordinated into a single Ministry of Public Enlightenment, as in Nazi Germany under Dr. Goebbels. But the trend is certainly in that direction. The irony is that the more we propagandize our own people, in a manner essentially un-American, the more we fulminate about the anti-American propaganda of the communists.

Every Washington correspondent and radio commentator can cite instances of official pressure brought to report governmental policies and activities in a continuously favorable light. But the most comprehensive evidence is found in the published hearings on "Availability of Information from Federal Departments and Agencies," conducted since November 7, 1955, by a special subcommittee of the House Committee on Government Operations. This committee has throughout keyed its inquiry to the incontrovertible thesis of James Madison: "A popular government without popular information or the means of acquiring it is but a prologue to a farce or a tragedy, or perhaps both." And the testimony it has elicited certainly shows that the United States today is in this prologue stage.

Of particular interest is the statement made at the opening hearing by James Reston, the highly regarded chief of the Washington bureau of the New York *Times*. He then observed that reporters confront a condition quite as insidious as the official "suppression of news." This is "a growing tendency to manage the news." Mr. Reston gave as an illustration, first the State Department's effort to play up the 1955 Summit Conference at Geneva as a great American diplomatic triumph, and then the subsequent effort to blame Soviet Russia for its failure because "the people in the Western countries were letting down their guard. . . ." [4]

Much later in these hearings, on July 8, 1957, an interesting bit of testimony came from General

Arno H. Luehman, Director of the Office of Information Services, Department of the Air Force. In answer to some acute questioning on the guided missiles program, from Representative John E. Moss of California,[5] General Luehman said: "We feel, in our service, again speaking for the Air Force only, that the progress we have made, that the country has made in this missile development firings, has reached the point that maybe we ought to consider telling a little more about it."

Just four months later, after the *Sputniks* had made "telling a little more about it" a political necessity, President Eisenhower himself gave a green light in this particular channel.

For this Federal Republic there is a very serious threat in the combination of undisputed power and calculated secrecy now exercised by the executive branch of the central government.[6] Indeed it may and should be questioned whether the Russian military threat, which of course encourages the centralizing trend here, is the more serious danger. Care must be taken, however not to concentrate the blame on those harassed officials who, like the rest of us, are caught in the swiftly running tide of world events. The fundamental problem is not of their making but is an inevitable consequence of the fallacious theory of a general will.

If there is anything on which the people of the U.S.A. and the U.S.S.R. are mutually agreed we may be sure that it is horror at the thought of their reciprocal mass murder by intercontinental missiles with atomic warheads. Yet the highly centralized governments of both countries, each claiming to be a "people's democracy" and each claiming to act in self-defense, have been moving steadily towards a smash for which a balance of terror has become the sole deterrent. For the Russians, who have never known self-government and free enterprise, the tragedy is far less poignant than it is for us.

Under the fatal illusion of strongly nationalized power the United States has now geared its economy to preparation for war and if those gears were unmeshed the immediate effect would be catastrophic. Instead of plenty of work at high wages there would be, for a time at least, much less work at much lower wages. Gradually, the dislocation would rectify itself. Taxes could be cut to a fraction of the present scale. Production costs would then come down, stimulating renewed economic activity and employment for the cold-war workers. The dollar would regain, instead of ever steadily losing, purchasing power. But the transition to a peace economy could not be made overnight. It would be accompanied by hardships which many Americans are no longer prepared to accept. Like Frankenstein's monster the general will to live luxuriously would turn on those who have animated it. And this fate officials who are nominally in the seat of power believe they must at all costs avert, even though the present course portends the fall of the Republic.

It was difficult, evidently, to solve the "re-entry problem" for guided missiles. But the problem of re-entry to American constitutional government is every bit as difficult.

THIRTEEN

The States and the Presidency

In spite of facility in adaptation and innovation, most Americans of Anglo-Saxon origin are strongly traditionalist at heart. This is not to say that those of the original breed are in any way superior people. They merely recognize that our institutions were developed by their ancestors, and that the preservation of this inheritance is therefore something of a personal responsibility.

Nowhere is this stubborn sense of tradition stronger than in the field of politics. There we adhere to inherited practices which are literally senseless if our true objective is to centralize power in behalf of world leadership. Of course it could be argued that this conservatism roots in ignorance. Harry Hopkins thought that most Americans are "too damn dumb" to appreciate the efforts made for them by an elite in Washington. But the tendency to cling to "horse and buggy" procedures in politics could also be intelligently based. It could reveal a determination to preserve our federal system in spite of the obstacles it raises for bureaucratic planners. The issue deserves analysis. And it is logical to focus that analysis on our most important collective political undertaking, which is the choosing of the Chief Executive.

The procedure of a Presidential election is certainly not democratic, and nobody will pretend that it is efficient from any overall national viewpoint. One knows in advance that no aspirant from a State with a small electoral vote has any chance of nomination, no matter how ideal his qualifications. One also knows that to be successful—to date at least—a candidate must be a white man of Anglo-Saxon extraction and a definite church affiliation. The laws to this effect are not less binding because unwritten. Moreover, the conditions controlling a candidate's campaign are as well defined as are the personal qualifications.

For months before the election, dispassionate and objective consideration of any national issue is all but ruled out. The candidate is expected to appear personally in as many States as possible, and to slant his speeches towards the dominant interest of the locality, regardless of the resulting inconsistencies which partisan critics will be on the *qui vive* to detect. In moderating these conditions somewhat, radio and television have simultaneously established new ones. The candidate now must be nicely groomed, reasonably photogenic and something of an actor to boot. Possibly a Robert Montgomery could make another Abraham Lincoln an acceptable candidate today. But it would require a lot of make-up, in every sense of the word.

The staging of the Presidential campaign is also stereotyped. There must be countless rallies, with a heavy concentration on banalities, platitudes, histrionics and double-talk. The formula further demands that tons of newsprint be consumed in reporting these largely meaningless garrulities. Expenditure of money is almost as lavish as the waste of time, for a major purpose of each camp is to cancel whatever political effect has been achieved by the other. The incongruous antithesis of elephant and donkey is well chosen. They never come to grips with each other in natural life, and not much more so in politics.

Behind all this façade, however, a number of shrewd professionals are operating with keen intelligence. This dexterous political manipulation is readily apparent at the precinct level, where fanfare and window dressing are at a minimum. There the concentration is on the machine and not the man. As its operation moves up to the culminating circus of the national convention the party machine is progressively concealed by the panoply of showmanship. But we all know that the strategy is determined in hotel suites, controlling the tactics followed on the floor of Convention Hall. Of course, as in all big battles, the high command sometimes loses control.

What should be better appreciated is the fact that the farther we get from the local community, the more gaudy and the less democratic our politics become. It is at the grass roots, or in the city blocks, that they have the greatest reality. There politics are truly popular, or can be made so. On the national level there is much stimulated sound and fury —indeed an approximation of bedlam—but the significance so far as democracy is concerned diminishes. To be a ward or precinct leader you do not have to be an Anglo-Saxon Protestant; you need not dress well, look well or speak well. Indeed such attributes are likely to be handicaps. The characteristics necessary for a President are decidedly not the ones of those who are most influential in selecting the candidates for that office.

There is nothing even remotely cynical in this realistic appraisal of our major political enterprise. As a wise Frenchman said: *"On se moque de ce qu'on aime."* Those who have learned political folkways as city hall reporters are not those who love them least. Like all folkways, there is good practical reason for cherishing them. To examine a tradition closely is to find that, though possibly outworn, it is at least logical and reasonable in origin.[1]

If you consider the United States as a federal union of fifty largely self-governing republics, then the protracted carnival of a Presidential year makes plenty of sense. The overall expenditure of time and money and energy on politics must be divided by the number of States to get a true proportion. It isn't a President of the American *people* that is being chosen, but a President of the United *States*. So it is altogether fitting and proper that Rhode Island should try to put on as much of a show as Texas; that Nevada as well as New York should desire visits by the candidates. A vitally important part of the quadrennial election is the choosing of the local officials. And the union of the self-governing commonwealths in a compound republic is given nationwide recognition by the fuss and fun and frolic over the rival aspirants to the White House.

In each State, moreover, the campaign objective is not so much the election of the President as it is party control over the electoral vote of that State. This point is fundamental, yet easily overlooked. It is made clear by turning from the method of nomination to the very definite rules, completely undemocratic in nature, that govern the election of a President of the United States.

Although many think otherwise, no American has ever voted directly for any Presidential candidate. The vote, by States, is only for the unduplicated Presidential electors nominated separately in each State. These electors are equal in number to the total Congressional representation of each State and so cannot be less than three, which is currently the case for Alaska, Delaware, Hawaii, Nevada, Vermont and Wyoming. The minimum of electors for a State is three, but there is no set maximum, since population determines the size of each State's representation in the House, and even when the total number is not increased there is a reapportionment after every decennial census. This necessarily brings some States up, and others down, in the number of electoral votes and therefore in the scale of political importance.

At present, New York has the largest electoral vote—45—followed by California and Pennsylvania with 32 each. In 1948, New York had 47 electoral votes, Pennsylvania 35, Illinois 28 (now 27), while California was then only tied with Ohio for fourth place, at 25 electoral votes. It is, of course, a matter of great political significance that California gained seven electoral votes by the 1950 census, while New York lost 2, Pennsylvania lost 3 and Illinois lost 1. The 1960 census seems destined to give California a bloc of electoral votes not far short of that of New York, though this further shift of political power to the West Coast will not take full effect until the Presidential election of 1964.[2]

Since there are currently 100 Senators and 437 members of the lower House the total membership of the Electoral College is 537. A majority of this figure, meaning a minimum of 269 electoral votes, is necessary to elect a President by what has come to be regarded as normal procedure. But if no candidate secures this majority the election is thrown into the House of Representatives, under the provisions of Article II, Section 1 of the Constitution, as revised by the Twelfth Amendment. This happened in 1800 and 1824. We should examine the latter occasion closely, because its repetition is always possible. Indeed, the founding fathers expected the President to be elected "frequently" by the House of Representatives. In No. 66 of the *Federalist* papers Hamilton predicted this and further observed that "this ultimate though contingent power" of the House might well operate "to outweigh all the peculiar attributes of the Senate."

With only two major candidates, and as long as the total of the Electoral College is an odd number, a President obviously must be elected, if only by a bare majority of the electors, on the appointed day.[3] But whenever there is a third strong candidate, likely to win a sizable number of electoral votes, the situation is altogether different. Then there is no certainty that any one candidate will get a majority and a distinct possibility that the front-runner will have only a plurality. That is not less likely because the six most populous States together currently have 34.5 per cent of the electoral vote; the next six States together have 17.1 per cent; the remaining 38 States (counting Alaska and Hawaii) together have only 48.4 per cent, which is a minority of the Electoral College. So, in a three-cornered Presidential campaign, it is arithmetically possible for a candidate to win more than three-quarters of the States on election day, but not be elected until the House has acted, on the purely federal basis of one State one vote. Something like this happened in the Election of 1824, which had momentous consequences.

That, which was the tenth Presidential election, was the first in which any attempt was made to count the popular vote. This had previously been impossible to tabulate, by candidates, because then only the names of the electors appeared on the ballots and these electors were originally uncommitted. In the Election of 1824, for instance, two of Louisiana's five electors voted for John Quincy Adams and three for Andrew Jackson, a division regarded as black ingratitude by the hero of New Orleans.

The elasticity of the original system extended to the time and method of choosing the electors. For the election of 1824, Congress had stipulated that they be chosen between October 27 and December 1. In Ohio and Pennsylvania the choice was made by the voters, who went to the polls on October 29. In Louisiana and South Carolina the State legislatures chose the electors and did not act until November 22. Thus the first stage of the 1824 election of the electors—was spread out over a period of more than three weeks and even so was wholly inconclusive, except for the easy triumph of John C. Calhoun as Vice-President. For the Presidency itself the Electoral College divided, 99 for Jackson, 84 for Adams, 41 for William Crawford, and 37 for Henry Clay. None had a majority, so nobody was elected.

This, of course, was wholly in accord with the Constitution, as it stood and still stands. Article II, Section 1, permits each State to appoint its electors "in such manner as the Legislature thereof may direct," the only limitations being that nobody holding office under the national government, nor any member of the Congress, shall be an elector. The objective was to have the President chosen by non-political community leaders—thoughtful men in a "detached situation" to quote from the analysis of this highly undemocratic procedure made by Alexander Hamilton.[4] "It was desirable," Hamilton concedes, "that the sense of the people should operate in the choice of the person to whom so important a trust [the Presidency] was to be confided." But:

> It was equally desirable that the immediate election should be made by men most capable of analyzing the qualities adapted to the station, and acting under circumstances favorable to deliberation, and to a judicious combination of all the reasons and inducements which were proper to govern their choice.

Furthermore, it was deemed "peculiarly desirable" to safeguard the choice of the President against "democratic passion." The localized selection of many electors, Hamilton concluded, "will be much less apt to convulse the community with any extraordinary or violent movements, than the choice of *one* who was himself to be the final object of public wishes."

Hamilton's defense of this federalized electoral system is the more interesting because he himself was a nationalist, usually very luke-warm to the whole theory of federalism. But if nationalism implied democracy he was for federalism as much the lesser evil. And there was general agreement on the indirect election of the President, through the medium of an independent Electoral College. The result is that this vital choice is even now not really a national election but rather a collective election by the States, which were and still remain its indispensable basis.

The professional politicians, who have to make this complicated system work, have therefore from the beginning concentrated on the *electoral* rather than on the popular vote. For a long time that meant concentration on State almost to the exclusion of national politics, since some of the State legislatures appointed their electors until the Civil War and in the South especially were jealous of the prerogative. In the quadrennial Presidential election one might reasonably expect domestic politics to be national rather than local in emphasis. But due to the device of the Electoral College, often criticized but still inviolate, local considerations remain paramount. This was demonstrated in the 1956 election, when President Eisenhower himself won easily, but was unable to carry either House of Congress for his party. The reverse anomaly, for Mr. Stevenson, was of course equally pronounced.

Up to a point, the development of party organization has modified Presidential election procedure. Manifestly, such organization would have been futile if the original conception of a wholly independent Electoral College had endured. Political parties must by their very nature endeavor "to convulse the community with" those "extraordinary or violent movements" against which the Electoral College seemed to Alexander Hamilton reliable insurance. There was certainly no point in organizing the electorate to vote for a Presidential candidate when the popular vote was not even tabulated. And the only way in which a vote for an elector could be counted as a vote for a President was first to have the electors presented as party nominees and then to get each state-wide bloc of electors pledged to the party candidate.

That did not come overnight, and it is important to realize that there is still absolutely no legal compulsion for an elector to vote as pledged. In 1948, Truman polled 270,402 votes in Tennessee, Dewey 202,914 and Thurmond only 73,815. But an independent-minded Tennessee elector named Parks nevertheless cast his conclusive ballot for the "Dixiecrat" candidate. The right of Mr. Parks to do so could not be questioned and the official records show that in this election Truman got 11 electoral votes in Tennessee, Thurmond one and Dewey none. Even more noteworthy was the action of an Alabama elector, Mr. W. F. Turner, in 1956. Instead of casting his electoral vote for Stevenson, who had carried all but eleven of Alabama's 67 counties, Mr. Turner voted in the Electoral College for Circuit Judge Walter B. Jones, who was not even a Presidential nominee in Alabama or in any other State.

There are many other instances of electoral independence. In 1916 Woodrow Wilson received one electoral vote from West Virginia, although Charles E. Hughes carried the State. In 1904 Maryland gave one of its electoral votes to Theodore Roosevelt and the other seven to Alton B. Parker. Before the turn of the century divisions of a State's electoral vote were frequent. In 1892, North Dakota gave one of its three electoral votes to the Democratic, one to the Republican and one to the Populist candidate.

Every historian of Jackson's era has noted the "swelling demand," as Marquis James describes it, for some measure of political democracy which marked that period. The application of a greater degree of democracy to Presidential elections began to be urged when James Monroe, running for his second term in 1820, received 231 of the then total of 235 electoral votes, a victory almost as disproportionate from any representative viewpoint as Roosevelt's 523 to 8 triumph over Landon in 1936. This virtual unanimity of Monroe's second election stimulated the rise of party organization, and the introduction of a certain measure of democratic practice following the bitter election of 1824. Also, the leadership of the Revolutionary period had by then served its time; the frontier had been pushed beyond the Mississippi; new interests and new problems occupied the minds of the electorate, and new electoral methods were desired to deal with them. The stage was set for change when Monroe, the last of the "Virginia dynasty," made it plain that he had no intention of challenging the already firm two-term tradition.

There were at first five avowed candidates, all strong men but none with a binding party label, for one must remember that there were then no established parties in the modern sense of the word. Calhoun, however, shrewdly switched his candidacy to the Vice-Presidency when a Pennsylvania Convention, on March 4, 1824, abandoned his cause to endorse Andrew Jackson, the newly elected junior Senator from Tennessee. At this State convention, significantly, "all sound Democrats" were urged to vote for electors favoring Jackson, who at the time was still calling himself a Republican.[5] So were the other three candidates, John Quincy Adams, heir to the anti-democratic, Federalist tradition of his father, most appropriately by modern standards; Henry Clay, the debonair, clever, unscrupulous Speaker of the House, a serious threat to Jackson's Western support; William H. Crawford, of Georgia, Monroe's Secretary of the Treasury, at the outset a leading contender, but in the fall of 1823 stricken with paralysis.

This was a fateful illness for American politics, because it helped to destroy the old system of nomination by Congressional caucus. Crawford, like Senator Taft in 1952, was the most popular of the candidates in Congress. But the caucus method of nomination was for that very reason under vehement attack by all his rivals. When the caucus attempted to nominate the obviously incapacitated Crawford this criticism burst all bounds. In the upshot a majority of the members boycotted the gathering, and jeered from the gallery of the House when Crawford, and Albert Gallatin for Vice-President, were nominated by a rump group of 66.[6]

It took some time to build the system of national nominating conventions on the ruins of the caucus. Separate state conventions, of which our present Presidential primaries are the heritage, filled the gap. But the old system of nomination by Congressional caucus had its death blow when Crawford was fruitlessly named on February 14, 1824. "The caucus," said the then Representative Daniel Webster shrewdly, "has hurt nobody but its friends. . . . Mr. Adams and General Jackson are likely to be the real competitors at last." [7]

And so they were, Jackson carried 11 of the 24 States to seven for Adams, with Crawford and Clay leading in three apiece. But the electoral vote was divided in many of the States, and Jackson's total of 99 electoral votes was under 40 per cent of the total of 261. So a House run-off election was necessary, between the first three contenders, as provided in the Twelfth Amendment. The crippled Crawford stayed in the fight, for he had won 4 more electoral votes than Henry Clay. The Speaker of the House had been eliminated as a possible President, but not as a President-maker.

There are various accounts of the deal negotiated between John Quincy Adams and Henry Clay. In the mind of Marquis James, Jackson's most careful biographer, there is no doubt that Clay sold his great influence in the House to Adams in return for a promise that the "Kentucky gamester" would be made Secretary of State. James traces the secret agreement to the night of January 9, 1825, exactly one month before the run-off election.[8] The indisputable fact is that in this election the tables turned sharply and surprisingly in Adams' favor. He had won in only 7 States at the polls, but received the support of 13 under the unit rule by which the House voted on February 9. Jackson now had only 7 States behind him, and Crawford 4. So John Quincy Adams, by a bare majority of the then 24 States, was elected and duly inaugurated on March 4. And it is a further fact that Clay had by then already been named as Secretary of State, and that 14 Senators out of 48 resentfully voted against his confirmation.

That historic election of 1824 deserves remembrance, not only because of its intrinsic interest but also because its salient features could easily be re-enacted. Indeed, in 1948 the election was not far from being thrown into the House for the third time, as we shall now recall.

FOURTEEN

The Tenacity of Tradition

At the 1948 Democratic National Convention, in Philadelphia, the delegations of Alabama, Louisiana, Mississippi and South Carolina walked out to the tune of "Dixie," in dramatic protest against the Civil Rights plank adopted for the party platform. They later nominated their own States' Rights Democratic candidate, Governor (later Senator) J. Strom Thurmond of South Carolina for the Presidency, with Governor Fielding L. Wright of Mississippi as his running mate.

Thus, six years before the Supreme Court decision on Integration, there was a significant political crystallization of the incompatibility between the theories of James Madison and those of Jean Jacques Rousseau. For there can be little doubt that the "general will" of the American people as a whole has developed so as to oppose any legal discrimination within the United States on the grounds of color or race. A national plebiscite on this issue would almost certainly go strongly in favor of full social democracy. But it is far less certain that such a plebiscite would favor the enforcement of social democracy in accordance with the theory of unbridled political democracy, as was attempted by President Eisenhower at Little Rock.[1]

The temporary withdrawal of the States' Rights Democrats in 1948 was not an attempt to establish a third party. There was no open division between this faction and the "loyal" Democrats in Congress, and therefore no disturbance of seniority rights there. But Democratic opposition to the regular Democratic Presidential candidates, Truman and Barkley, was nevertheless intense throughout the South. They were eliminated from the ballot in Alabama and ran far behind in other rebellious States, which together rolled up 38 electoral votes for Thurmond. To this was later added that one independent electoral vote from Tennessee.

President Truman nevertheless won re-election, capturing twenty-eight States with 303 electoral votes, as against sixteen States with 189 electoral votes for Governor Dewey and four States, 39 electoral votes, for Governor Thurmond. But what impressed close students of American politics at the time was this: "If Thurmond had been first in only four more Southern States, Florida, Georgia, North Carolina and Virginia—in all of which there was a strong "Dixiecrat" poll—President Truman would not have been re-elected. And if the Republican candidate had on this assumption run exactly as he did, nobody would have been elected at the polls in 1948. For Truman would then have had 258 electoral votes; Dewey his 189 and (in the circumstances envisaged) Thurmond 84. The requisite number for election was then, prior to Alaskan and Hawaiian Statehood—266.

This outcome would have forced a House run-off election, with its result as unpredictable, and as conducive to devious dealing, as in the case of the Adams-Jackson contest.[2] For if the Republicans in 1948 had kept their sixteen States, and if the Dixiecrats had won eight instead of four, the national Democrats would have controlled only twenty-four States, which then lacked one of the majority necessary to elect. It is not difficult to imagine the hectic competition for House delegations that would have ensued, especially since in the States of Delaware, Nevada, Vermont and Wyoming one single Congressman, in each of these four States, would have had the individual power to cast the vote of the State. With Alaska and Hawaii in the Union there are now six one-Congressman States.

It may also be noted that the electoral vote is not tabulated, by present law, until the first Monday after the second Wednesday in December.[3] In 1956 that was December 17, almost six weeks after the election on November 6. The almanacs for 1957, going to press between these dates, assert that in 1956 Eisenhower got 457 electoral votes and Stevenson 74. That is incorrect. The official tally was Eisenhower 457, Stevenson 73, Jones 1. The error points up the fact that under our electoral system a whole Presidential election can be upset a month or more after it is apparently decided.

All this is by no means idle theorizing. In 1948 the switch of the one Tennessee elector, weeks after the election, made no real difference. It reduced Truman's electoral vote from 304 to 303; increased Thurmond's from 38 to 39, and elicited a certain amount of professional political criticism. That was all.

But suppose Thurmond on November 2, 1948, had won seven of the Southern States mentioned, allowing Florida's eight electoral votes to Truman, who actually took them. On that hypothesis Thurmond would apparently have had 75 electoral votes, Dewey his 189 and Truman 267, or one more than the minimum necessary for election. Then suppose that six weeks later not only Mr. Parks but also just one other Tennessee elector had decided that he preferred the States' Rights Democrat to the national Democrat. Then Truman's election would have been announced on November 2, and necessarily denied on December 13. The shock to this country would have been terrific, and that to the world at large even greater.

Of course this is only a picture of "what might have been." But it is worth drawing as an illustration of the divergence between our actual constitutional law and the often wholly erroneous contemporary idea of the American political system.

After the dual Democratic candidacy in 1948 some obvious hard feeling between the two factions remained. But its intensity seemed to fade with the emergency of the Korean War. In 1952 there was no repetition of the "Dixiecrat" split. As a placatory move, Alabama's Senator John J. Sparkman was nominated as Adlai Stevenson's running mate, and superficially it seemed that the former Illinois Governor had a united party behind him. Yet signs to the contrary were not lacking. Shortly before the 1952 election, influential Senator Byrd of Virginia announced that he could not endorse Stevenson's candidacy. The extent of Southern discontent with the socialistic leadership of the Democratic Party was revealed when General Eisenhower carried Florida, Texas and Virginia, as well as the border States of Missouri and Tennessee, all five of which had gone Democratic four years earlier. In 1956 the

Republicans added Louisiana to this list, though they then narrowly lost Missouri.

The assumption that the "Solid South" had lost cohesiveness under the warmth of President Eisenhower's personality was clearly premature. It was an unwarranted conclusion from the evidence that many Southerners preferred him to the leadership of the Northern Democrats. But as the President's doctrine of "modern Republicanism" became scarcely distinguishable from the centralizing philosophy of Northern Democracy, the Southern divergence from both of them became apparent. From the day of the Supreme Court's unanimous ruling against racial segregation in the public schools, May 17, 1954, a resurgence of political movement in behalf of States' Rights became probable. It became a certainty when President Eisenhower ordered troops of the central government to Little Rock to enforce integration, on September 24, 1957.

If the situation which has resulted is to be constructively resolved, there must be a separation of the social and political aspects of the problem. Like oil and water these different issues simply cannot be "integrated" and no helpful purpose is served by muddling them together. From the social viewpoint one is perhaps entitled to conclude that the South is reactionary, benighted, feudalistic or what-have-you in the way of self-righteous, denunciatory epithets. But from the separated political viewpoint one must then also conclude that a very considerable section of the Republic, perhaps holding a balance of power in the Electoral College, does not believe in unqualified majority rule; does not, in short, concede the theory of a dictatorial general will.

The positive faith of the South clearly favors something quite different from and antagonistic to totalitarian democracy. It favors the federal principle, which in all but clearly delegated powers definitely protects each constituent State against subservience to the majority will of the nation as a whole. The unsavory story of the Fourteenth Amendment, far better known in the South than elsewhere, helps to strengthen the loyalty of that section to authentic federalism.

Thus the Democratic Party is torn between those who put democracy ahead of States' Rights, and those who put States' Rights ahead of democracy. But if the issue should irrevocably split this party, that outcome would by no means necessarily favor the Republicans. The two divisions were weakened in 1956 by vain efforts to find a successful compromise ticket, yet still were strong enough to elect a Democratic Congress. In 1958, the Democratic factions, striking from right and left, mowed down Republicans whose leadership seemed to the electorate to have no real convictions on any issue. If the Democratic Party should separate again there would certainly be a closing of the ranks in each of the divided camps. The Southern Democrats would line up solidly behind their constitutional candidate; the Northern and Western Democrats no less solidly behind a more socialistic nominee. Faced with this opposition on two fronts the Republican Party would reap an advantage only in those border states where right- and left-wing Democrats tend to cancel each other. Wherever one or the other wing proved clearly dominant, holding undisputed control of the State organization, the Republican nominee would fail to gain substantially from Democratic dissension.

That holds true because our Presidential election is, at the risk of repetition, really a sum total of fifty separate and distinct State elections now for reasons of convenience held on the same day—as was not originally the case. Anything but a straight two-party contest is of dubious outcome, and may have to be resolved by the House, especially if a third candidate has a sectional strength which has been consolidated by coercive external pressure. In such a three-man fight Candidates A, B, and C would not oppose each other on an equal basis throughout the country. In one section it would be primarily A versus B; in another B versus C; in the third, A versus C. That situation increases the possibility of an inconclusive popular vote.

If the simple theory of political democracy— majority triumph—were acceptable to most Americans, one would certainly expect a fundamental revision of this highly complicated, and highly undemocratic, electoral system. Doubtless, if a Presidential election should again go to the House for decision, to the complete surprise and bewilderment of many, such a revision would be attempted. At present, however, there is no apparent popular demand for changing the Constitution in respect to Presidential elections, and there has not been such demand since the adoption of the Twelfth Amendment in 1804. Since Presidential elections began to be tabulated, no less than thirteen have been won by a candidate who secured only a minority of the popular vote. But few Americans have been disturbed by this, though many continue to misname the Republic a democracy just the same.

There have, certainly, been many suggestions for a revision of Presidential election procedure. The original plan of the founding fathers was that the electors should be chosen individually by Congressional districts, with the two extra ones for each State selected "at large" from that State as a whole. But the matter was left to the State legislatures to decide and the district plan never was universally established.[4] Then, after the rise of organized political parties, the custom arose of naming mere figureheads as electors, loyal but undistinguished party workers pledged in advance to support the party slate. Because there is nothing other than party discipline to enforce that pledge, any severe dissension within a party will weaken its influence on independent-minded electors.

This application of a unit rule, in all the States, of course accentuates the inevitable disproportion between the popular vote and the electoral vote. In the 1956 Presidential election, for instance, Eisenhower received 457 electoral votes, Stevenson 73 and Jones 1. Had the electoral vote been divided in the same proportion as the popular vote, Eisenhower's score would have been 305 and Stevenson's 223. Minor candidates would have divided the remaining 3 votes needed to fill out the then electoral college total of 531. Judge Jones, who had no popular vote, but one electoral vote from Alabama, would have lost the latter. The extreme anomaly of the electoral system is found when it defeats a Presidential candidate who has actually polled more popular votes than the one elected. This happened not only in the case of Adams and Jackson, but also when Hayes was dubiously chosen over Tilden in 1876, and when

Harrison got more electoral, though fewer popular, votes than Cleveland in 1888.[5]

The results of the system in individual States are even more devoid of logic or democratic propriety. In the 1948 Presidential election the Republicans in New York State polled 45 per cent of the popular vote; the Democrats 44 per cent. Yet by this trifling plurality, and on a minority of the popular vote, the Republican Presidential candidate obtained all of New York's 47 electoral votes (as the number was then), a figure which of itself was almost 9 per cent of the entire Electoral College. In New York, on that same day, the same ballots of the same voters sent more Democrats than Republicans to Congress from the same State that was in effect voting unanimously for a Republican President.

The principles of democracy and of federalism are alike flouted when a minority of ballots can so easily be taken as expressing the will of the State. The arrangement gives a wholly undesirable influence to the political boss who, by controlling 2 or 3 per cent of the registration in a State, is yet able to deliver its solid bloc of electoral votes to the Presidential candidate who knows he must secure them to be elected. Aside from the inevitable corruption thus promoted, the situation gives easily organized metropolitan districts a substantial advantage over the suburbs and rural areas.

There have been various proposals to correct this undesirable arrangement. The most enduring and logical is the proposed Constitutional Amendment, originally sponsored by Senator Mundt (S.D.) and Representative Coudert (N.Y.), prescribing that electors be chosen by Congressional districts, with the two corresponding to the Senators named from each State as a whole, as the founding fathers anticipated would be the case. The essential, and admirable, feature of the Mundt-Coudert plan is that it ties the elector to the verdict of his Congressional district, thus permitting a reasonably accurate reflection of the popular will, without doing any injury to the federal basis of our Republic. Under this plan, in the 1952 election Eisenhower would have received 375 electoral votes to 156 for Stevenson—a good deal more accurate reflection of the popular division than was the electoral vote as then cast: Eisenhower 442; Stevenson 89.

But neither the Mundt-Coudert Amendment, nor any of several proposed alternatives, seems to have any chance of adoption. No revision plan has as yet passed both Houses of Congress, let alone going before the States for ratification, and none has been pressed by any recent President. This steadfast refusal to bring some real democracy into our Presidential elections certainly suggests that, in spite of all their lip service to the word, political democracy is actually neither valued nor desired by the politicians.[6]

Political inertia could, of course, account for our failure to revise a Presidential election system which certainly has little to command it from the viewpoints of simplicity, efficiency or democracy. But Americans are not an inert people. It is not merely in mechanical matters that we are quick to adopt new devices and welcome any gadgets which, rightly or wrongly, can be said to show "progress." Changes in styling, design, architecture and even educational methods are readily accepted. "Novelties" are al-

ways popular and from fiction to flower arrangements that which is latest is also likely to be that
which is fashionable.

Therefore it is difficult to believe that an inconsistent apathy adequately explains the public indifference to political improvement in so basic a matter
as the selection of the nation's Chief Executive. No
corporation, no women's club, no sandlot baseball
team, would choose its captain in so implausible a
manner. And certainly there is no sign of public
indifference as to the character, capacity and commitments of Presidential candidates. It applies only
to the archaic method by which one is selected
over another.

Clearly there is a missing ingredient somewhere
in this picture, and it would seem to be the stubborn
American sense of tradition in political matters.
In spite of our zest for experimentalism we have
surrounded the Constitution with much of that
divinity which doth hedge a king. The sad results
of the Fourteenth Amendment, forced into the
Constitution in a most unconstitutional manner,
have not been altogether pernicious. The outrages
springing from the Sixteenth Amendment have also
strengthened conservatism. It seems most unlikely
that we shall again attempt to destroy the essence
of our organic law by direct amendment.

The essence of the Constitution is, of course, the
federal system which it established. Every provision
of the organic law is based on the fundamental concept of these *United States*. They are not and cannot
be merged into a single state as long as the Constitution stands. And so, for all who revere the Constitution, States' Rights is a vital issue, whereas

political democracy decidedly is not. If, as and when democracy runs sharply counter to States' Rights, then many Americans will rally to oppose democracy. It should be obvious to all that an organic law which specifically safeguards minorities is for that very reason antagonistic to unqualified majority rule. But where reasoning power is lacking, the reverential attitude comes in to support our constitutional form of government. And where reason and reverence alike support a tradition, it is sure to be strong.

This strong tradition, and not inertia, explains why efforts to reform the method of Presidential election have failed, even though it is obvious that some reform is on many counts desirable. And one should note that the most democratic reform suggested is the one that has met with the least favorable response. Senators Humphrey (Democrat of Minnesota) and Langer (Republican of North Dakota) together proposed that the President and Vice-President be elected by direct vote of the people. If we believe in democracy that is obviously the most appropriate procedure. The fact that it would eliminate the electoral vote, and therefore the States as such as factors, should be secondary. Actually the proposal when made fell flat on its face, and neither in Congress nor in the country as a whole is there any apparent strength behind it.

Even the Mundt-Coudert proposal, in thorough consonance with both the letter and spirit of the Constitution, lacks popular support. The tradition in favor of the federal system is so strong that any reform here is regarded as tampering with the Constitution, despite the most convincing proof that there is no such intent, and would be no such result.

FIFTEEN

The Revival of Interposition

The primary characteristic of every federal system is a specified division of sovereignty between the local governments establishing the federation and the general government established thereby. Consequently, as noted in the first chapter of this study, every federation must have a supreme court, the essential role of which is to resolve conflicting claims of sovereign power in particular cases.

Decisions of this court are from its nature primarily interpretive. And constitutional interpretation is more subtle than that of a will, or deed, or contract. It must take cognizance of changing circumstance as well as of the collective purpose of the authors and of all amendment of their original work. Nevertheless, the interpretation must be in reasonable accord with the basic principles of the constitution. Otherwise this "organic law" is left without significance and the political form of the organism created is undermined.

This general rule for federation is made applicable to the United States by the first two sections of Article III of the Constitution, defining the judicial power, and by Article VI, Section 2, which subordinates both national and State judiciary to the Constitution in the following explicit language:

This Constitution, and the laws of the United States which shall be made in pursuance thereof; and all treaties made, or which shall be made, under the authority of the United States, shall be the supreme law of the land; and the Judges in every State shall be bound thereby, anything in the Constitution or laws of any State to the contrary notwithstanding.

There is, of course, an essentially undemocratic flavor to any court which is thus empowered to override the actions of representative legislatures. These laws presumably represent majority opinion, whether local or national. To strike down a majority opinion is in no sense arbitrary, if the negation is in accord with all parts of the organic law. But such a negation is always likely to be undemocratic. It is for this reason that a unitary government, having no need for a supreme court, can be politically more democratic than a federal government.

It follows that a federation which is moving towards political democracy, and which is widely acclaimed as a political democracy, will necessarily in some way reveal a weakening of the power and authority of its supreme court. Broadly speaking, there are two ways in which this judicial degeneracy would become apparent: either by active infringement upon the independence of the court by other governmental agencies, or by passive subservience of the court to those other agencies. Of course these two tendencies might, and probably would, be simultaneously apparent. Such improper subordination of a no longer truly supreme court would easily influence it towards arbitrary, arrogant and erratic judgments, illustrative of what in the case of an individual would be called an "inferiority complex."

In the case of the United States the prestige, and even the authority, of the Supreme Court has not infrequently been temporarily debased. We have noted its subservience to the Radical Congress when the Fourteenth Amendment was forced into the Constitution. Prestige was again injured, this time by executive criticism, in the "nine old men" attack from President Roosevelt. In 1954, the influence of the Court was again adversely affected, also by the executive in the name of democracy, as a result of pressures which certainly owed some of their strength to communist gibes about racial discrimination in the United States.

One must sympathize with the hard-pressed members of the Court, no longer able to disregard the many exigencies of the Administration's foreign and domestic policy. And one may sympathize the more because some of the decisions have been, in effect, suicidal. In recent years the Supreme Court has seemed to many almost an instrument in the effort to shift the United States away from a federal form of government.[1] Yet if complete centralization can be made permanent there will no longer be any good reason for keeping the Supreme Court as an institution. It could be dismantled, along with the superfluous machinery of State governments.

The possibly superfluous character of the Supreme Court is paradoxically emphasized by assertion that its decisions are in themselves "the law of the land." This tends to suggest that law-making power can properly be usurped both from Congress and from the State legislatures. The fact that the Supreme Court, in deciding specific cases, has implicit authority to nullify statutes, both national and State,

does not mean that it has power to legislate in sub-
stitution. It means, rather, that new, or different,
legislation is necessary to meet constitutional requirements as interpreted by the Court. And should it
ever become accepted national purpose to substitute
decrees for legislation, this cumbersome Court would
scarcely be chosen to formulate the edicts. In all
the totalitarian democracies it is always the administrative officers who define the "general will." The
courts are kept merely for disciplinary matters, for
window dressing and to draw a veil over the
arrogance of naked dictatorship.

Respect for the Supreme Court's interpretations
of the Constitution, whether welcome or unwel-
come, is of course a fundamental obligation of
citizenship. There can be no sympathy whatsoever
with the contempt attributed to President Andrew
Jackson in the case of *Worcester v. Georgia:* "John
Marshall has made his decision; now let him enforce
it." [2] But a proper deference towards the Court
does not imply exaggeration of its constitutional
function.

The distinction has been made time and again,
but never with greater clarity than by Viscount
Bryce in his classic study of *The American Commonwealth.* Indeed this British authority almost
labors "the fact that the judiciary of the United
States are not the masters of the Constitution but
merely its interpreters. . . ." And this emphasis is
the more interesting because Bryce was a profound
admirer of the centralizing decisions of Chief Justice
Marshall, partly because he "did not forget the duty
of a judge to decide nothing more than the suit

before him requires. . . ."³ As Bryce sums it up, the sole and whole duty of Supreme Court Justices is "to construe the law":

> And if it be suggested that they may overstep their duty, and may, seeking to make themselves not the exponents but the masters of the Constitution, twist and pervert it to suit their own political views, the answer is that such an exercise of judicial will would arouse the distrust and displeasure of the nation, and might, if persisted in, provoke resistance to the law as laid down by the court, possibly an onslaught upon the court itself.⁴

Such "an onslaught upon the court itself," as foreseen by James Bryce in 1888, was produced two generations later precisely because its members seemed to many to "twist and pervert" the Constitution "to suit their own political views." There are various illustrations of this tendency, but because of its outstandingly momentous consequences consideration here is limited to the consolidated opinion (*Brown v. Board of Education*) affecting the public school systems of Kansas, South Carolina, Virginia and Delaware.

This famous decision in behalf of racial integration, handed down by Chief Justice Warren on May 17, 1954, produced as one of its earlier consequences the Congressional Manifesto of March 11, 1956. In this nineteen Democratic Senators and seventy-seven Democratic Representatives pledged themselves "to use all lawful means" to reverse the verdict, which they defined as "a clear abuse of judicial power . . . contrary to the Constitution." The indictment by this large section of the Congress, supported by a

strong legal opinion by no means entirely confined
to the South, was bolstered by the following arguments:

First, the Court assumed too lightly that the key
phrase in the Fourteenth Amendment—"the equal
protection of the laws"—is adversely affected by
segregation in the public schools. Furthermore, the
Court was in error when it called evidence to the
contrary "at best . . . inconclusive."

It is recalled that the same session of Congress
which initiated the Fourteenth Amendment simultaneously passed legislation establishing segregated
schools in the District of Columbia "for the sole
use of . . . colored children." Moreover, in twelve
of the States that ratified the Fourteenth Amendment the same legislatures made provision for segregated schools. Within two years after adoption of
this Amendment two more States, Indiana and Maryland, also established racially separate schools. In
seven other States pre-existent segregated schools
were maintained after ratification of the Fourteenth
Amendment. Clearly the practice was not then
regarded as unconstitutional. And the evidence that
changing circumstance has made it so can also be
called "at best inconclusive." [5]

Second, the Court went beyond its proper function, and espoused questionable doctrine, when it
said: "In approaching this problem, we cannot turn
the clock back to 1868 when the Amendment was
adopted. . . ."

It is of course true that in this case the Supreme
Court had to interpret wording of 1868 in the light
of conditions in 1954. But in so doing it had also to

give due consideration to the federal formula as written in 1787 and still essentially unaltered. If the clock cannot be turned back to 1868, then it could follow that there is still less validity in principles laid down even earlier. On that assumption, there would be no constitutional guarantee which could be held immune from destruction in the light of current conditions, or current sociological opinions.

It should be noted, however, that Chief Justice Warren was not the first to suggest the relativity of those principles which the Constitution was designed to safeguard. The permanence of all values was questioned even more sharply by Chief Justice Vinson when, on June 4, 1951, in *Dennis v. United States*, he said: "Nothing is more certain in modern society than the principle that there are no absolutes. . . . To those who would paralyze our Government in the face of impending threat by encasing it in a semantic straightjacket we must reply that all concepts are relative." Back of this viewpoint, in turn, stands the highly influential pragmatism of Justice Oliver Wendell Holmes, who said: "When it comes to the development of a *corpus juris*, the ultimate question is what do the dominant forces of the community want and do they want it hard enough to disregard whatever inhibitions may stand in the way." This is sincere flattery for Rousseau's assertion that we are all "under the supreme direction of the general will." [6]

It is not a new idea that the Supreme Court should interpret the Constitution in the light of what the dominant forces of the community seem to want. Unfortunately for the prestige of this organ, the guess made on May 17, 1954 was clearly wrong, so far as a great many American communities are concerned.

Third, the Court, in *Brown v. Board of Education*, relied on what it was pleased to call "modern authority" to bolster its assertion that "segregation . . . has a detrimental effect upon the colored children."

Whether this conclusion is true or false, it seems questionable in a Supreme Court decision, where the issue is, or should be, one of constitutional law. Prominent in the list of "modern authority" cited by the Court was that of the Swedish sociologist, Gunnar Myrdal. Other European authorities of socialistic persuasion could be found to advocate nationalization of the American steel industry, quite possibly on the grounds that the high wages it pays have a detrimental effect on the morale of school teachers. That would not justify the Supreme Court in demanding nationalization, unless there had been previous legislation on the subject, previously found constitutional on some test case brought thereunder. In a case subsequent to the one at issue the Court itself in effect admitted the validity of this point, saying: "It has not been deemed relevant to discussion of our problem to consider dubious English precedents . . . because they reflect a power of discretion vested in English judges not relevant to the constitutional law of our federalism." [7]

Fourth, there was not, and still is not, any national legislative act to implement the claim that the Fourteenth Amendment itself outlaws racial segregation in the public schools.

This legislative omission in no way affects the

judicial power and duty of final interpretation. But it is nevertheless notable because the closing section of the Fourteenth Amendment goes out of its way to state: "The Congress shall have power to enforce, by appropriate legislation, the provisions of this article." We have noted that this specification, now found at the close of four Amendments, is dubious. But, once enshrined in the Constitution, it necessarily cuts two ways. If legislative action is desirable to enforce, it follows that no legislative action means no effective desire to enforce.

In the matter of racial integration in the public schools there has never been any attempt by Congress to enforce, and if there had ever been such a law it is quite possible that it would have been declared unconstitutional, since the regulation of education has always been a field reserved to the States. It was at least partly in recognition of States' Rights that the Supreme Court, on six different occasions prior to 1954, had ruled that the provision of "separate but equal" public facilities met all the requirements of the Fourteenth Amendment. So we have a situation where the Supreme Court has itself decreed what it might well have overruled if proposed by statute law.[8]

Fifth, and finally, the illogic of the *Brown v. Board of Education* opinion is not confined to abstruse points, but is in places apparent to everyone, as in Chief Justice Warren's flat assertion: "Separate educational facilities are inherently unequal." That is obviously only a personal opinion, not less so because of the concurrence of the other Justices. If true, it must also be true that boys' schools and girls' schools are at an "inherent" disadvantage compared with co-educational institutions—a proposition completely unsusceptible of proof.

It can be, and sometimes is, argued that the entire Fourteenth Amendment is unconstitutional. But, waiving this extreme ground, it is clear that a tortured interpretation by the Supreme Court has not compelled, and cannot compel racial integration in areas where public opinion will not tolerate it. All that the Court has decided is that a State may not deny to any person on account of race the right to attend any school that it maintains. As a last recourse this could mean, over large areas, abandonment of public education as a State function.[9] In that eventuality, however, it may be anticipated that the central government would move to establish national schools in such areas, thus driving another nail into the coffin of federalism. This possibility, plus the cumulative strength of the five general criticisms that have been summarized, gave determination to the "onslaught upon the court."

This reaction appropriately took the form of a revival of Interposition, a doctrine sanctioned by frequent use in the early days of the Republic, and one calculated to maintain formidable obstacles to any nation-wide enforcement of the judgment of May 17, 1954. The word "inherent" may properly be used for the association of the doctrine of Interposition with the federal form of government. Its connection with the racial issue, however, is wholly fortuitous. As the Attorney General of Texas has pointed out, Interposition could just as appropriately be invoked by a State to block intra-State regulation of gas and oil production by an agency of the central government. Revival of the doctrine is therefore a striking illustration of the tenacity of the federal tradition in American thinking, and a powerful weapon in the armory of those who seek to maintain the Republic.

Interposition is an official action on the part of a State Government to question the constitutionality of a policy established by the central government. The action at least temporarily interposes the sovereignty of the State between its citizens and the distant authority of Washington. Customarily there is some sort of formal declaration to the effect that the objectionable national policy will be opposed until or unless the moot issue of its constitutionality is satisfactorily resolved. The device has been used both to demand that the Supreme Court rule on the constitutionality of an Act of Congress and, as currently, to demand that Congress clarify the constitutionality of a dubious Supreme Court decision.

The justification for Interposition is strengthened by the fact that without it the constitutional system of check and balance would be in one vital respect deficient. The President is subject to check by both Court and Congress; the Congress is subject to check by both President and Court. *Sed quis custodiet custodes?* The right to challenge any usurpation of power on the part of the Supreme Court must by lack of alternative, if for no other reason, devolve upon the States.

Even so ardent a nationalist as Alexander Hamilton suggested this, before final ratification of the Constitution. In 1788 he cited the necessity of State consent to suit by an individual "as one of the attributes of sovereignty . . . now enjoyed by the government of every State in the Union." [10] To the extent that the States have "attributes of sovereignty" they are of course entitled to act in defense of those attributes, which is what John C. Calhoun had in mind when he said: "This right of Interposition . . . I conceive to be the fundamental principle of our system, resting on facts as historically certain as our revolution itself."

One of these historically certain facts is, of course, the Tenth Amendment, which rounds out the Bill of Rights by making it a constitutional assertion of States' Rights as well as those of individuals. The courts may be relied upon to protect the individual, but what governmental agency is there to safeguard the rights of a State? In particular, how can one or more States peacefully defend the powers "reserved" to it or them against encroachment on the part of the Supreme Court? It would seem that the assertion of State sovereignty must also be the defense of it—in a word, Interposition.

Ironically enough, Interposition was first found necessary in regard to the very point on which Hamilton had said State sovereignty was not endangered. Even more ironically, it was immediately after the adoption of the Bill of Rights that the Supreme Court, in *Chisholm v. Georgia*, ruled that a State could be sued by a citizen of another State. Although a summons was served on the then Governor of Georgia, as many years later on Governor Faubus of Arkansas, the former refused to appear before the Court. Not content with passive resistance, the hot-blooded Georgia House of Representatives passed a resolution providing that any United States Marshal attempting to levy on the property of Georgia under the court order "shall suffer death, without the benefit of clergy, by being hanged." [11] Other States chimed in, the Congress took action and the result was the Eleventh Amendment, declaring the States immune from suits "by citizens of another State, or by citizens or subjects of any foreign State." [12] Not for the last time, the Supreme Court was backed off the boards.

The next important use of Interposition was prompted not by any overt act on the part of the Supreme Court, but by a fear that the Court would fail to act in a manner contrary to the executive will. The Fifth Congress, disturbed by the effects of the French Revolution, in 1798 adopted three drastic laws, known as the Alien and Sedition Acts. The third of these made it a crime "to write, print, utter or publish" anything that might bring either the President or Congress "into contempt or disrepute." This was clearly in violation of the constitutional guarantee of free speech and free press. But it was not so sure that the Supreme Court, under the influence of the Federalist Party, would so decide.

Therefore a delegation from the newly admitted State of Kentucky prevailed on Thomas Jefferson, then Vice-President, to draft anonymously a Kentucky Resolution of Interposition, questioning the constitutionality of these Alien and Sedition Acts. It was in this first Kentucky Resolution, adopted November 16, 1798, that Jefferson used the oft quoted slogan: "In questions of power, let no more be heard of confidence in man, but bind him down from mischief by the chains of the Constitution."

A month later the Virginia legislature adopted a similar, but somewhat milder, resolution, drafted by James Madison. This was the model used by the

Virginia General Assembly in its equally historic Interposition resolution approved by the State Senate 36 to 2, and by the House of Delegates 90 to 5, on February 1, 1956. The Madison resolution called on other states to "concur with Virginia in declaring, as it does hereby declare, that the acts aforesaid are unconstitutional." Kentucky then responded with a second, more aggressive, resolution, asserting "that a nullification, by those sovereignties [the States] of all unauthorized acts done under color of that instrument [the Constitution], is the rightful remedy." Here was illustrated the important difference between a Resolution of Interposition and an Act of Nullification, such as that adopted by South Carolina in 1832 against the federal tariff laws. Interposition may threaten Nullification but of itself does nothing to nullify and is orderly protest as distinct from rebellion.[13]

Since the Kentucky and Virginia Resolutions of 1798, Interposition has been many times invoked against Supreme Court decisions. Following the Dred Scott case a total of twenty-two States declared that judgment without binding authority. One of these instances may be examined because it shows how Wisconsin, in 1859, used the device of Interposition in exactly opposite but complementary manner to that employed by most of the Southern States, following the leadership of Virginia, in 1956.

Under the Fugitive Slave Law, as confirmed by the Supreme Court in the Dred Scott decision, a runaway Negro named Joshua Glover was arrested in Racine by a United States Marshal. The law prescribed his return to slavery. But Glover was forcefully freed from custody by abolitionists, whom the Wisconsin courts refused to prosecute. To give this local attitude at least a semblance of legality the Wisconsin legislature, on March 19, 1859, adopted a resolution of Interposition. It denounced the Supreme Court for "assumption of power" and declared "that the several States . . . have the unquestionable right" to exercise "positive defiance" in behalf of their interpretation of the powers reserved to the States by the Constitution.[14]

This was much stronger wording than anything found in the resolutions adopted by Virginia and nine other Southern States nearly a century later. But, no matter how moderately worded, a resolution of Interposition must by its very nature run counter to national authority, and also very possibly to the majority will of the nation as a whole, though obviously not to that of the State which adopts Interposition. So here is another outstanding instance in which federal and democratic doctrine, nationally interpreted, clash head-on.

When Interposition is attempted four reasonable outcomes are possible. The central government may tacitly back down; the State government may abandon the stand it has taken; there may be a mutually acceptable compromise between the two positions; or a solution may be found by clear-cut Constitutional Amendment. In the cases cited the position taken by the interposing States was successfully maintained. In the school issue good will and common sense may eventually bring a token integration which will satisfy both the prestige of the Court and the sovereignty of the recalcitrant State. Such a compromise would not mean that "democratic centralism" has overcome the basic principles of federalism.

Indeed it was scarcely accidental that, with the revival of Interposition, the Supreme Court opinions began to demonstrate a much more favorable attitude toward federal doctrine. A striking illustration is found in the case of *Bartkus v. Illinois*, mentioned above. In this "double jeopardy" case the Court divided 6 to 3 (Chief Justice Warren dissenting) in favor of the right of a State to prosecute and sentence, in the robbery of a federally insured savings and loan association, despite prior acquittal of the petitioner for the same offense in a federal court. Shortly thereafter, on June 8, 1959, the Court ruled (Warren again dissenting) that the controversial Steve Nelson case had not prevented a State from bringing "prosecutions for sedition against the State itself."

In *Bartkus v. Illinois* Justice Frankfurter emphasized that the case "raised a substantial question concerning the application of the Fourteenth Amendment"—the Due Process Clause—and based the decision not so much on precedents, strongly attacked by the dissenting opinion, as on the principle of dual sovereignty. Here Justice Frankfurter did not hesitate to "turn back the clock." He derided "some recent suggestions that the Constitution was in reality a deft device for establishing a centralized government. . . ." He approved the remark of Justice Brandeis that separation of powers was adopted "not to promote efficiency but to preclude the exercise of arbitrary power." And Justice Frankfurter then concluded: "Time has not lessened the concern of the Founders in devising a federal system which would likewise be a safeguard against arbitrary government. The greatest self-restraint is necessary when that federal system yields results with which a court is in little sympathy."

That wording could be used to justify the recalcitrance of the South on the Integration issue, and certainly suggests that this is not wholly, or even primarily, a matter of racial prejudice. Undoubtedly that is a factor, for people in general are uninterested in abstract ideas unless they are clarified by connection with daily experience. On the other hand, mere prejudice, completely unfortified by principle, has low vitality in any community which is open to the competition of broader thinking. A prejudice must have some measure of reasoned conviction behind it in order to survive.

Such a conviction was behind the stand which the South took in 1861, and a similar conviction is clearly present today. The defense of slavery as an institution was certainly a factor in Southern thinking a century ago, but many who were personally strongly opposed to slavery espoused the Southern cause. That cause had moral validity, and was stubbornly maintained against great odds, because it was grounded on the characteristically American belief in home rule, which was and is both sanctioned and sanctified in the Constitution. That organic law says nothing about democracy. But it has a great deal to say about States' Rights.

As already emphasized, the Civil War did not destroy, but on the contrary reaffirmed, the federal character of our government. It was not fought primarily to free the slaves, but to prevent the disruption of the Union. The legal outcome of the conflict did not destroy State citizenship, which is specifically re-emphasized in the first sentence of the Fourteenth Amendment. The South abandoned the theory of secession, and no serious claim to that previously alleged right has been made since Appomattox. But it is wholly natural that, in yielding this extreme claim, the resolution to safeguard States' Rights short of secession should have gained strength. And as the South has regained economic power its political philosophy has also naturally become more potent.

Tradition is strong in the South for many reasons. To justify their part in the "War Between the States" Southerners have had to study our constitutional history, and they are generally more familiar with it than are many in other sections of the country. Then there is the increasingly idealized glamor and romance of the Lost Cause and the civilization for which it stood. Finally, a great deal of highly important economic and social self-interest is now involved. Against the combined strength of these factors the advocates of political democracy have as yet made no great headway.

It is not for a moment suggested that this attitude is morally justifiable. But unquestionably it is a traditionalist position not likely to be rapidly undermined; which may indeed grow stronger rather than weaker under what is regarded as external coercion. It is another, very important, illustration of the fact that tradition still counts strongly in the United States, and can operate to the detriment of what may quite properly be called "the national interest."

And the tradition is the stronger because its roots

go back a long way. Indeed the Southern protest against the Supreme Court decision on Integration traces directly to action taken by the English Parliament in 1641. It was then that the King's Court of Star Chamber was abolished because, in the words of the statute, its judges "have undertaken to punish where no law doth warrant and to make decrees for things, having no such authority." [15]

There was no racial problem in England when Parliament refused to tolerate government by court decree. And the racial problem is by no means the only element in the similar Southern protest today. As much as anything, the protest is directed against any tendency towards restoration of the tyrannical judge-made law which, under King Charles I, gave the phrase "star-chamber methods" to our language.

SIXTEEN

Factors for Federalism

Although the centralizing trend in the United States is very powerful, it has as yet made little impression on the State-based system of American politics.

This is most obviously demonstrated in the amorphous character of both major parties, as seen from any national viewpoint. There is no single accepted or acceptable party line for the Democrats of Mississippi and those of Minnesota. Republican variations, from State to State, are scarcely less pronounced. Those who lack both sympathy and understanding in regard to federal doctrine would like to see firmer party discipline and direction. It is well to realize that these characteristics are most highly developed where the theory of the general will has gained complete control and where one single party, such as the Communist, is alone entitled to dictate in the name of "the people."

The localized character of American politics, however, is by no means the only factor operating to maintain the federal system. There are two other countervailing forces that remain to be considered. One is the institutional and cultural pattern that was established when federalism was virile, which in every case involves local loyalties and therefore does not readily yield to a shift in direction at the top. The other factor is the disillusion that springs from the all but inevitable failure of socialism to fulfill its glittering promises. This second factor does not of itself strengthen federalism, since it is at most a dissipation of the force that seeks to destroy the traditional American system. Yet a negative factor may easily prove important in a positive manner.

Extravagant promises were made by President Franklin D. Roosevelt in behalf of his "Economic Bill of Rights." Everyone was assured "the right to a useful and remunerative job"; adequate earnings; protection in old age, sickness and unemployment; a "decent home"; a "good education"; free "medical care" and so on. And all these "rights" were set forth without any balancing of conjunct responsibilities, though a right without an attendant responsibility is as unreal as a sheet of paper which has only one side.

A fallacious philosophy must draw fallacious reasoning to its support. Inevitably, the most uneconomic measures have been used in the effort to provide "rights." Among the results are ever-mounting governmental costs, a precariously balanced national budget, enforced wage increases unrelated to productivity, a mistrust of an undermined and weakened currency, and in spite of grinding taxes, a continuous rise in prices. At the expense of the community as a whole a section of organized labor is partially protected by escalator clauses against the effects of inflation. Shrewd speculators can similarly safeguard themselves by special skills and inside knowledge. But the greater part of the population is not and cannot be automatically carried up as the cost of living rises. Most are in the position of the Red Queen. They must run ever harder if they are not to lose ground.

In this situation every type of governmental subsidy, without exception, tends steadily to diminish
in purchasing power. Even if the nominal amounts
paid out are steadily raised, there is little, if any,
net gain in groceries. Social security benefits, for
instance, have nominally been increased by Congress
in every election year since 1948—five separate times
to date. When these payments began, in 1940, the
maximum for a single retired worker was $60 a
month. This was raised by stages to $127 a month
in 1958. During this period, however, the cost of
living doubled. Inflation swallowed practically all
of the nominal gain. And the situation is worse for
those innocents who complied with the Treasury's
exhortations to "invest" in "E" Bonds, for on their
maturity taxes have to be paid on an alleged gain
in value which has been largely if not completely
fictitious.

Few people are any longer unaware of an erosion
so pronounced that it has to be admitted. In the
words of the Advisory Council on Social Security
Financing, this system

> has created for millions of Americans expectations
> regarding their future place in economic society.
> These expectations could be defeated by discharg-
> ing the system's obligations in dollars having a sub-
> stantially lesser command of goods and services
> than the beneficiaries have come to count upon
> in their personal planning. . . . the trusteeship is
> so large and the number of people involved so
> great that the defeat of beneficiaries' expectations
> through inflation would gravely imperil the stabil-
> ity of our social, political and economic institu-
> tions.[1]

In this context Uncle Sam begins to assume a very different aspect from the benevolent and rather rustic old gentleman of bygone days. He seems the more of a sharper because his earlier promises were so lavish and unlimited. And with this disillusionment comes a skepticism, if nothing worse, towards all the silver-tongued advocacy of the Service State. To predict that this reaction will "gravely imperil" national stability is, one may hope, excessive. That would be the danger if there were no alternative to totalitarian democracy. But the well-tested machinery of federalism is as yet by no means dismantled and, there is reason to think, will again be utilized more actively, if only consideration is given to its remarkable values.

Another socialistic promise that has gone badly askew, in spite of the effort to maintain it by fantastic governmental expenditure, is that of "full employment." Under communism some sort of a job can doubtless be assured to everyone who is physically able to dig and hew.[2] But in a free market economy, which this country is clearly not yet ready to abandon, a fluctuating amount of unemployment has got to be accepted as the shadow side of the profit-and-loss system. Unemployment relief, as distinct from its subsidization, may be called a proper charge on government, though under federalism primarily on local authorities. But at present national policies are actually encouraging unemployment. For many workers on his payroll the employer now pays a social security tax of $120 a year, scheduled to rise to $216 by 1969. This tax alone tends to create unemployment. When the burden of all the taxes on production is added to high wages and fringe benefits, the rapid development of automation is explained. If profits are to be made, labor costs must be cut in a manner which means fewer jobs, available in large part only to those who are both willing and able to contribute to efficient operation.

For a time it was popular to emphasize "built-in" safeguards against unemployment, without consideration of the self-defeating element present in many of them. The unreliability of these safeguards was indicated by the 1957-58 recession, even though relatively slight and transient. A more serious sign was the failure of employment to recover in proportion, as production resumed its interrupted upward course. Of course it could be, and was, argued that the remedy was more relief, more governmental spending, an ever-larger deficit. But the national debt has now reached a level at which the interest charge alone amounts to nearly ten billion dollars a year. And, like any other wastrel, the government finds that it costs more to borrow as its credit grows suspect. The situation does not promise that inflation can be held to a "creeping" rate. The faster its rate, the greater the disillusion with the Service State.

In the fiscal year 1865, which saw the close of the Civil War, the expenditures of the national government for the first time time mounted above the billion dollar level. Then they receded sharply, not passing this figure again until fiscal 1917, during which the United States entered World War I. In fiscal 1960 it is anticipated that the mere storage and loan charges on surplus farm commodities will pass the billion dollar mark. The comparison, even allowing for the change in dollar value and the gain in productivity, suggests how the attitude towards government spending has altered, within the memory of all who are now eligible for social security benefits.

But the very rapidity of that change, and the speed with which price supports have built up an unmanageable, $9-billion food surplus, suggests that policies of subsidization have passed the point where diminishing returns set in. What seems to be gained on one sector is now definitely lost on others. No group of beneficiaries is immune from a dollar devaluation which has reached such serious proportions that "reasonable price stability" has been coupled with "maximum employment" as an "explicit goal" of economic policy.[3] If this disillusionment had developed earlier the social planners, as in Great Britain, might well have turned to the nationalization of industry as a last resource. But the lugubrious English experience with government monopolies, together with the unquestionable efficiency of free enterprise here, has checked that counsel of desperation. Moreover, it is difficult openly to adopt socialist techniques while vehemently maintaining that the communists, who have carried those techniques to perfection, are therefore our mortal enemies.

The net of it is a growing skepticism towards the Service State and, more importantly, towards the fiction of the general will on which the whole tottering structure of centralized paternalism has been built. With this revulsion, if not too long delayed, could come a fair reappraisal, and then an active reanimation, of traditional American values. And this is not a matter of nostalgia but of intelligent choice. Let us consider some of the evidence showing that institutions which evolved under federation, and which would make no sense in a centralized unitary state, are not losing but rather gaining in contemporary esteem.

One such illustration is the privately endowed small college, a characteristically American institution which would have no excuse for being were it not for our decentralized system of government. There is nothing accidental in the fact that while the unitary states of Europe possess many great universities they have nothing akin to the essentially parochial small colleges which are scattered in such profusion over the length and breadth of the United States. From the educational viewpoint many of these colleges are second-rate. Their libraries and laboratories are inadequate. The quality of instruction is often mediocre and few graduates carry away a zest for learning in any intellectual field. Better results might be obtained by closing several hundred of these feeble academies and locating their more promising students in centers of instruction with high standards, a category in which a very few of the State universities may be said to belong.

If the United States were losing their federal character this educational centralization would be entirely natural, and might well extend to conversion to more useful purposes of those State universities which have little more than a semi-professional football team to make them distinctive. One enormous provincial university in each of the twelve Federal Reserve Districts could adequately handle public education at the higher level, using TV and correspondence courses as desired. The great private universities, from Harvard to Leland Stanford, could then be expanded to care for serious students, with government scholarships as needed. In such concentrated centers of learning there could be a far more intensive concentration on that training for world leadership which successful imperial development certainly demands.

Yet it seems unlikely that any State will permit its own university to be closed down, and equally improbable that the parochial small colleges, barring a few whose financial position is hopeless, will be allowed by their loyal clientele to go under. In the service that the small college has always given to its particular community lies the strength of the institution in this time of trouble. Trustees and faculties alike make great sacrifices to keep these local organizations going. Annual giving by the alumni has become standardized practice. Business is approached on a State-wide basis to meet the campus emergencies. And a generally merciless tax system is so arranged, both on the national and the State levels, as to allow generous deductability for all who contribute to an educational system bound in with the concept of federalism. Unfortunately, few of the colleges give either adequate or animated instruction in the subject as a return.

In many ways, such as the financing of military research, loans for dormitory construction, even the direct subvention of students, the central government is unquestionably getting more of a grip on higher, as well as on secondary, education. It could be that the destiny of the small colleges, as well as of the universities, both private and public, is, like that of the banks, to become local agencies of policies directed from Washington. That is what happened to them temporarily during World War II. But, partly because of that experience, the determination to remain decentralized is still vital in the field of education. The opposition to bureaucratic encroachment grows stronger as its threat intensifies and a loyalty that is essentially local is as yet by no means undermined.

For the small colleges this localism is notably reinforced by religious support. Originally these institutions were almost without exception church-established, with ministerial training a primary part of their original purpose. Only the Roman Catholic church has successfully maintained this connection and, in general, separated seminaries have come to handle clerical education, on a post-graduate basis. In a manner which would have seemed dangerous to George Washington, separation of church and state has come to mean a definite elimination of religious instruction from Protestant education.[4] But here too a healthy reaction is apparent. At the elementary and secondary levels church-related schools are increasing in numbers, with a merger of religion and education which seems to give more vitality to both.[5] It is unlikely that the Protestant churches will recapture the major responsibility for education they once possessed in the United States. But any ground regained in this direction is in the interest of a decentralized political system.

Many factors can be discerned behind the restoration of church-connected education. Widespread parental dissatisfaction with the results of present-day public school training is certainly one. Another is compulsory integration in areas which predominantly resent this development. But there is also the factor of what is broadly called religious revival. The political import of a spiritual movement is not to be minimized because it cannot be measured statistically, by increasing church membership, attendance or financial contribution. The effect is seen more clearly in such activities as voluntary welfare work, well maintained by the churches and other private agencies in spite of the pressures to have all this channeled through official agencies.[6] Here again it is noteworthy that tax arrangements are helpful to those who seek to fortify the churches as that first line of defense against governmental aggrandizement which they have so often, and so logically, proved to be. Those who are loyal to God are always reluctant to render unto Caesar any more than his rightful due.

Church organization in the United States generally conforms to State divisions and in very few cases has it been thought desirable to focus religious direction in the national capital. Other important congregations, such as business and professional associations and labor unions, are also usually organized on a State basis, even when federated nationally. It is significant that the labor unions, generally socialistic in their outlook, have been centering their powerful executive leadership in Washington, much more so than other types of private organization. In many unions, as the investigations of the McClellan Committee have demonstrated, democratic control of the unit organization has been abandoned in favor of strongly centralized direction.[7] It follows naturally that those who direct union policies should locate where national policies are planned and most easily subject to persuasive influence.

None who has watched the spectacular growth of Washington over the past half-century will minimize its development from a small and sleepy city into a great and very beautiful metropolis. Yet, partly because of the wise prohibition of large-scale industry, it is still only the political capital of the United States. The growth of Washington is a measure of the growth of governmental activity and centralization. It has become a mecca for those who must deal with the central government in any of its myriad manifestations, for all who would do scholarly research in the social sciences, and for casual visitors in countless numbers. Washington has many amenities, but many of those who live there do not consider it a permanent home. It is still far from being an all-inclusive national center in the sense that London and Paris are.

Washington, for instance, has never possessed either an outstanding university or a nationally circulated newspaper. Its art galleries are dominating as is, of course, the Library of Congress. But it draws no visitors for music and the theatre. In the cultural field as a whole the capital trails several other American cities, and would be lower in the scale except for the stimulus from a diplomatic corps which now almost rivals that of an army in numbers. Famous men die in Washington—many more than are born there. But, excepting those who rest in Arlington, it is to their own localities that American leaders return for burial. A Westminister Abbey in Washington is unthinkable.

That is because the emotional response of the American people, despite their mobility and fre-

quent deracination, remains strongly localized. Nowhere is this more clearly apparent than at meetings
of the various "State Societies" in the national
capital. Here the rank-and-file employees of the
central government gather for sociability, not along
functional lines but according to the States of their
origin; and there is none so poor as not to be thus
honored. At these affairs the sense of commonwealth
seems to redress the balance lost in routine bureaucratic duties that treat the Federal Republic as an
accomplished amalgamation. Always the State flag
is on display, and the State song in demand. Old
Fletcher, of Saltoun, was somewhat reckless in saying: "Let me make the songs of a people and you
shall make its laws." But it is nevertheless significant
that American folksongs are so strongly localized.
Not even in the more national anthems is there that
identification of the individual with centralized control so obvious in *Deutschland, Deutschland Über
Alles*; in *Allons Enfants de la Patrie,* or even in *Rule
Brittania*. And for all its haunting beauty there is
something completely alien to American thought in
Rupert Brooke's idea of sublimation:

> If I should die, think only this of me:
> That there's some corner of a foreign field
> That is forever England.

Into whatever phase of American life one looks,
the State is still the unit. On that basis the countless
civic and citizens' associations cooperate; the increasingly active historical associations are organized; on that basis flora and fauna are listed; on that
basis the State universities prepare their publication

lists. The Federal Reserve System, as an exception to prove the rule, ignored State lines in establishing its twelve districts. When Alaska achieved Statehood it became merely part of the Seattle branch territory of the district where San Francisco is the Reserve Bank city. But it is to be noted that these districts for the most part absorb States as units, and that where this is not the case the financial boundaries follow the lines of counties, townships or parishes as constituent parts of the States. The State, or its subdivisions, continues to provide the basis on which nearly every national statistical compilation is computed. And short as the United States Treasury is for cash, there is little likelihood that the tax-exempt feature in local government obligations will be eliminated.

The underlying reason for all this is brought home most strongly to anyone who flies criss-cross over the nation, as it has been my good fortune to do on a chamber of commerce "aircade." What one comes to realize, far more sharply than on a direct transcontinental flight, is the enormous climatic and physical variation within the United States. With that realization comes a deeper appreciation of the wisdom of those who endowed us with a political system tailored to this variation, designed to prevent monopolization of power by national officers inevitably ignorant of many local customs and characteristics. It has been wisely said that there are very few matters on which a parliament can legislate simultaneously for Esquimaux and Hottentots. That comes to mind when one moves on the same Febru-

ary day from 15 below zero in Minnesota to 75
above in Arizona.

The changes in cultural background are no less
pronounced. English characteristics linger in Boston
very much as do those of Germany in Milwaukee.
The heritage from France is not least among the
attractions of New Orleans while El Paso retains a
Spanish impress in more than name. In Europe such
differences have blocked political unification. Here,
the principle of home rule has permitted union without a stultifying uniformity.

Contrasts in physical environment combine with
racial variations to validate the system of State
sovereignty. Even identical twins will develop very
different political outlooks if one lives in a well-
watered area, the other on land which requires constant irrigation.[8] Contrasting geophysical features—
upland and lowland, desert and swampland, prairies
and rivers, mountains and oceans—continuously
press differing characteristics into men, who in controlling nature are also influenced by her many
manifestations. We assume far too easily that such
variations are ironed out by speed of communication, by uniformity of stereotypes or by standardi-
zation of gadgets.

The founding fathers never had opportunity to fly
over even the relatively meagre territory of the
thirteen original States. They nevertheless realized
what the airplane makes dramatically obvious—that
a country of sharp physical contrasts cannot be
successfully pressed into the mold of strongly centralized government. The last place to assume a
general will is in a population of heterogeneous

origin, constantly affected by varying natural conditions. And so it was written into the Bill of Rights: "The powers not delegated to the United States by the Constitution, nor prohibited by it to the States, are reserved to the States respectively, or to the people."

Nobody can maintain, however, that powers originally reserved to the States have been lost merely because of centralized usurpation, tolerated or encouraged by the Supreme Court. To a large extent the attrition of federalism has come by default in the localities.

A solemn warning against this outcome was voiced by Elihu Root, then Secretary of State, as far back as December 12, 1906. It may be noted that this was half-way through a fiscal year in which the expenditures of the national government were $579,128,842, or less than one per cent of the annual dollar figure they reached just half a century later. In a brief but notable address to the Pennsylvania Society in New York, Mr. Root said:

> It is useless for the advocates of State rights to inveigh against the supremacy of the constitutional laws of the United States, or against the extension of national authority in the fields of necessary control where the States themseles fail in the performance of their duty. The instinct for self-government among the people of the United States is too strong to permit them long to respect anyone's right to exercise a power which he fails to exercise. The governmental control which they deem just and necessary they will have. It may be that such control would better be exercised in particular instances by the governments of the States, but the people will have the control they need, either

from the States or from the National Government; and if the States fail to furnish it in due measure, sooner or later constructions of the Constitution will be found to vest the power where it will be exercised—in the National Government.[9]

State governments, with a few honorable exceptions, are both ill-designed and ill-equipped to cope with the problems which a dynamic society cannot, or will not, solve for itself. State Constitutions are in many cases unduly restrictive. Their legislatures meet too briefly and have the most meagre technical assistance. The cities are usually grossly under-represented, as compared with the rural areas, so that hard-pressed municipal officials now habitually turn to Washington rather than to the State capital for help. Governors generally have inadequate executive control over a pattern of local government unnecessarily complex and confusing. As has been well said, the State pattern shows "too many local governments, not enough local government." [10]

Various agencies, public and private, struggle heroically to improve this situation, which is of course a constant invitation for the extension of centralized planning and command. The Council of State Governments[11] has proved itself an efficient medium for inter-State cooperation, acts as a clearing house for the exchange of information among State officials, and has done much to tone up local administrative practice. The unofficial Governmental Research Association coordinates the activities of countless civic leagues, municipal study groups and taxpayers' organizations. The steadily mounting cost of local government is giving a healthy stimulus to the demand for greater efficiency and economy. The theory of federalism is regaining some vitality as a result.

Speaking to the forty-ninth annual Conference of Governors, at colonial Williamsburg in June, 1957, President Eisenhower capitalized on the setting to urge the return of governmental responsibilities to the States. "I believe," he said, "that the preservation of our States as vigorous, powerful governmental units is essential to permanent individual freedom and to the growth of our national strength."

Since then there have been definite moves for the relinquishment of certain specified tax revenues to the States, coincident with their assumption of full responsibility for programs now financed with "federal aid." It is noticeable, however, that these plans have aroused a virtual chorus of protest from professional social workers, and rather indifferent support from local citizen's groups. One would expect that with all our talk about "democracy" there would be general eagerness to see it in operation where public opinion always has most reality—at the local level. On the contrary, many who talk eloquently in terms of "the people" obviously favor nationalized social services, with local participation limited to the unquestioning payment of "federal" taxes.

Where Mr. Root erred was in thinking that "the instinct for self-government" would survive, once it had operated to institute government by remote control. Like any other talent, the less self-government is practiced, the more it atrophies. In the words of Secretary of the Treasury Robert B. Anderson, co-chairman of the "Federal-State Action Committee" in this field: "There must be willingness and a desire on the part of the people of the State and local governments to have the responsibility for these programs." [12]

SEVENTEEN

The Vitality of Federalism

One of the sharpest of history's many ironies is the spread of the federal idea throughout the world coincident with its decline in the United States, the country that proved its value for mankind.

Paradoxically, this development overseas has often been actively promoted and assisted by agencies of the central government in Washington, as in the case of the establishment of the German *Bundesrepublik*. While the executive branch was drawing ever more power to itself from the States of the American Union, its officials were simultaneously advising the post-war leaders of West Germany to prevent such concentration.

For at least three reasons the defeated Germans, given freedom to do so, would in any case have adopted a federal constitution. Such a system was a direct repudiation of the extreme centralization practiced by the Nazis. With Prussian overlordship destroyed, it promised restoration of much of the autonomy reluctantly yielded by Bavaria and the lesser States under the first Reich. And it was the formula best adapted to the hope of eventual reunification of the broken and divided German nation. So the solicitude of the American political advisers was superfluous, yet none the less praiseworthy in view of the way German federation has paid off in dividends for all the so-called Free World.

Of course there is no way to determine accurately how much of the "miracle" of German recovery is attributable to the federal system set up in 1949. The free market maintained by Dr. Ludwig Erhard from the day he became Minister of Economics is rightly given a large measure of the credit. So also is the indefatigable persistence of the German workers, the skill of their scientists and technicians, the ability of industrial management.[1] But in the federal republic these factors received a maximum of encouragement from the political decentralization, as compared with a maximum of discouragement for all but a small proportion of their fellow countrymen under the centralized socialism of the Russian zone. In post-war Western Germany, as everywhere that climate does not enervate, the less oppressive the control of government, the more energetic the individual activity of the governed.

The Constitution of the German Federal Republic became effective on May 23, 1949. Soon thereafter the government headed by Chancellor Adenauer was firmly established and was admitted to full membership in the Organization for European Economic Cooperation, the European Payments Union, the Coal and Steel Community, and the Council of Europe. All these bureaucratic organizations, in their different ways, were attempts to achieve greater economic and political unification in that part of Europe not under, but clearly threatened by, communist domination.[2]

This unification movement was from the beginning

strongly supported from below, and indeed to a large extent guided, by active unofficial pro-federalism organizations in most of the Western European countries. By March 25, 1957, the federal trend had reached the stage where two very significant diplomatic instruments could be signed in Rome. They were the Common Market and Euratom Treaties, the second of which pools ownership, among the six participating governments, of all fissionable materials that are not diverted to military use.[3]

The same six governments—of France, Italy, Western Germany, Netherlands, Belgium and Luxembourg—compose the much more broadly important European Economic Community. This Common Market grouping was really built on the success of the Coal and Steel Community, which by the end of 1953 had gone far to eliminate tariff and trade restrictions among the six in those two basic products. In the origin of this undertaking there was undoubtedly some punitive animus against the Germans. They should be compelled to share their coal and steel with countries the Nazi legions had overrun. But this hangover of nationalistic resentment evaporated as it came to be realized that the elimination of trade restrictions in these basic commodities was operating in the mutual interest of all concerned.

Consequently, in June, 1955, the foreign ministers of the above-mentioned six national governments, meeting at Messina, decided in principle to merge the economies of their countries, in much the same way as the economies of the States in our own Union are merged. The major decisions taken at this historic, yet contemporaneously little noticed, meeting were to eliminate all tariffs among the six states, to re-establish free convertibility of their respective currencies, to permit the unrestricted movement of labor across their frontiers, to harmonize and coordinate their respective social security systems and to create common investment institutions for economic development. The step was somewhat the less epoch-making because the little Benelux combination—Belgium, Netherlands and Luxembourg—had already achieved some preliminary success along these lines.

The Common Market Treaty, quickly ratified by all six national parliaments, established a somewhat elastic timetable, spotted with escape clauses, for accomplishment of this far-reaching plan. It became nominally effective on January 1, 1958, and a year later a definite start was made, both in the direction of free currency convertibility and of actual tariff consolidation and reduction within the six-country grouping, which Greece is disposed to join.

There can be no assured prediction as to the eventual outcome of this long-range undertaking. In economic matters it is working much more clearly in the direction of a federated Europe than is the case with the political arrangements. The Council of Ministers, which has the executive power for the Common Market, is composed of governmental appointees, four each from France, West Germany and Italy, two each from Belgium and the Netherlands, one from Luxembourg. Any decision, within the terms of the treaty, can be taken by a vote of twelve of these seventeen members, provided that in certain cases the twelve votes must be provided by four of the national delegations. This means that, unlike the Council of the United Nations, no single government can exercise a veto power.

The Common Market Council operates through a full-time commission of nine members, serving renewable terms of four years, during which they may engage in no other professional activity, remunerated or not. All members of this commission must be nationals of the Common Market countries, and no more than two may have the same nationality. Any proposed commission member can be blackballed by any one of the participating governments, but once installed in office "they shall neither solicit nor accept instruction from any government nor from any organization" other than the Council which they serve (Art. 157). In other words, the civil service of the Common Market is, like the secretariat of the U.N., designed as a professional and non-political body.

The organization also has a Consultative Assembly, though this has been given no more governmental power than the name indicates. Not even this body has any direct connection with the electorate of the Common Market countries. Members of the Assembly, in assigned numbers, are chosen by the six national parliaments from among their own memberships, in proportion to party representation there. Finally, the financing is by annual grants requested in set proportions from these parliaments. Seemingly any country could secede from the Common Market merely by withholding its contributory grant.

At present, therefore, the organization cannot be classified as a federation, but rather as a limited league of nations, designed to promote the economic integration of its membership. Nevertheless, "Little Europe," as this six-nation grouping is often called, bears a close and suggestive structural resemblance to the Confederation of American States, during the period between the Revolution and adoption of the Constitution of 1787.

On the one hand, common economic interest, especially the virtual necessity of unimpeded transport, communication and power transmission, is working constantly to bind the Common Market countries into "a more perfect Union." On the other hand, political factors tend to retard this development. Even before the Rome treaties were signed, the British Government had found "substantial reasons why the United Kingdom could not become a member of such a Union," arising "in particular from the United Kingdom's interests and responsibilities in the Commonwealth." The Conservative Government therefore, in 1957, suggested an alternative "Grand Design" providing for a larger free trade area in Western Europe, though one which in the interest of the Commonwealth would exclude agricultural production, and for a vaguely adumbrated European Parliament, with which the United States and Canada might, if they so choose, be associated.[4] The nebulous political part of this "plan" gave temporary encouragement to the advocates of "Union Now" among the North Atlantic "democracies." But the "Grand Design" wilted under opposition from the Council of Europe. And the much more explicit free trade area proposal did not deter the restricted Common Market movement from forging ahead along its own limited lines.

Problems which are intrinsically French and German are calculated to prove more of a handicap than British opposition to the development of real federation in "Little Europe."

The British, though distinctly worried by the potential competitive strength of the Common Market, have concluded that imperial interests preclude their membership in it. The French decision was exactly opposite. All of the remaining African dependencies of France, including Algeria as an integral though rebellious part of the country, have been brought into the Common Market grouping as part of the larger French "community." While this attempted fusion of a colonial empire with a central European customs union offers obvious economic advantages it is also politically anomalous. What if these French African dependencies, whether predominantly Arab or Negro, should prefer not to be attached to a European grouping? The Common Market will certainly not develop further towards federation if its members, aside from France and Belgium, think that thereby they will incur any responsibility to maintain a colonial system for others. And this mistrust was increased by the accession to quasi-dictatorial power of General de Gaulle, more clearly imbued with nationalistic mystique than with any apparent desire to subordinate French independence to European federation.

Uncertainty as to the future of divided Germany raises another imponderable. While the *Bundesrepublik* under Adenauer has been a leader for European federation, it could be quite otherwise if and when Germany is reunited. This involves agreement with Soviet Russia for which German neutrality is certainly the minimum price. That development would be more of a threat to the predominantly military organization of NATO than to the predominantly economic organization of the Common Market. But it would tend to keep the latter from acquiring any real political unity.

So any evolution of the still embryonic Common Market towards federal structure is doubtful, to say the least. Nevertheless, it is significant that in the continuous consideration given to this step no single authority on unification has been quoted more frequently than the *Federalist* papers. And of those essays the closing passages of No. 11, by Alexander Hamilton, are now better known in Europe than in the United States. Especially apt for the problems of Western Europe, judging by the frequency of its quotation there, is Hamilton's closely reasoned paragraph beginning: "An unrestrained intercourse between the States themselves will advance the trade of each by an interchange of their respective productions, not only for the supply of reciprocal wants at home, but for exportation to foreign markets."

The closing sentence of this memorable essay is also frequently cited in Europe, as apposite—in reverse—to its current problems: "Let the thirteen States, bound together in a strict and indissoluble Union, concur in erecting one great American system, superior to the control of all transatlantic force or influence, and able to dictate the terms of the connection between the old and the new world!"

Only in similar fashion, suggests Professor Bruno Leoni dryly in a study of *The Actuality of Federal-*

ism, can Europe in its turn hope to build a political system "superior to the control of all transatlantic force or influence." [5]

Within Europe, progress towards federalism is slowed by deep-rooted nationalistic prejudice, by interests of many kinds vested in the nationalistic traditions, to some extent by the paradoxical effort to prevent the rise of other nationalisms in crumbling overseas empires.

The liquidation of colonialism, on the other hand, has given notable stimulus to a widespread application of federal method to former dependencies. British, much more than American, statesmanship has taken the lead in this. For instance, the independent Republic of the Philippines, proclaimed with the sanction of the United States on July 4, 1946, is unitary and not federal. Members of the Senate are all chosen "at large" and not by the "provinces," which have little or no autonomy. Whenever the word "state" is used in the Philippines' Constitution it means the national government alone. Indeed, this Constitution is worthy of careful examination, as an open proclamation of the system which many Americans would like to see established here. Section 6 of Article XIII will serve as an illustration. It reads:

> The State may, in the interest of national welfare and defense, establish and operate industries and means of transportation and communication, and, upon payment of just compensation, transfer to public ownership utilities and other private enterprises to be operated by the government.

By contrast the nearby Federation of Malaya, since August, 1957, a self-governing nation (excluding Singapore) within the British Commonwealth, conforms in more than mere name to federal definition. The Senate is appointed by the "Paramount Ruler," who is elected by the local Sultans among themselves. But its members are definitely supposed to represent sectional and minority interests. Moreover, all powers not reserved to the central government vest in the Councils of the constituent States.

The Federation of the West Indies is a more recent illustration, within the British Commonwealth, its newly elected Parliament having been formally opened by Princess Margaret on April 22, 1958. It is composed of ten former crown colonies strung in a loose arc of far-flung tropical islands, including Jamaica and Trinidad at either end. For the present a British Governor-General fills the role which could eventually be that of President, and he appoints the Senate, two from each of the amalgamated crown colonies except Montserrat, which provides only one. In the European parliamentary tradition, the Prime Minister of the West Indies is the choice of the dominant party in the freely elected House of Representatives, from forty-five constituencies in all the federating islands. His power is limited both by the functions reserved for the local control of the ten former colonies and by those (defense, foreign affairs and currency) kept in the hands of the British Governor-General.

The British are generally supposed to have learned the value of the federal formula the hard way—by not having it in time to apply to the continental American colonies when revolution might thereby have been averted. The Leeward Islands, however, practiced a crude form of federalism as early as the

reign of Queen Anne, and it has been suggested that
Alexander Hamilton, who was born there, was
influenced by this background when he helped to
draft the Constitution of the United States.[6] But
there is little or no supporting evidence for this
theory in any of Hamilton's voluminous political
writings. What is less disputable is the fact that
the British have recently found the federal form
of government as suitable for racially heterogeneous
equatorial territories, on opposite sides of the globe,
as they did in the past for "all-white" Australia and
Anglo-French Canada.

Many other current illustrations of the vitality of
federalism could be cited. The union of Egypt and
Syria is widely regarded as only a first step in the
building of a federated Arab Republic. The French
have loosely federated both their West African and
equatorial colonies, as the British have not too
successfully attempted in Nigeria and East Africa.[7]
Relations between the new African republics of
Ghana (formerly British) and Guinea (formerly
French) suggest that the idea of federation may
spread rapidly among new Negro nations formed out
of emancipated European colonies.[8] Indeed, fear of
that development is one reason for the strength of
the "apartheid" movement in the Union of South
Africa, itself a well-designed federation dating back
to the days when the little Dutch republics, Trans-
vaal and Orange Free State, joined forces to resist
the British in the so-called Boer War. There is
something reminiscent of that Boer coalition in the
consultative "Nordic Council" currently maintained
by the governments of Denmark, Finland, Norway

and Sweden, which some would like to see expanded into a Scandinavian Federation.[9]

These illustrations certainly indicate that the federal form of government is adaptable to the greatest diversity of cultural and climatic conditions. They further show that it is far from "obsolescent," as Professor Harold Laski asserted in 1939 and as more cautious socialists, English and American, have been affirming since. On the other hand, it must be noted that federalism is constantly threatened by centrifugal as well as centripetal tendencies. The pronounced trend towards centralization of all political authority in Washington is the outstanding illustration of the latter force. Examples of the centrifugal tendency can be found in dissolution of the former dynastic unions of Norway and Sweden; of Holland and Belgium; of Austria and Hungary.

Another illustration is found in the splintering into five separate republics of the Central American Federation formed when these Spanish provinces jointly obtained their independence in 1821. These five (Costa Rica, Guatemala, Honduras, Nicaragua, El Salvador) are nevertheless showing a definite tendency towards reunification, currently in the establishment of a customs union.

It is often asserted that federalism is only a political way-station on the road to the strongly integrated nation-state. The argument here is that the division of sovereignty which is the essence of federalism is reasonable during a period of national probation, so to speak, but cannot be tolerated in a "Great Power." Countries which have achieved that allegedly desirable status must, it is said, have strongly unitary governments able to act vigorously and promptly in their foreign relations and empowered to standardize domestic practices in the interest of efficiency, economy and public welfare. The reasons for the growth of that seductive yet specious reasoning, together with many of its flaws, have been examined in the course of this study. Here it is sufficient to point to the inevitable end of this mode of thinking.

If Great Power status is actually the final goal of political evolution it follows logically that one nation should eventually rise triumphant over all its rivals. This has been the objective, never attained and probably never attainable, of all the conquerors of recorded history. It is widely believed to be the aim of the Russian leadership today, though some uncertainty creeps in from evidence that communist China might in the future be quite as interested in world domination as is Soviet Russia.

All American energies are therefore being increasingly concentrated by centralized government, at the expense of the American tradition, to block the supposed objectives of the communist leadership. Yet in this literally suicidal effort the ultimate weapon of all-out war is denied us. For if there is one certainty about an atomic war it is that the result would be the complete destruction of major aspects of freedom in the United States. Win, lose or draw —in the military sense—the simple, dictatorial methods of communism, whether directed by Americans, Russians or Chinese, would displace the free market from the moment the first atomic bomb was dropped.

Since this is realized by all thinking people, and furthermore since we ourselves deny any disposition to run the world from Washington, it would seem logical to give far more positive and continuous support to the principles of federalism, both at home and abroad. The case for such policy is strengthened by the evidence that mankind is in any case groping towards the adoption and development of a political formula which was first thoroughly thought out by American statesmanship and which has certainly proved beneficial to all who have employed it.

Among the men who planned the federal system the most practical and prosaic, the least inclined to indulge in rhapsody of any kind, was undoubtedly James Madison. Yet even Madison, when the fate of the newly drafted Constitution hung in the balance, could not refrain from that rare type of emotional appeal, firmly based upon the most careful observation and reasoning, which characterized the Hebrew prophets of old. "Hearken not," he advised, "to the voice which petulantly tells you that the form of government recommended for your adoption is a novelty in the political world; that it has never yet had a place in the theories of the wildest projectors; that it rashly attempts what it is impossible to accomplish. No, my countrymen, shut your ears against this unhallowed language." [10]

They did so. And it may be hoped that Americans of today will with equal conviction shut their ears to the even more unhallowed language of those who maintain that in less than two centuries the Federal Republic has necessarily run its course. This suggests that the end of the road for the United States is just one more tombstone of the type that tells the lifespan of the countless centralized despotisms of the past. Yet, all too clearly, that could be the outcome.

In this same *Federalist* essay Madison answers the doubts of those who say that while federalism may be a suitable system for a small and compact country, like Switzerland, it will not serve larger areas as well as strongly centralized government. On the contrary, he says, for so long as the jurisdiction of the central government "is limited to certain enumerated objects" the natural limit of a federal republic "is that distance from the centre which will barely allow the representatives to meet as often as may be necessary for the administration of public affairs. Can it be said that the limits of the United States exceed this distance?"

The question was merely rhetorical, when posed by Madison in 1787, and is far more so today. With the development of air transport there is indeed no longer any "natural limit" to a federation. Nor is the interposition of the ocean, or of territory under another soverignty, any longer an obstacle, as shown by the entry of Hawaii and Alaska into the American Union, and by the wide separation of Jamaica from its sister States in the Federation of the West Indies.

Those who plead for "world federalism" may therefore be far more politically realistic, much more closely attuned to the realities of our age, than many who regard them as the "wild projectors" that Franklin, Hamilton, Madison, Washington and their colleagues were once deemed to be. Certain it is that two world organizations, composed primarily of unitary states with concentrated sovereignty, have both bogged down since World War I. With the extreme polarization of power, as now between U.S.A. and U.S.S.R. the problem of world stabilization has become insoluble through further concentration of governmental strengths. Nationalism is clearly anachronistic when it is shot through the earth's atmosphere to compete in outer space.

Unlimited concentration of governmental power encourages both internal and external tension. The increase in both has been clearly apparent as our own country has moved towards empire from its federal basis. By its division and separation of powers, federation tends to relieve both types of tensions. There is nothing accidental in the fact that wars between federations are most unusual, nor in the fact that where federalism is really practiced, changes of government by free election are both frequent and orderly.

So the resurgent vitality of federalism, weakened though the doctrine is in its American birthplace, is encouraging to all who look for something better than "cold war" ad infinitum. For through the gradual formation of perhaps a dozen great federations, of which the United States and Russia would certainly be two, those polarized enemies would be disengaged, a balance of power would be re-established, the backward nations might look forward to some such blossoming as came to our own backward States when they federated, and above all a better basis of less recriminatory international cooperation might well be laid.

The present government of Russia, of course, is not in reality federal. And that of the United States is ceasing to be worthy of the definition. But there are many signs that Americans are unhappy about the loss of this distinctive national form. And other signs are not lacking that Russia, if peace were stabilized, might develop towards federalism, with less concentration of power in Moscow and consequently more freedom in the constituent units.

One point is not speculative. The world, as a result of the breakdown of the European system of nation-states, has been thrown into a political melting pot at least as liquefying as was the French Revolution. So much has been shattered that no reformation in the old mold is conceivable. The changes that have taken place since 1945 are undoubtedly only a portent of those still to come, even on the assumption that there will not be atomic war.

In such a period, regardless of the course of others, it is of the first importance for Americans to hold fast to those tested principles of government which have served them so well; to give far more consideration to the assets of federalism than is now generally rendered—even to realize, for reasons now to be noted, that once again, in Alexander Hamilton's words, "It belongs to us to vindicate the honor of the human race." [11]

EIGHTEEN

Freedom and Federalism

"Words"—says Joseph Conrad, at the outset of the novel in which he sought "to capture the very soul of things Russian"—"are the great foes of reality." [1] That is certainly true of the word "democracy." It is also true of another abstract political term that must be confronted with equal resolution —"freedom."

Precision is the more necessary because these two vague words are so often closely associated. It is commonly asserted that the more democratic a system of government, the more free will be those whom it governs. The assumption is baseless. If democracy is at variance with federalism, and if federalism is conducive to freedom, it could follow that, far from maintaining freedom, democracy is inimical to it.

The first part of this hypothesis has been established. By its very nature a federal system is an impediment to that unrestricted triumph of the majority will which is the essence of political democracy. The distribution of power characteristic of a federation is an obstruction to any "general will" in all matters reserved to the control of the autonomous localities. In the federation of the United States this obstruction is intensified, because the Constitution reserves certain specified rights to the

259

people and prohibits any governmental infringement of these rights, whether by the national or by the State authorities. But to prove that democracy is at odds with federalism is not to demonstrate that federalism is conducive to freedom, the nature of which must now be explored.

Our officials constantly assure us that we are a "free nation," joined with like-minded Allies in "the Free World"—meaning that part of the planet which is not subservient to Moscow and Peiping. Such assertions have little reality at best and are the more suspect because they seek to make freedom collective. Political government can certainly discourage or encourage the condition of freedom. But, in the deeper sense, men are not free unless they make their own decisions, for themselves.

It has already been remarked that there is a subtle difference between what we mean by "freedom" and what we mean by "liberty," even though the dictionary seems to sanction their interchangeable use. It has also been pointed out that "freedom" has come to be used where "security" is meant, a corruption much more difficult in the case of "liberty," which more clearly implies the element of choice and the uncertainty that frequently goes with it. In this final chapter we endeavor to isolate the abstract quality which both freedom and liberty seek to define. The effort is imperative because this quality is the very heart and substance of what we seek to defend against communism. And if the quality cannot be successfully defined it is most doubtful that it can be successfully defended.

We start from the simple fact that "freedom" is a noun of Anglo-Saxon origin, while "liberty" is derived from the Latin. It is a fair assumption that any difference in meaning traces to the different social concepts held by the Romans and by the northern "barbarians" whom their legions were never able to subdue. Since the Romans were much the more civilized people one would expect the word they used to have the more refined conception.

This expectation is substantiated by considering the customary verbal use of the two words. One may free a house from a mortgage, a boat from a sandbar or a pole from a log-jam. One would not "liberate" these inanimate objects. Release from physical restraint is in both cases the objective. But we think more naturally of *people* as being liberated; of *things* as being freed. For wild animals, however, either verb seems appropriate. Also, in this intermediate area on the scale of life, we use either the personal or the impersonal pronoun. To free a vixen from a trap is to liberate her—or it.

The associated prepositions are also suggestive of a transition from the impersonal to the personal. We obtain freedom "for" or "from" something—a preliminary condition which is confirmed by the dictionary definition of "free" as being "*at liberty*." If freedom is essentially an absence of external restraint, liberty stands forth as a more positive condition, involving a measure of personal choice which is less inherent in freedom.

The more the evidence accumulates, the more a strongly individual flavor in liberty is indicated. It is a condition of the mind rather than the body, so that Byron could properly speak of the Prisoner of Chillon as having liberty while confined by chains in a dungeon. Alternatively, one may be largely free from any physical coercion—as Patrick Henry certainly was when he declaimed "give me liberty, or give me death!"—and still feel deeply that some quality essential to a desirable life is lacking. This higher quality, however, implies a form of restraint as clearly as the lower form of freedom implies its absence. When we say that "liberty is not license" we mean that it involves self-denial as well as self-assertion. Certainly in most American political thought it has been agreed that, as Daniel Webster put it, "Liberty exists in proportion to wholesome restraint." [2]

The most wholesome restraint, from any ethical viewpoint, is that which the individual applies to himself. And it is because of this necessary element of self-control that spiritual overtones, largely lacking in the case of freedom, creep in whenever we speak of liberty. In the words of St. Paul: "Where the Spirit of the Lord is, there is Liberty." [3] This means that liberty is something far more elevated than the mere condition of mundane freedom. And this is not disputed by the beautiful phrase in the Collect for Peace which defines the service of God as "perfect freedom." Liberty is depicted by these definitions as earthly freedom perfected by faith in values which are not of this earth.[4]

We are now in a position to examine more closely the opinion of the late Chief Justice Vinson: "Nothing is more certain in modern society than the principle that there are no absolutes. . . ." The assertion, in the first place, is logically fallacious. If there are no absolutes then there is no such thing as truth and consequently there are no principles, which do not exist without some truth to give them backing.

Therefore, it is a contradiction in terms to speak of "the principle that there are no absolutes." It is tantamount to proclaiming "the truth that there is no truth."

But disagreement with this observation by a former Chief Justice goes very much deeper than mere logic-chopping. Our whole system of government is based on the assumption that there *are* certain absolutes, referred to in the Declaration of Independence as "the Laws of Nature and of Nature's God." This maintains that there *is* a God, not less so because we may not fully appreciate His laws, nor fully understand His *logos*. If there are no absolutes, then the concept of God must be merely relative, which is precisely what the communists maintain. If there are no absolutes then Americans, identically with the communists, have no firm basis whatsoever for either their political or their religious faith.

Furthermore, to say that "there are no absolutes" and that "all concepts are relative" is to affirm, in so many words, the unlimited power of political government. It is to say that the definition of freedom is to be determined by the spokesman for the "general will." Therefore it is to deny any valid case for free enterprise as against governmental regimentation. And it is additionally to suggest that habeas corpus, trial by jury and even the right to counsel are mere political luxuries, to be eliminated if they become inconvenient to political authority.

Of course this doctrine was not original with Chief Justice Vinson. It stems back to Justice Oliver Wendell Holmes and before him to the "positivist" school of philosophy, chiefly promoted in this country by Professor John Dewey. That philosophy, like

Marxism, discards faith in favor of observable phenomena and mathematically demonstrable facts. It is probably helpful to scientific achievement, as the communist success in this field strongly suggests. But positivism is toxic to the traditional concept of freedom. And precisely because of the success of positivism it is essential to emphasize that there is a quality, distinct from freedom, which cannot possibly be packaged and dispensed by government bureaus. That is the quality which we are calling "liberty."

When Sir Isaac Newton first used a prism to break sunlight into its component colors, there was considerable overlap in the resulting spectrum. Yet only the color-blind can fail to observe the difference between the violet, at one end of the scale, and the red at the other. Similarly, there is overlap in that spectrum which shades from the mere absence of physical restraint up to the voluntary acceptance of moral prohibitions. But this does not mean that freedom, at the former end of the scale, and liberty, at the latter, are indistinguishable. Liberty has a religious association which freedom lacks. And because of this religious association individual liberty has long been a most deeply prized concept, a valuation that extends down to generalized freedom because it is difficult to locate the boundary between the two. Any damage done to the liberty of one may prove to be an infringement on freedom for all.

The Common Law, in English-speaking countries, has long recognized this close association between liberty and freedom. And by protecting liberty, in countless individual cases, the Common Law has operated, and continues to operate, in behalf of freedom. Judicial unwillingness to differentiate between the two is doubtless one reason why the distinction remains shadowy. But the tremendous growth of statutory and administrative law, progressively cutting into the discretion of Common-Law judges, has steadily tended to put first the protection and now the control of freedom back into the hands of the executive branch of government, which is precisely what Patrick Henry and his fellows rebelled against. It is this process of centralization which adds emphasis to the importance of our written Constitution, as a last bulwark for the liberty of the individual. In a number of recent cases the Supreme Court has strongly defended this redoubt, incurring sharp criticism for being tender to communists in so doing. But the defense has been weakened by the "no absolutes" conception, since without absolutes there is no substantial basis on which to defend liberty.

Nor can liberty be defended, no matter what the form of government, nor how independent and enlightened the courts, unless the citizen himself is willing to give it value. He may not know the truth in any particular issue, but he must be sure that absolute truth exists and that to it, and not to any mundane authority, his ultimate loyalty is due. Indeed the transition from generalized freedom to individual liberty may be said to come at that point on the moral scale or spectrum where a person decides that certain absolute values, which may run contrary to the laws of his land, mean more to him than life itself. He will have the Crucifixion to justify him. And long before that, witness the Hebrew prophets, men were seeking to make the formal laws conform to higher spiritual values which they, at least, considered absolutes. "Truths of the spirit are true always. The greatest teachers of the Old Testament understood them as no men have more, and in their pages we can find ourselves." [5]

As Dean Roscoe Pound so cogently reminds us, the English language slurs the clear distinction which is made in French between *droit* and *loi*, in German between *Recht* and *Gesetz*, and similarly in other tongues. We can only distinguish between law and a law, which fails to point the contrast between the ethical conception of what is right and the legal conception of a right established by statute or decree. Our need to differentiate between liberty and freedom is the greater because the former cannot possibly be promoted by a law and the condition of freedom can be so advanced. Law as such, on the other hand, is not merely "reason unaffected by desire." [6] It is further deeply concerned with the moral element which characterizes liberty.

The Romans, under the Republic, also made clear distinction between *ius* and *lex*, the Latin nouns from which we derive justice and law. And by far the greater part of their law, to which we owe so much, was magisterial rather than legislative. It is helpful to realize that until recent years no connection was drawn between the conception of justice and that of democratic action. Justice was a divine conception. It was the natural law, to which all man-made laws should conform. In Cicero's words: "Law is neither a thing contrived by the genius of man nor established by any decree of the people, but a certain eternal principle which governs the entire universe, wisely commanding what is right and prohibiting what is wrong." [7]

This means that if liberty is good, which we hold to be a self-evident truth—an absolute, in spite of Chief Justice Vinson—then it has nothing to do with any decree of, or in the name of, the people. *Vox populi* is not *vox dei*, and may indeed be its very opposite. Alexander Hamilton brought the point into the context of the American Constitution when, quoting Montesquieu, he said: "There is no liberty if the power of judging be not separated from the legislative and executive powers." [8]

But this separation of powers merely facilitates, and cannot create, the spirit of liberty, which comes to men from sources outside human control. The mechanical perfection of a political system cannot compensate for the loss of spiritual values among those whom it governs. Undue reliance on mechanism, however, is less likely with realization that law is something much more than the composite of all the laws currently in force. It is, rather, the body of at least relatively constant principles and permanent values that underlie the social contract and hold a society together by reason rather than by force. Law is even more basic than a written constitution, which after all can be no more than a heroic endeavor to set forth these underlying values and principles in an enduring codification. In the somewhat metaphysical language of Oswald Spengler: "In every healthy state the letter of the written constitution is of small importance compared with the practice of the living constitution, the 'form' (*Gestalt*) . . . which has developed of itself out of the experience of time, the situation, and, above all, the race-properties of the nation." [9]

"The beginnings of law," says Dean Pound, "are in

custom," whereas "the beginnings of legislation are in police regulation." [10] Here, from another angle, we see the separate forms of restraint that help to differentiate liberty from its lower form which we have called freedom. In primitive societies there is little of either. The restraint necessary for cooperative life is enforced by superstition, which is the prototype of both law and laws, of *ius* and *lex*, of *droit* and *loi*. The word itself tells the story, since *superstition* is simply that body of customary belief that "stands over" men and thereby commands submission.

In due course, though not contemporaneously in different places, superstition divides into two more highly developed branches of restraint. One of these continues to be spiritual, confronting the mysterious forces of nature with the import of which a priesthood is assumed to be most familiar. The other branch of restraint becomes temporal, dealing with social problems under a leadership which is called aristocratic because it has the "monopoly of legal knowledge." [11] In many places, and for a long time, there is no clear distinction between the prophetic and the political authority. After Rome loses the latter it continues to hold the former, among most Christianized peoples. The struggle between Empire and Papacy is bitter, in spite of Christ's explicit statement: "My kingdom is not of this world." The boundary between the restraints of spiritual and temporal authority are not defined until the rise of the modern nation-state, and the consequent breakdown of the universal church. Then, instead of balance between them, the temporal restraint comes to dominate the spiritual, which loses its once freely accepted influence.

Well before the establishment of the United States, however, the issue had been resolved, and nowhere more in the interest of stabilizing balance than in the American colonies. After the Revolution, spiritual authority was here accepted as the dominion of independent churches; temporal authority was a matter for civil government. Willing obedience to religious authority had been far too important in the American story to let it be jeopardized by political encroachment. And it was logically reasoned that politics should be equally immune from religious encroachment. The Declaration of Independence naturally cited every conceivable grievance, justified or not, against a king pilloried as "unfit to be the ruler of a free people." But it made no reference whatever to any objectionable action by the Anglican Church; nor to any interference with any American church on the part of the British government.

When they came to draft the Constitution the founding fathers therefore had a great advantage which they utilized to the full. They could rely on the self-restraint in which an independent and influential clergy had trained their parishoners. This in turn meant that the Constitution could dispense with those centralized governmental restraints which are necessarily an encroachment on the condition of freedom. Though often lawless in regard to man-made laws, Americans were for the most part loyal to law in its fundamental, moral, Ciceronian sense. Madison says as much in No. 39 of the *Federalist*, where he speaks of "that honorable determination which animates every votary of freedom, to rest all our political experiments on the capacity of mankind for self-government." And the evidence is confirmed by De Tocqueville, who as late as the Jacksonian era said: "The Americans combine the notions of Christianity and of liberty so intimately in their minds that it is impossible to make them conceive the one without the other." [12]

Indeed, the political import of religious faith was emphasized by nearly all of the founding fathers, and by none more earnestly than that stalwart old free-thinker, Ben Franklin. Asking that the sessions of the Constitutional Convention should be opened with prayer, and addressing George Washington as its president, Franklin said: "I have lived, Sir, a long time, and the longer I live the more convincing proofs I see of this truth: that *God* governs in the affairs of men. . . . without His concurring aid we shall succeed in this political building no better than the builders of Babel." [13] And the originally Christian character of the American government was more than perfunctorily embodied in the original Constitution by the statement, just above the signatures of the signers, that this was: "Done in convention . . . in the year of our Lord one thousand seven hundred and eighty-seven. . . ."

Religious conviction, however much it may have waned in recent years, was certainly at the beginning a part of the "living constitution" of the United States. And since religious conviction demands the element of faith, it is clear that faith is inextricably associated with those "blessings of liberty" which our federal form of government originally set itself to secure. Faith brings to the condition of freedom that spiritual quality which gives life and animation, and which alone justifies us in using the words freedom and liberty interchangeably.

Conversely, when the element of faith is withdrawn the condition of freedom is devitalized, being cut from its stimulative connection with the Kingdom of God. And with this debasement comes an almost chemical change in the character of freedom. In place of a moral idea comes identification with material condition. A man is not free unless his circumstances are prosperous. And he feebly believes that even though that prosperity stems from deficit government spending, he still is free! Thus the unity of a quality is denatured into a divisible quantity— four or some other number of "freedoms"—to be extended or withheld as the political leadership may deem expedient. Separation of church and state becomes subordination of church to state. With us, too, the concept of a balance of power is lost. And so freedom, divorced from faith, ceases altogether to be the absolute value as which it was once regarded, and with the change loses both constant meaning and intrinsic permanence.

This decay of a concept means that freedom can no longer be regarded as the clear-cut opposite of slavery. Indeed, the two ideas are perceptibly beginning to merge, as anticipated in George Orwell's horribly prescient *Nineteen Eighty-Four*. There (or then) the Party Slogan inscribed "in elegant lettering" on the huge building of the Ministry of Truth was: FREEDOM IS SLAVERY. Orwell explains the purpose behind this prostitution in his appendix on

Newspeak, "the official language . . . devised to meet the ideological needs of Ingsoc, or English Socialism."

> Its vocabulary was so constructed as to give exact and often very subtle expression to every meaning that a Party member could properly wish to express, while excluding all other meanings and also the possibility of arriving at them by indirect methods. . . . The word *free* still existed in Newspeak, but it could only be used in such statements as "This dog is free from lice" or "This field is free from weeds." It could not be used in its old sense of "politically free" or "intellectually free," since political and intellectual freedom no longer existed even as concepts, and were therefore of necessity nameless.

A comparable, if less deliberate, procedure is being followed in the United States as we move towards 1984 and the presumable triumph of Amlib, or American liberalism. It was a long step backwards so to degrade freedom as to equate it with security. This degradation permits the nationalization of freedom, so that official pronouncements now no longer refer to the United States as "a free people" but almost invariably as "a free nation." Yet there is still a difference between the Oceania and the Eurasia of Orwell's biting satire. The Western socialist believes that security, miscalled freedom, can be obtained from the state without the surrender of individual liberty. This the communist categorically denies. To him dependence on the state is really and wholly that. When the state supplies freedom it necessarily denies liberty. The latter is indeed only a captious claim to the non-existent right of opposing the general will. To the communist, in short, individual liberty is treason.

Thus we see that to distinguish between freedom and liberty is no mere semantic exercise. The differentiation is forced upon us by the claim of centralized government that it can provide freedom, and the all too reasonable expectation that what officials provide they will soon begin to define selectively. Indeed President Franklin D. Roosevelt said as much in his "Four Freedoms" message, when he denounced "trouble makers" and asserted that "a free nation has the right to expect full cooperation from all groups." That is exactly what Rousseau meant in stating that "whosoever refuses to obey the general will . . . is forced to be free."

But if the meaning of freedom has been debased into a commodity now dispensable by a bureaucracy, in return for good behavior, the same cannot be said of individualized liberty. That quality cannot be allocated by any Ministry of Truth or by any Department of Health, Education and Welfare. On the contrary it is an elusive flame, continuously rekindling, in unexpected places and among all sorts of "trouble makers," regardless of the will and generally contrary to the wishes of Big Government. And to seek the source of this flame is to find it, with Saint Paul, "where the spirit of the Lord is."

Far from being an intellectual tour de force, the distinction between freedom and liberty accurately locates the highwater mark of totalitarian democracy. That murky tide may rise to submerge the rock of freedom. But it can never overwhelm the wingèd spirit of liberty.

A truth now disagreeably self-evident is that the authoritarian state can, and is prone to, extend its physical control over every aspect of a free society, of course including free enterprise. Slowly but surely, in less than a century, Americans have witnessed first the nationalization of rights, then the nationalization of power, now the nationalization of the concept of freedom itself. With such a well-established trend it is futile to expect that a mere mechanism like the free market will remain immune. For all the volumes that have been written about free enterprise it is, after all, only one of many emanations from the basic concept of freedom. Therefore it will disappear if its source is eliminated. Once freedom itself has been nationalized, it is only mopping up to nationalize a particular industry.

In this context, the value of federalism, in preventing the prostitution of freedom, becomes more clear. It has, first, the negative advantage of blocking the thoughtless extension of national power. The word "no," used as a direct restraint on government, occurs twenty-six times in the original seven Articles of the Constitution, five times more in the Bill of Rights. Had President Truman been living in 1787 he could quite reasonably have called it a "Do-Nothing" Constitution. But to do so would be to forget that the founding fathers put restraints on government so that the governed might be free.

In addition to limiting governmental power, the Constitution most delicately balances its exercise. And the balance of power, like the limitation of power, has worked admirably. In the course of this survey we have seen the Congress dominant under

Thaddeus Stevens; the Executive dictating under F.D.R.; the Judiciary in the saddle under Chief Justice Marshall and, very briefly, under Chief Justice Warren. Yet always, so far, balance has been restored; fortunately so, since without balance there are only the alternatives of anarchy on the one hand or autocracy on the other.

That is why it is plain absurdity to talk of democracy as though unhampered majority rule could ever be itself an objective of good government. The aim must be balance, which is achieved when local affairs are handled locally, and lost when government becomes so omnipotent as to turn the citizen into a mere ward of a unitary state. Democracy, in the social sense of the brotherhood of man, can only be maintained, as Aristotle said, in local groupings. Interpreted in national terms, as the triumph of Rousseau's *volonté générale*, democracy becomes perverted and as such perverts freedom.

And finally, the Constitution, while "the supreme law of the land," was in its original form and still essentially remains a valiant attempt to reflect the even more fundamental Natural Law which men will endeavor to observe as long as they believe in those enduring moral values without which civilization would be impossible. Our organic law seeks to harmonize all governmental action with the talent of a truly free people from self-government. They remain free only as long as they maintain this spiritual aspiration. Without faith, the Constitution falls.

When or not our Federal Republic will be maintained is therefore at bottom a moral issue. It depends as much on the churches and the synagogues as on the legislatures and the law courts. The growth of Big Government goes hand in hand with the loss of Big Conviction.

When Caesar stood on the banks of the Rubicon, deciding whether or not to strike down the sadly corrupted Roman Republic, he argued to himself that the issue was really already settled. "It is nothing," he said, "to be a republic, now a mere name without substance or character." [14]

If that is the way we have come to feel about federalism, then is our Republic also, in less than two centuries of history, on the way out.

Notes

CHAPTER 1

1. The Constitution of the Union of Soviet Socialist Republics (1958 edition) lists 24 separate "spheres" (Article 14, paragraphs a to x inclusive) in which the central government is all-powerful. These cover almost ever conceivable governmental activity, including (i) "Safeguarding the security of the state"; (p) "Contracting and granting of loans"; (r) "Determination of the basic principles in the spheres of education and public health"; (t) "Determination of the principles of labor legislation"; (w) "Determination of the principles of legislation concerning marriage and the family." Article 20 further stipulates that "In the event of divergence between a law of a Union Republic and a law of the Union, the Union law prevails." Nevertheless Article 15 maintains that "Outside of these spheres [as listed in Article 14] each Union Republic exercises state authority independently." See also, John N. Hazard, *The Soviet System of Government*. Univ. of Chicago Press (Chicago 1957) esp. Ch. 6.

2. Alexis de Tocqueville, *Democracy in America*, Alfred A. Knopf edn. (New York 1945) Vol. 1, pp. 166 and 95.

3. Madison, in the *Federalist*, No. 39, argues that no government where power is concentrated and absolute should be called a Republic. "We may . . . bestow that name," he says, "on a government which derives all its powers directly or indirectly from the great body of the people, and is administered by persons holding their offices during pleasure, for a limited period, or during good behavior."

4. *Const.*, Art. II, Sect. 2, Par. 2. The Senate's power to reject Presidential appointments is a sharp check on the authority of the Executive.

5. In two ponderous volumes on *Politics and the Constitution*, Professor William W. Crosskey, propounds "a unitary theory of the Constitution" maintaining, *inter alia*, that the intent of the commerce clause was to give Congress the power to regulate "all gainful activity" throughout the country. Professor Crosskey is highly intolerant of the States' Rights viewpoint. The value of his research is lessened by a vehemence of unsupported asseveration, as when he says "it is virtually certain that much of the *Federalist* was written only to fill up space in the New York 'federal' newspapers and thereby to make less obvious the exclusion therefrom of opposing views." *Op. cit.*, Univ. of Chicago Press (Chicago 1953) Vol. I, p. 9.

6. Quoted, David Shub, *Lenin*, Doubleday & Co. (New York 1948) p. 369.

7. The Farewell Address.

CHAPTER 2

1. The *Federalist*, No. 10.

2. Quoted, Claude G. Bowers, *Jefferson and Hamilton*, Houghton Mifflin Co. (Boston and New York 1953) p. 322.

3. *America in Midpassage*, The Macmillan Co. (New York 1939) p. 922.

4. The Common Law, most ably sustained and developed, is of course a safeguard against legislative dictation in Great Britain.

5. *Records of the Federal Convention of 1787*, Max Farrand, editor, Yale University Press (New Haven 1937) Vol. I, p. 57 and pp. 134-5.

6. *Democracy in America*, Vol. I, pp. 289-90.

CHAPTER 3

1. By "departments" Madison here means the division into executive, judicial and legislative branches, not departments of the executive branch in the sense of Department of State, etc.

2. *Politics*, Bk. I, Ch. 2 (Jowett translation).

3. Sir Frederick Pollock, *Introduction to the History of the Science of Politics*, Macmillan & Co. (London 1919) p. 79.

4. *Du Contrat Social*, Livre Premier, Ch. 6me.

5. *Ibid.*, Ch. 7me. Voltaire's comment on this passage: "Tout cela n'est pas exposé assez nettement."

6. Quoted, Pollock, *op. cit.*, p. 94.

7. First Letter "On a Regicide Peace," *Works* of Edmund Burke, Little, Brown & Co. (Boston 1869) Vol. V., p. 285.

8. *Op. cit.*, Livre Deuxième, Ch. 3me. Bertrand de Jouvenel, in his comprehensive *Essai sur la Politique de Rousseau*, argues that to Rousseau himself the general will meant no more than a general conception of the moral law. But that generous judgment only intensifies the danger of tyranny when the concept is made applicable to political life, as it was almost immediately.

9. To understand the almost psychopathic character of Rousseau one should read his own *Confessions*, since 1953 available in English in a well-translated *Penguin* edition. Rousseau begins this uninhibited autobiography with the statement: "I am like no one in the whole world." Nature, he says, broke "the mold in which she formed me." It is of the irony of history that Rousseau himself then proceeded to design a political mold into which men everywhere are now being involuntarily compressed.

10. *Du Contrat Social*, Livre Premier, Ch. 1er.

CHAPTER 4

1. In his *Jefferson and Hamilton*, Claude G. Bowers finds "the shrieks of protest from the Federalists" against the Jacobin Clubs" "inexplicable to the twentieth century." (p. 223.) But that was written in 1925, before the communists had shown the power of cellular organization in its modern form. Mr. Bowers agrees that the principles of the French Revolution have had far more lasting political significance for the United States than is generally realized. *Op. cit.*, pp. 208-9.

2. From the *Theses on Feuerbach* (1845). Ludwig

Feuerbach, today remembered largely for his apothegm: "Mann ist was er isst"—"Man is what he eats"—had stimulated Marx by his *Essence of Christianity* published the same year (1841) that Marx wrote his doctoral thesis at Jena.

3. Quoted by George Catlin in his *Story of the Political Philosophers*, Whittlesey House (New York 1939) p. 589. Professor Catlin comments: "The thesis, then, of Marx is precisely the old one of the revolutionary French Jacobins."

4. This sequence is carefully traced by J. L. Talmon in *The Rise of Totalitarian Democracy*, The Beacon Press (Boston 1952). Professor Talmon concludes: "Nothing would be easier than to translate the original Jacobin conception of a conflict endemic in society, between those of virtue and those of selfishness, into the Marxist idea of class warfare." (p. 252).

5. British disillusionment, resulting from hodgepodge nationalization of industry, hurried into effect by democratic procedures, is minutely and objectively described by R. Kelf-Cohen in his *Nationalisation in Britain: The End of a Dogma*, Macmillan & Co. (London 1958).

6. *Politics*, Bk. I, Ch. 5.

CHAPTER 5

1. For Hamilton's draft constitution see Farrand, *Records of the Federal Convention*, Vol. III, pp. 617-30 (Appendix F).

2. Farrand, *op. cit.*, Vol. I, p. 299. The quotation is from the notes of Judge Yates, less condensed in this particular passage than those of Madison, *ibid.*, p. 288.

3. Letter to Dr. James Brown, Oct. 27, 1808. Commenting on this, Professor Gilbert Chinard says: "if this episode can serve to illustrate the inconsistency of the philosopher, it constitutes also a most striking refutation of the accusations of Jacobinism so often launched against Jefferson, for only the Jacobin is perfectly consistent in all circumstances." *Thomas Jefferson, Apostle of Americanism*, Little, Brown & Co. (Boston 1929) p. 438.

4. James Bryce, *The American Commonwealth,* 3rd edn., The Macmillan Co. (New York 1897) Vol. II, p. 177.

5. The biographies of the two most utilized are Charles M. Wiltse, *John C. Calhoun—Nationalist, Nullifier, Sectionalist* (3 vols.) Bobbs-Merrill Co. (Indianapolis 1944, '49, '51), and Marquis James, *The Life of Andrew Jackson,* Bobbs-Merrill Co. (Indianapolis 1938).

6. This point is comprehensively sustained, *inter alia,* by Avery Craven, *The Coming of the Civil War,* 2nd edn., Univ. of Chicago Press (Chicago 1957).

7. James defines the proclamation as "one of the greatest [state papers] to bear the name of an American President." *Op. cit.,* pp. 611-2.

8. This speech (of Feb. 15-16, 1833) is printed in full in *Calhoun, Basic Documents,* John M. Anderson, editor, Bald Eagle Press (State College, Pa. 1952); see esp. pp. 181, 183-5. This collection also contains Calhoun's brilliant *Disquisition on Government,* which gives his conception of federalism in detail.

CHAPTER 6

1. Claude G. Bowers, *The Tragic Era,* Blue Ribbon Books (New York 1929) p. 67. This is easily the most readable, and probably the most useful, general survey of what, in his sub-title, Mr. Bowers calls *"The Revolution After Lincoln.* It covers the period from Lincoln's assassination to the end of military government in the Southern States (1865-77).

2. Quoted, Samuel Eliot Morison and Henry Steele Commager, *The Growth of the American Republic* 4th edn., Oxford Univ. Press (New York 1956) Vol. II, p. 33.

3. The classic, blow-by-blow, account is Horace Edgar Flack's *The Adoption of the Fourteenth Amendment,* The Johns Hopkins Press (Baltimore 1908). Dr. Flack's meticulously careful and comprehensive study is the more valuable because it long antedates present-day controversy over this Amendment. It has been heavily utilized in writing this chapter. Also useful is *The Fram-*

ing of the Fourteenth Amendment, Joseph B. James, Univ. of Illinois Press (Urbana, Ill. 1956).

4. Morison and Commager, *op. cit.*, Vol. II, p. 39.

5. Flack, *op. cit.*, pp. 98-9, 126 and *passim*.

6. *Congressional Globe*, 39th Cong., 1st Sess. pp. 2542-3.

7. The point is made by Dr. Flack, *op. cit.*, p. 80.

8. Cf. Charles A. Beard, *The Rise of American Civilization*, The Macmillan Co. (New York 1927) Vol. II, pp. 112-4.

9. "The Fourteenth Amendment Reconsidered," *Michigan Law Review*, Vol. 54, No. 8, June 1956, p. 1084.

10. "The Dubious Origin of the Fourteenth Amendment," *Tulane Law Review*, Vol. XXVIII, 22-44, December 1953, pp. 24-26. The entire article deserves the most careful study.

11. In his *Personal Memoirs* (Vol. II, p. 523) General Ulysses S. Grant admits that "much of" the Reconstruction legislation to which he gave military administration "no doubt was unconstitutional; but it was hoped that the laws enacted would serve their purpose before the question of constitutionality could be submitted to the judiciary and a decision obtained." As noted in this chapter, the Supreme Court ducked that responsibility.

CHAPTER 7

1. Charles E. Hughes, *The Supreme Court of the United States*, Columbia Univ. Press (New York 1928) p. 180.

2. Carl B. Swisher, *Stephen J. Field, Craftsman of the Law*, Brookings Institution (Washington 1930) p. 424.

3. Edward S. Corwin, *The Twilight of the Supreme Court*, 4th prtg., Yale Univ. Press (New Haven 1937) pp. 77-8.

4. Charles A. Beard, *Basic History of the United States*, New Home Library (New York 1944) p. 318.

5. Professor Gottfried Dietze is outspoken on this point: "The Supreme Court seems to have abdicated its former position as the guardian of the Constitution and free government with its capitulation before the American *volanté générale* in 1937 and through its reluctance

to exercise judicial review in the following decades." *Virginia Laws Review,* Vol. 44, No. 8, December 1958, p. 1260.

6. The compromise reached, preserving the theory of dual sovereignty, was well defined by Justice Cardozo, in *Palko v. Connecticut* "immunities that are valid as against the federal government by force of the specific pledges of particular amendments have been found to be implicit in the concept of ordered liberty and thus, through the Fourteenth Amendment, become valid as against the States."

7. John W. Burgess, *Recent Changes in American Constitutional Theory,* Columbia Univ. Press (New York 1923) p. 54.

8. Opinions on what has been called "plutocracy" in this period differ greatly. That of James Bryce was not merely contemporaneous, but certainly as well-informed and objective as any. In 1888 (*The American Commonwealth,* Vol. 11, p. 591) he wrote: "It is not, however, only in the way of bribery at popular elections that the influence of wealth is felt. It taints the election of Federal senators by State legislatures. It induces officials who ought to guard the purity of the ballot box to tamper with returns. It procures legislation in the interests of commercial undertakings. It supplies the funds for maintaining party organizations and defraying the enormous costs of electoral campaigns, and demands in return sometimes a high administrative post, sometimes a foreign mission, sometimes favours for a railroad, sometimes a clause in a tariff bill, sometimes a lucrative contract. . . . One thing alone it can scarcely ever buy, —impunity for detected guilt."

9. The definitive biography of Bryan is not yet written. Helpful in regard to him, aside from personal acquaintance and periodical literature, have been Paxton Hibben's *The Peerless Leader* and M. R. Werner's *Bryan,* Harcourt, Brace (New York 1929). Mark Sullivan's *Our Times: The Turn of the Century* has also been utilized.

10. I follow the lead of Dean Roscoe Pound in preferring "Service State" to the more familiar term "Wel-

fare State" because, as he says, governments of every description "have always held that they were set up to promote and conserve public welfare.

CHAPTER 8

1. V. I. Lenin, *State and Revolution*, 3rd prtg., International Publishers (New York 1935) p. 83.

2. *Ibid.*, p. 74.

3. Beard, *Basic History*, p. 340.

4. *Ibid.*, p. 342.

5. This triumph of Senate over Administration is well told by Allan Nevins in his biography of *Hamilton Fish*, Dodd, Mead & Co. (New York 1936) Ch. XIV.

6. Professor Burgess calls the enforced separation of Panama from Colombia "one of the most unqualified and arrogant violations of international law known to the modern history of man." *Recent Changes in American Constitutional Theory*, p. 39.

7. The outstanding account of President Wilson's effort for the League is found in Herbert Hoover's *The Ordeal of Woodrow Wilson*, McGraw-Hill Book Co. (New York 1958).

8. *The Peloponnesian War* (Crowley translation) Book V, Ch. 17, The Modern Library (New York 1934) pp. 330 ff.

9. In Miami, Fla., Dept. of State *Press Release*, Oct. 10, 1955, No. 597.

10. Arnold J. Toynbee, *A Study of History*, Oxford Univ. Press (London 1939) Vol. IV, p. 504.

CHAPTER 9

1. A condensed but comprehensive survey is found in my *Foreign Policy of the United States*, Alfred A. Knopf (New York 1951).

2. Farrand, *Records of the Federal Convention*, Vol. I, p. 402. The ms., in Pinckney's handwriting, is in the Library of Congress.

3. Incomparably the best documented and most objective study of the Doctrine is the Department of State's

own *Memorandum on the Monroe Doctrine,* prepared by J. Reuben Clark, Undersecretary of State, dated Dec. 17, 1928, Govt. Printing Office (Washington, 1930).

4. Letter to Governeur Morris, March 12, 1793.

5. *Democracy in America,* Vol. I, pp. 166 and 168-9.

6. The Farewell Address.

7. Reasons for the amorality of the state are examined in my *Power in the People,* Van Nostrand (New York 1949) Ch. V.

8. This was argued by Theodore Roosevelt, then Governor of New York and Republican candidate for the Vice-Presidency, as far back as 1900: "It may be the highest duty to oppose a war before it is brought on, but once the country is at war the man who fails to support it with all possible heartiness comes perilously near being a traitor. . . ." *The Works of Theodore Roosevelt,* Memorial Edition, Charles Scribner's Sons (New York 1923) Vol. XIII, p. 406. This is a considerable expansion of the Constitutional definition: "Treason against the United States shall consist only in levying war against them, or in adhering to their enemies, giving them aid and comfort." (Art. III, Sect. 3, Par. 1)

CHAPTER 10

1. Lord Charnwood, whose biography of Lincoln is the more interesting because written from the viewpoint of an English nobleman, says of the martyred President: "He was a citizen of that far country where there is neither aristocrat nor democrat." *Abraham Lincoln,* Henry Holt & Co. (New York 1917) see esp. pp. 455-6.

2. There is as yet no fully adequate study of the inception, purpose, implementation and collapse of the National Industrial Recovery Act and Administration. A good summary is found in: Leverett S. Lyon and Victor Abramson, *Government and Economic Life,* Brookings Institution (Washington 1940) Vol. II, Ch. 27. As here observed: "The legislative process of code making in the NRA . . . was in large degree entrusted to representatives of special interest groups, chosen by these groups and charged with preserving and improving the

competitive advantages of those groups." (p. 1041.)
This well describes the way that many developments
described as "democratic" work out in actual practice.

3. An excellent summary account, written contemporaneously, is by Merlo J. Pusey, *The Supreme Court
Crisis*, The Macmillan Co. (New York 1937).

4. James A. Farley, *Jim Farley's Story—The Roosevelt Years*, McGraw-Hill Book Co. (New York 1948)
pp. 186 ff., esp. p. 190.

5. A clear summary of techniques used by the New
Deal to solve nine "problems" of centralization, in a
federal republic, is given by Garet Garrett, *The Revolution Was*, The Caxton Printers, Ltd. (Caldwell, Idaho
1944).

CHAPTER 11

1. In his *Collected Works* (123 edn.) Vol. XVII, pp.
321-2, used as a text by all communist theoreticians,
Lenin asks: "Is there such a thing as Communist morality?" Replying in the affirmative he inquires: "In what
sense do we [communists] repudiate ethics and morality?" His answer: "In the sense that they were preached
by the bourgeoisie who declared that ethics were God's
commandments. We, of course, say that we do not
believe in God, and that we know perfectly well that
the clergy . . . spoke in the name of God in order to
pursue their own exploiters' interests. . . . We say:
Morality is that which serves to destroy the old exploiting society and to unite all the toilers around the proletariat, which is creating a new Communist society."

2. For antecedents of the Employment Act of 1946,
see Edwin G. Nourse, *Economics in the Public Service*,
Harcourt, Brace & Co. (New York 1953) Chs. 4-6. Dr.
Nourse was the first chairman of the Council of Economic Advisers. This Act of 1946 is also well summarized by Lewis A. Kimmel, *Federal Budget and Fiscal
Policy, 1789-1958*, The Brookings Institution (Washington 1959) pp. 237-40.

3. *The Growth of the American Republic*, Vol. I,
p. 641. Professor Commager in particular has shown him-

self a strong advocate of highly centralized government. Yet, in February, 1959, he was sent by the Department of State to participate in a lecture series on "Federal Principles" in the newly established Federation of the West Indies (Dept. of State *Press Release*, Feb. 20, 1959, No. 132).

4. The Roosevelt Administration was strongly influential in the drafting of these provisions. Cf. the Dept. of State's Publication 3580, *Post-War Foreign Policy Preparation, 1939-45*, U.S. Government Printing Office (Washington 1950) esp. Appendices 12-14, pp. 470-85.

5. All these "rights" and "freedoms," described in more detail, are "assured" by Articles 119-125 of the present Russian Constitution.

6. The Bricker Amendment is analyzed in my pamphlet *Treaty Law and the Constitution*, American Enterprise Ass'n (Washington 1953).

7. The basis of this Report was "an expert survey of recent Supreme Court decisions" in the field of federal relationships. This survey is available in a *Special Supplement* to the *Law School Record* of the Univ. of Chicago, Vol. 8, No. 1, Autumn 1958.

CHAPTER 12

1. Eph. 6:12 (King James Version).

2. Niccolo Machiavelli, *Discourses*, Ch. XLI, The Modern Library (New York 1940) p. 528.

3. *Congressional Record*, of Sept. 12, 1958, pp. A 8347 ff., lists 2422 names of those who in the preceding fiscal year received more than $10,000 each for *not* producing on "soil bank" acreage. On March 2, 1959, Senator John Williams of Delaware told the Senate that during the same period three agricultural corporations had received almost $3,500,000, and 51 other "farmers" in excess of $100,000 apiece, in price-support payments.

4. 84th Cong., 2nd Sess., *House Report* No. 2947, p. 5.

5. It was also Mr. Moss who, on Feb. 12, 1958, drew from the Department of the Army a reluctant admission that some experimentation with bows and arrows had

been labeled "silent flashless weapons"; was regarded as
involving a "security factor"; was classified first "Confidential," then "Restricted," then "Confidential" again;
until finally "reviewed and declassified" on Jan. 31, 1958
—three days after the inquiry from Congressman Moss.
(85th Cong., 2nd. Sess., *House Report* No. 1884, pp.
174-5.)

6. Senator Thomas C. Hennings, Jr., of Missouri,
Chairman of the Senate Constitutional Rights Subcommittee, said in a statement released Jan. 28, 1959, that
this committee also "has come across many instances of
what have appeared to be completely unwarranted withholdings of information from both the public and the
Congress."

CHAPTER 13

1. This is well brought out by Frank R. Kent in *The
Great Game of Politics*, William Morrow & Co. (New
York 1923). See also his *Political Behavior* (New York,
1928).

2. Hawaii, with only one Representative to start, will
obtain another by the 1960 reappointment.

3. A tie vote between two candidates is barely possible
in the case of an even number of total electoral votes.

4. The *Federalist*, No. 68.

5. James, *Andrew Jackson*, p. 390. See also Wiltse,
Calhoun, Vol. I, pp. 282-4.

6. The nomination was not unanimous, though Crawford, counting the two proxies, received 64 of the 68
votes cast. Albert Gallatin received 57 votes for the Vice-Presidential nomination. The desperation of those backing the stricken Crawford was evidenced by selection of
the foreign-born Gallatin as his running mate and presumable successor, Gallatin, one of the lesser known
but most able of American statesmen, was born in
Geneva in 1761, almost half a century after Rousseau,
who unquestionably influenced the younger man's thinking. (See Raymond Walters, Jr., *Albert Gallatin*, The
Macmillan Co. (New York 1957) p. 8 and p. 318. Gallatin was nineteen when he emigrated to America,

towards the close of the Revolutionary War. His "foreignness" was the more of a political handicap in 1824 because he had then only recently returned from ten years of almost uninterrupted diplomatic service in Europe. Gallatin did not die until 1849, when he was 88.

7. Quoted by James, *op. cit.*, p. 389.

8. *Ibid.*, pp. 427 ff. See also p. 852.

CHAPTER 14

1. On February 11, 1959, the Department of Justice released the text of a telegram sent to President Eisenhower by Mayor W. W. Mann, of Little Rock, on September 24, 1957. This telegram urged the immediate dispatch of national troops to Arkansas "in the interest of humanity, law and order *and the cause of democracy world-wide . . .* " A.P. *Report* of Feb. 11, 1959 (emphasis supplied). Mayor Mann was later quoted as saying: "Even in the United States, force cannot and will not make people submit to a way of life that they are not willing to accept." (*U.S. News and World Report,* Feb. 27, 1959, p. 103.) Why "even"?

2. The hectic political maneuvering at that time is vividly described in James, *Andrew Jackson*, pp. 428-40. For strategems in one newly admitted State (Missouri) see William Nisbet Chambers, *Old Bullion Benton, Senator from the West*, Little, Brown & Co. (Boston 1956) pp. 129-30.

3. 3 USC 7; 62 Stat. 672.

4. No subject before the Constitutional Convention aroused more protracted debate than the procedure for election of the President. The entire discussion is of course summarized in Farrand, *Records of the Federal Convention, seriatim*. It may more conveniently be examined in the one-volume *Documents illustrative of the Formation of the Union of the American States*, selected, arranged and indexed by Dr. Charles C. Tansill, 69 Cong. 1st Sess., House Document No. 398, Govt. Printing Office (Washington 1927), Index, p. 1080.

5. Morison and Commager see "little reason to doubt" that "the will of the people" was overborne by the out-

come of the Hayes-Tilden election (*The Growth of the American Republic*, Vol. II, p. 78). Full contemporary accounts, by men deeply concerned in the contest, are found in James G. Blaine, *Twenty Years of Congress*, The Henry Hill Publishing Co. (Norwich, Conn. 1886) Vol. II, Ch. 25, and in John Sherman's *Recollections of Forty Years in The House, Senate and Cabinet*, The Werner Co. (Chicago 1895) Vol. I, Ch. 28.

6. Some of the older States retain equally undemocratic arrangements for State elections. In Maryland, for instance, primary contests for State-wide office are not decided by popular vote, but by a "unit system" comparable with that of the Electoral College. The 23 counties of Maryland divide 110 electoral votes in the State convention in set proportions, while Baltimore City is allotted 42 electoral votes to make the total of 152. The city, which is approximately one-half the population of the State, controls less than one-third of the electoral votes. Consequently a candidate for Governor or Senator not infrequently gets a majority of his party's popular vote but fails to obtain the party nomination.

CHAPTER 15

1. Constitutional lawyers are almost unanimous on this point. The following comments are taken from the Autumn 1958, *Special Supplement* of the Univ. of Chicago *Law School Record*: Professor Allison Dunham: "since 1940 the Supreme Court and the Congress between them have drastically reduced a State's ability to deal with its own social order and economic enterprise as it wishes." (p. 55.) Asst. Prof. Roger C. Cramton: "the Court's frequent use in recent years of preemption doctrine to effect broad displacements of State authority reopens the important question of the soundness of preemption doctrine as it has been developed by the Court." (p. 25).

2. Quoted by Beveridge, *John Marshall*, Vol. IV, p. 551.

3. Bryce, *The American Commonwealth*, Vol. I, p. 385.

4. *Ibid.*, p. 253.

5. Cf. James J. Kilpatrick, *The Sovereign States*, Henry Regnery Co. (Chicago 1957) pp. 269-70.

6. Professor Edward S. Corwin comments: "Justice Holmes became the mouthpiece of a new gospel of *laissez-faire*, namely of *laissez-faire* for legislative power, because legislative power represents, or under a democratic dispensation ought to represent, what he termed 'the dominant power of society.'" *Court Over Constitution*, Princeton Univ. Press (Princeton, N.J., 1938) p. 119.

7. *Bartkus v. Illinois*, March 30, 1959.

8. The rule of *stare decisis*—"to stand by decisions" already handed down—is of course not immutable. But reasonably flexibility is very different from complete reversibility, which can easily produce a legal chaos.

9. On June 2, 1959, the Board of Supervisors of Prince Edward County, Virginia, "with profound regret" eliminated all appropriations for the operation of public schools from its 1959-60 budget. The county had previously maintained 3 public high schools and 18 elementary schools. It was one of the five localities directly involved in the Supreme Court decision of May 17, 1954.

10. The *Federalist*, No. 81. In the same essay Hamilton argues that the legislative authority will not be endangered by encroachment from the judiciary because, *inter alia*, of the latter's "total incapacity to support its usurpations by force." This ignores the support that the executive may be expected to give to judicial decisions.

11. Quoted, Kilpatrick, *op. cit.*, p. 57.

12. Cf. Beveridge, *op. cit.*, Vol. II, p. 84n.

13. It has been maintained (cf. Claude G. Bowers, *Jefferson and Hamilton*, pp. 409-11) that the Kentucky and Virginia Resolutions were primarily protests against governmental interference with freedom of speech and press; were only incidentally concerned with federal theory. This argument draws a distinction without a difference.

14. Quoted, Kilpatrick, *op. cit.*, p. 215.

15. *17 Car. I, cap. 10*. The full text is given by Samuel Rawson Gardiner, editor, *Constitutional Documents of the Puritan Revolution 1625-1660*, Clarendon Press (Oxford 1906) pp. 179-86.

CHAPTER 16

1. *Report* to the Trustees, Jan. 1, 1959, U.S. Govt. Printing Office (Washington 1959) p. 2.

2. The "full employment" of which the communists boast is only achieved (a) by actual forced labor in prison camps or (b) by maintaining at public expense individual plants, or if need be whole industries, which operate continuously at a deficit. This aspect of Marxism is emphasized by Milovan Djilas, the former Vice-President of Yugoslavia who was expelled from the Party in 1954 for heresy, in his study of *The New Class*. Uneconomic military production of course helps communist governments to maintain the fiction of full employment, as also to some extent (see Ch. 12) in the United States. But here the inflationary effects of deficit financing cannot, as yet, be concealed by outright expropriation, as in Russia.

3. *Economic Report of the President*, January, 1959, U.S. Govt. Printing Office (Washington 1959) p. vi and *passim*.

4. In his Farewell Address Washington said: "Of all the dispositions and habits which lead to political prosperity, Religion and morality are indispenable supports. . . . And let us with caution indulge the supposition that morality can be maintained without religion."

5. "The essence of education," in the opinion of Alfred North Whitehead, "is that it be religious." A religious education he defines as "an education which inculcates duty and reverence." But Professor Whitehead also warns against "the inculcation of morals as a set of isolated prohibitions" saying, in this connection: "The vitality of religion is shown by the way in which the religious spirit has survived the ordeal of religious education." *The Aims of Education* (7th prtg.), Williams & Norgate (London 1951) p. 23 and p. 62.

6. Under the title *Grass Roots Private Welfare* the Foundation for Voluntary Welfare has published an interesting collection of 50 factual reports on as many private welfare undertakings currently operating through-

out the United States. Alfred de Grazia, editor, New York Univ. Press. (New York 1957).

7. 85th Cong., 2nd Sess., *Senate Report* No. 1417, Govt. Printing Office (Washington 1958) p. 4 and *passim*.

8. "Historical conditions being equal, a major natural difference [is] the possible cause of decisive institutional differences." Karl A. Wittfogel, *Oriental Despotism*, Yale Univ. Press (New Haven 1957) p. 13.

9. *Address on Government and Citizenship* (collected and edited by Robert Bacon and James Brown Scott) Harvard Univ. Press (Cambridge, Mass. 1916) pp. 369-70.

10. Commission on Intergovernmental Relations, *Report to the President*, U.S. Govt. Printing Office (Washington 1955) p. 47. The whole report is worthy of careful study by those interested in the preservation of federalism in the United States.

11. Founded in 1925 as the American Legislators' Association. It assumed its present name, with expanded functions, in 1935.

12. Interview in *Nation's Business*, March 1958, p. 85.

CHAPTER 17

1. Dr. Erhard himself makes the important point that the German genius can be great either for destruction or construction. It was the former when harnessed to monopolistic power. It has been the latter since, in Western Germany, it was wedded to the system of free, competitive enterprise, with the objective of market rather than military victories. As Nazi Germany strengthened Autarky everywhere, so the Federal Republic can strengthen free trade everywhere. Classical economics are important because they reflect the classical concept of liberalism, and therefore of liberty itself. See his Foreword, on "The Spiritual Fundamentals of Healthy Foreign Trade," to *Deutschlands Rueckkehr zum Weltmarkt*, Econ-Verlag GMBH (Duesseldorf 1953). The reasoning is equally applicable to the U.S.A.

2. For a compact summary of these, and subordinate, moves towards European federalism see *Dix ans d'efforts*

pour unir l'Europe, Bureau de Liason Franco-Allemand (Paris 1955).

3. The official French texts of these treaties have been utilized: *Textes Diplomatique,* CLXXI and CLXXII respectively, *Le Documentation Française* Nos. 2279 and 2280, Ministry of Foreign Affairs (Paris 1957).

4. *A European Free Trade Area,* Her Majesty's Stationery Office (London 1957) mmd. 72.

5. *Il Politico,* Univ. of Pavia, Vol. XXIII, No. 1, March 1958 (English translation).

6. *British Affairs,* official organ of British Information Service (New York), September 1957.

7. Reporting to the President on his circuit of Africa, in March, 1957, Vice-President Nixon said not a word about incipient federalism there. On January 17, 1959, however, Asst. Sec. of State Joseph C. Satterthwaite, addressing the Southern Assembly at Biloxi, Miss., said that "the United States views with favor" the development of "the general concept of federation or regional association in Africa." Dept. of State *Press Release,* Jan. 17, 1959, No. 38. The contrast suggests the rapid growth of the federal idea in Africa during the intervening period.

8. On May 1, 1959, the Prime Minister of Ghana and the President of Guinea signed an agreement pledging themselves "immediately to lay the foundation" of a "Union of Independent African States," designed to possess a common "Union Economic Council" and "Union Bank of Issue."

9. Cf. *Scandinavia on the World Stage, The Economist* (London) Nov. 9, 1957, pp. 473-4.

10. The *Federalist,* No. 14.

11. *Idem.,* No. 11.

CHAPTER 18

1. *Under Western Eyes.*

2. Speech at Charleston Bar Dinner, May 10, 1847.

3. II Cor. 3:17 (King James Version).

4. The Latin original of this phrase in the Collect is *quem servare est regnare*—"to serve Whom is to reign."

Service implies restraint. The translator was obviously well aware that perfect freedom (or liberty) must be restrained.

5. Edith Hamilton, *Spokesmen for God*, W. W. Norton & Co. (New York 1949) p. 237.

6. Aristotle, *Politics*, Bk. III, Ch. 16.

7. *The Laws*, quoted by F. R. Cowell, *Cicero and the Roman Republic* (Pelican Books No. A-320) pp. 354-5. Cf. also Bertrand de Jouvenel, *Sovereignty:* "As I see it, the Rule of Law is a natural phenomenon. Men are inhibited from doing certain things, and offended when such things are done, by reason of shared feelings as to what is right and proper. Upon those feelings, the content of which changes over time but the nature of which is unchanging, rests the possibility of social cooperation. . . . enacted laws themselves are subjected to these deeplying convictions. That such convictions should be held strongly, and that they should be shared, constitutes the essence of the Rule of Law, which is actualized by the expression of moral approval or disapproval." J. F. Huntington trans., Univ. of Chicago Press (Chicago 1957) p. 298.

8. The *Federalist*, No. 78.

9. *The Decline of the West*, Geo. Allen & Unwin Ltd. (London 1928) Vol. II, p. 369.

10. "Why Law Day?" *Harvard Law School Bulletin,* Vol. 10, No. 3, Dec. 1958, p. 5.

11. Sir Henry Sumner Maine, *Ancient Law*, World's Classics Edn., Oxford Univ. Press (London 1950) p. 12. See also Sir James George Frazer, *The Golden Bought, passim.*

12. *Democracy in America*, Vol. I, p. 306.

13. Farrand, *Records of the Federal Convention*, Vol. I, p. 451. The word "God" is twice underscored in the original ms., now among the Franklin papers in the Library of Congress.

14. "Nihil esse rem publicam, appellationem modo sine corpore ac specie." Suetonius, *Vitae duodecim Caesarum.*

SUGGESTED READING LIST

Federalism is a complicated form of government. Appreciation of its value, for both freedom and security, requires some understanding of political theory. The writings mentioned hereunder have, for the most part, stood the test of time, and those familiar with them will know all of their principal arguments, either for or against the federal system.

Of first importance for American students is *The Federalist*, by Alexander Hamilton, John Jay, and James Madison. Not all of these essays are of equal importance, but those dealing with the fundamental principles of our government can be readily identified and are as timely today as when written in 1787-88. Very readable and thought-provoking is *The Great Rehearsal* by Carl Van Doren, an examination of the applicability of federalism to international organization.

George Washington's *Farewell Address* should also be carefully studied for its clear expression of the American purpose as seen by "the Father of his Country" when he retired from public life.

It is difficult to choose among the many good histories which sketch our national development since the colonial period. For comparison with the one or more with which the student is already familiar, mention may be made of *A Basic History of the United States*, by Charles A. Beard. This book is very condensed and stops with the Second World War. Far more comprehensive and up to date, but often prejudiced, is the two-volume *Growth of the American Republic*, by Samuel E. Morison and Henry S. Commager.

Thorough students will at least examine both *Democracy in America*, by Alexis de Tocqueville, and *The American Commonwealth*, by James Bryce. The former depicts the United States through the eyes of a shrewd French observer in the early 1830's; the latter is a minute description by the acute British Ambassador of the late

1880's. These books are invaluable for showing what is enduring, as well as what has changed, in American political and social thinking.

Among the many excellent biographies, two in particular illustrate the practical problems inherent in a federal form of government. These are *The Life of John Marshall*, by Albert J. Beveridge, and *John C. Calhoun*, by Charles M. Wiltse.

English writers have given most thought to the difficult reconciliation of Freedom and Order. The student should at least read *The Man Versus The State*, by Herbert Spencer, and the essays *On Liberty* and *Representative Government*, by John Stuart Mill.

The completely anti-federal theory of totalitarian government was brilliantly formulated by Jean Jacques Rousseau, as is described in this book. In addition to what is said here about *The Social Contract*, the student should also read the brief *Communist Manifesto*, by Karl Marx and Friedrich Engels. Two contemporary studies, both very readable, illustrate the chasm between the thinking of the "Free" and "Slave" worlds. These are *The Rise of Totalitarian Democracy*, by J. L. Talmon, and *The Road to Serfdom*, by F. A. Hayek.

Last, but not least, the student should read *The Idea of a Christian Society*, by Thomas S. Eliot. In this brilliant essay, the Anglo-American author focuses on the role of Christianity in the political life of the West.

The books mentioned above provide adequate historical and philosophic background for a thorough consideration of the assets and defects of federalism as a desirable and workable political system. The basic ideas they contain are, for the most part, merely rewritten or summarized by contemporary authors, myself included.